THE CELTIC
WHEEL OF
THE YEAR

First published by O Books, 2007
O Books is an imprint of John Hunt Publishing Ltd.,
The Bothy, Deershot Lodge, Park Lane, Ropley, Hants, SO24 0BE, UK
office1@o-books.net
www.o-books.net

Distribution in:

UK and Europe
Orca Book Services
orders@orcabookservices.co.uk
Tel: 01202 665432 Fax: 01202 666219 Int. code (44)

USA and Canada
NBN
custserv@nbnbooks.com
Tel: 1 800 462 6420 Fax: 1 800 338 4550

Australia and New Zealand
Brumby Books
sales@brumbybooks.com.au
Tel: 61 3 9761 5535 Fax: 61 3 9761 7095

Far East (offices in Singapore, Thailand, Hong Kong, Taiwan)
Pansing Distribution Pte Ltd
kemal@pansing.com
Tel: 65 6319 9939 Fax: 65 6462 5761

South Africa
Alternative Books
altbook@peterhyde.co.za
Tel: 021 447 5300 Fax: 021 447 1430

Design: Stuart Davies

ISBN: 978 1 905 04795 6

A CIP catalogue record for this book is available from the British Library.

Printed in Great Britain by CPI Antony Rowe, Chippenham, Wiltshire

THE CELTIC WHEEL OF THE YEAR

Celtic and Christian

Seasonal Prayers

TESS WARD

Illustrations by Clare Arnison-Newgass

BOOKS

Winchester, UK
Washington, USA

**For Pete, Eleanor, Callum
and Georgie the dog**
for loving through every season.

CONTENTS

Acknowledgements   vi

Introduction   1

January   12

February   32

March   52

April   71

May   94

June   117

July   138

August   159

September   180

October   204

November   225

December   247

ACKNOWLEDGEMENTS

There were many acts of love that went into the making of this book. My thanks are due to John Hunt of O Books for being a risk-taker.

The writing of this book was unthinkable without my dearest friend Amanda Miles. Not only did she pray through every month of prayers as they arrived and make suggestions but her unfaltering encouragement and hand-holding through the ups and downs of each "contraction" make her a true midwife of the soul. Gratitude for your with-craft, dear one.

With thanks to Clare Arnison-Newgass for her labour of love with the artwork. Her gift of drawing, her love of the outside world and for Celtic spirituality which infuses her own, all poured into her beautiful pictures. Gratitude for understanding and offering your gift.

My thanks to Kim Taplin whose poetry inspires and who helped with my writing when I could not see anymore. Thanks also to Lynne and Jo who pored over some details for me with their prayerful eyes and to Johnnie and Janet who pored over some Introductions with their trained eyes.

Gratitude to all my sisters on the journey: Kim, Deborah, Jeanie, Monika, and not forgetting Sherry, who have blessed me every month for seventeen years, for your unerring faithfulness through many many episodes, and creating a space where I can be known and loved and express my soul freely. What can I say? Gratitude for my solstice group Margot, Kate, Lesley, Lou, Ally and Jo. I searched for you and you were sent. Thank you for your earthed wisdom. My thanks to Penny, my spiritual accompanier for helping to keep me truthful with God. Gratitude to Henrietta for her deep loyalty from babies onwards and most recently, understanding the task of book-writing. Thanks to Rachel and Susannah for cheering from the side-lines, and taking me out drinking at regular intervals.

Many books are works of love and there were some that particularly helped me in the introductions to the months, which I came to know well as the year unfolded. I have listed them below and am grateful for each in different ways.[1] The websites visited are too numerous to mention but used throughout were www.wikipedia.org and www.bbc.co.uk. These were always reliable places to go to check information though the others were worth the detour.

Finally gratitude to Pete and our children Eleanor and Callum who have lived with the writing of this book and much more besides. Pete's cooking and all their love sustains all. Gratitude too, for discovering the woods and the rivers, the fields and the sea together. Finally, gratitude to Georgie, our untrained collie dog. Thank you for leading me to the natural world with your unbounded enthusiasm and for your unconditional love that taught me about God's love at a time I needed it. Thank you for sitting outside my shed as I wrote, come rain or shine, angel dog. Gratitude you lovely ones for sharing home and loving through the years.

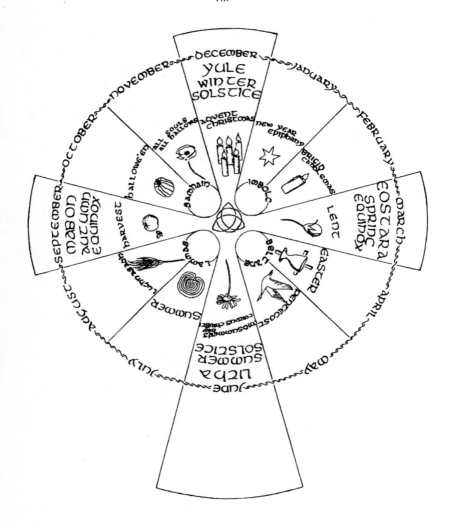

INTRODUCTION

The Wheel of the Year

The Celtic Wheel of the Year is a book of new and original prayers. It is contemporary spiritual writing which intertwines the two strands of Celtic Christian and Celtic pre-Christian traditions in a single pattern of prayer. In *The Celtic Way*, Ian Bradley defines the hallmarks of Celtic Christianity as the three Ps of "presence, poetry and pilgrimage".[2] Whilst this is not a book that is attempting to write in the style of those Celtic Christians I hope that it shares those same hallmarks: the presence of God in all things, poetry, and expression of our spiritual journeys as we walk our way into the heart of God, enfolded in all Love every day of our lives in the season's rhythms of each year.

It is well-known that the Christian festivals were overlaid on the pagan festivals that pre-dated them. In the British Isles and countries of the northern hemisphere, the themes of the Christian festivals fit seamlessly with the pagan cycle which was developed by rural communities in response to the agrarian seasons. So we celebrate the light of Christ's birth in the darkest month, his rising to new life after dying on the Cross as the land bursts into new growth for the year.

The wildlife and weather described are that of the British Isles. For those using this book, living in the southern hemisphere, some of the naturalistic references will not fit. Others could be creatively used at opposite times of the year, for example, swapping the equinox prayers. The effects of global warming influence our weather year by year. Even with the unpredictable nature of the weather in the British Isles, the seasons are distinct but their boundaries are changing. The blossoms arrive months before what we think of as spring, and the leaves can still be green in November. This book keeps to the traditional seasons, and so may not always be in line with the changes outside.

The seasons celebrated in the Celtic wheel of the year are being rediscovered in our time by different kinds of people. It has long been thought that the people of the British Isles celebrated the cycle of the seasons at eight points in the year. In the wheel, there are four fixed points forming a cross. These are the solar festivals. They are the winter solstice (December 20-23): the shortest day and longest night; the summer solstice (June 20-23): the longest day and shortest night; the spring equinox (March 20-23) and the autumn equinox (September 20-23) both of which are when the night and day are of equal length.

The word "solstice" is Latin for "the standing of the sun". As the earth travels along its orbit around the sun, the sun's rays hit the earth at different points. At the winter solstice the sun stops and commences the waxing cycle towards its peak on the longest day at the summer solstice. The sun seems to stop again and starts the waning cycle until the darkness reaches its peak again on the shortest day of the winter solstice. The equinoxes fall in the middle of those journeys and mark the turning of the season from summer to autumn (September) and from winter to spring (March).

Across these four points in the cycle are the quarter days. These are the lunar festivals celebrated at the full moon and often known as the fire festivals. Imbolc is at the beginning of February (often February 2), Beltane at the beginning of May (often May 1), Lammas or Lughnasadh at the beginning of August (often August 1) and Samhain at the beginning of November (often October 31).

The Celts

It must be said at this point that there has been a shift in archaeological and historical thinking in the last thirty years. Many would agree that there is little certain evidence about who the Celts were in the British Isles.[3] The only known self-defined tribe of Celts were a group of people in Europe from as early as 6th century BC. Much of the evidence about the Celts in Britain is from the classical writers (1st century BC). They used the term "Galli/Galatae" and this is likely to have been a term used to describe northern barbarians, among them the Celts. Some of the people who lived in Europe migrated to Britain. The language spoken by those known as the Atlantic Celts at this time is ancestral to the "Celtic" languages spoken in Brittany, Cornwall, Wales, Scotland and Ireland now. For this reason, these cultures can claim some Celtic roots in the pre-historic period. The caricature of the Celts as non-Mediterranean and barbarous (which means "strange" or "other") had some basis in fact. They were described as high-spirited, quick to battle and lovers of drink.

In "The Gallic War", Caesar records two higher classes of men: the knights and the Druids. The Druids had a priestly function, concerned with the worship of the gods, rituals and sacrifice and expounding religious matters and philosophy. They knew about the motion of the stars and the earth. There were also Bards and Seers who were poets and prophets. Music and literature were highly regarded. Unfortunately they practised in the oral tradition and did not write so we have no evidence of their beliefs and practise from the Druids themselves.

We do know that the Celts had a strong sense of the supernatural and of the life of the soul after death and that the Druids presided over religious ceremonies in the open. Sacredness of place was important; especially woods, groves, rivers and springs. Trees were particularly revered. Many of the Celtic healing sanctuaries focussed on a holy spring, seeing it as a source of healing and the worship of a deity. There were, of course, female goddesses as well as gods. One interesting feature is that there are tantalizing glimpses from archaeology, classical authors and vernacular myths of priestesses as well as priests and Druidesses, who were wise women and seers.

Druids were persecuted under the Roman Empire and there is little written testimony of them after the end of the first century. However thanks to the popularity of certain texts, both the Celts and the Druids were re-invented in Britain many centuries later. In the sixteenth century, the classical texts were re-discovered and, in the seventeenth and eighteenth centuries, antiquarians such as John Aubrey and William Stukely reconstructed the Druid order and linked it to stone circles like Stonehenge. In Wales, Iolo Morgannwg created some "traditions" for the enthroning of Bards at the National Eisteddfod which continue to this day. From the eighteenth century until now, the Druidic tradition has been maintained through various modern orders, for example the Order of Bards, Ovates and Druids. The website of the Druid Network[4] is a good place to discover modern druidry. Despite the robes and ceremonies, there is no real historical link between them and the Druids of classical antiquity.

The same is true of the Celtic wheel of the year. There is early Irish literature which suggests that the solstices and the quarter festivals were celebrated in Ireland though we do not know the extent or the nature of some of these festivals. There is evidence that the solstices, Beltane and some of the other festivals were celebrated in particular regions of the British Isles. What has held more sway than all of the history is that from the eighteenth century onwards the folklorists, historians and archaeologists including Sir James Frazer and his hugely popular "The Golden Bough" (1922)[5], asserted that these were our Celtic roots in the old religion before Christianity. They implied a certain uniformity of celebration across our isles. This was not seriously challenged until the 1980s. From the 1970s onwards interest in all things Celtic has once again been revived. Whatever it touches in British spiritual identity is clearly more powerful than historical facts.

The Wheel of the Year today

It is the spiritual quality of the wheel rather than the historicity that is of relevance for this book. As a priest and counsellor, I subscribe to the view that we are more motivated by our unconscious than by our conscious selves. Our spirituality must comprise of our inner life made up from past experience, knowledge, imagination, how our bodies "work" in the world, our sleeping dreams, our waking hopes, our sorrows and fears. These will be affected by our outer lives: the rhythm of the seasons, what is happening in love and work, in our world or our community, our age and stage. Our spirituality and our beliefs take in everything in our inner and outer lives.

I warmly commend the historian Ronald Hutton's book *The Stations of the Sun* to anybody who is captivated by the Celtic wheel. He speaks for my intentions when he says:

"It is one of the arguments of this book that the rhythms of the British year are timeless and impose certain perpetual patterns upon calendar customs: a yearning for light, greenery, warmth and joy in midwinter, a propensity to celebrate the spring with symbols of rebirth, an impulse to make merry in the sunlight and open air during the summer, and a tendency for thoughts to turn towards death and the uncanny at the onset of winter."[6]

The Celtic wheel might be attractive now for many reasons. The thought that it might connect to the past is immensely powerful. Roots strengthen our identity, especially if we perceive them to connect to who we are today. It also joins us to a community of other people, past people. Both roots and community are significant for most people either in their absence or presence.

The wheel of the year is a framework that is already on our spiritual radar because it is drawn from the world around us in the seasons in our land, so we are already in the realm of what is. The Welsh poet R S. Thomas called matter the "scaffolding of the spirit".[7] The natural world is spiritually significant for most people and has the capacity to affect our inner life. Indeed many people would identify their most spiritual moments as when they are caught up in nature. I am particularly indebted to the spiritual writings of Caitlin Matthews[8] and Glennie Kindred[9] that help us make those connections as we celebrate the Celtic wheel of the year.

Though the Celts lived in rural communities, the attraction to all things

Celtic is not particularly linked to a romantic ideal of living in the country. It is more about the new ecological awareness. It is about a growing responsibility to care for the earth and concern if we do not. Many people feel that the idea of power over the earth, or other people is outdated. This has long been true in feminist spirituality: that it is only by recognizing our inter-connectedness with all created things that we can move forwards, with each other and with the Earth.

The global political landscape has changed since 9-11. Those who were already intolerant of religion feel vindicated. This is a loud and powerful voice. However, it is not necessarily the most prophetic. For those who are aware and nurturing of their own spirituality, and certainly among mystics of different faiths, the opposite is true. Inter-faith dialogue has never felt more urgent. This is not only true between the world religions but also in the alternative spirituality world. Several established communities are keen to promote understanding between different faiths and spiritualities, for example Othona in Dorset, The Abbey in Oxfordshire, Findhorn in Scotland. Greenfire in Maine, US has been a particularly special place for me[10]. Breathing Space[11] in north London is a non-residential arts and spirituality space. It also holds a treasured place in my heart and would share these concerns. In these communities and others like them, both difference and inter-connectedness are celebrated and cherished.

This is not to say that the old enmity between pagan spirituality and Christianity is not alive and well in some quarters, but that in others, hospitality is offered to the other. For many of us, it is present in our own journey. Sometimes I wonder if hospitality might be the prophetic gift of our time: welcoming the other over the threshold and daring to walk over theirs only to realize that, as Maya Angelou once said, when describing what her work was about: "human beings are more alike than unlike".[12] The prayers in this book are offered in that spirit and it is not unique. Caitlin Matthews has written a Celtic prayer-book drawing from the Celtic pagan-Celtic Christian stream[13] and J. Philip Newell has done the same from the Christian-Jewish source.[14]

The Arrival of Christianity

If we look at the far greater testimony of belief and practice in Britain once Christianity arrived, (probably through the Romans in the second century), we will find that daggers were not immediately drawn between pagan and Christian.[15]

"Christ, the Word, was from the beginning our Teacher, and we never lost his teaching. Christianity was in Asia a new thing: but there never was a time when the Druids of Britain held not its doctrine."

- Taliesin, Welsh Bard 6th Century.[16]

The historicity of Taliesin's poetry is much in question but Christianity did graft onto Druidic culture and spread with missionary zeal across all the British Isles, especially through the monastic system and the idea of pilgrimage which was second nature to the wandering Celts. Both felt strongly the divine presence in the material and created world. The Celtic knots and patterns symbolized the interweaving of physical and spiritual, of earthly and eternal. This is called panentheism: God being within creation as well as creating it. Celtic prayers invoked saints and angels as pagans had invoked gods. Blessings and curses were common to both. The lorica, or breastplate, was a popular form of prayer, most famously St Patrick's:

"I arise today
Through the strength of heaven:
Light of sun,
Radiance of moon,
Splendour of fire,
Speed of lightning
Swiftness of wind,
Depth of sea,
Stability of earth,
Firmness of rock."[17]

Cairns or encircling prayers were also invocatory for protection. They called on God to protect them from evil forces without and within. The prayers in this book are written in this way.

Christian monks incorporated the veneration of nature and holy places within Christianity. Monasteries were built on Druid groves. Springs and wells associated with pagan gods were given saint's names and old rituals that celebrated creation like well dressing, harvest thanksgivings or the blessing of crops became part of the church's calendar. Of the beautiful standing crosses of Celtic Christianity, some like St Martin's in Iona had Bible stories one side and patterns of nature on the other.

Naturally there was also enmity between the two systems of belief and practice, especially as Christianity became more powerful. There was also tension between Celtic Christianity and Roman Christianity. The Celts saw the church in terms of loosely structured monastic communities. The Romans, who were from an urban background, saw bishops and priests as exercising pastoral and administrative authority in a fixed area. It has long been said that things came to a head at the Synod of Whitby in AD 664 when the Roman church was favoured.

However, the Celtic church survived in some areas of Britain for the next five hundred years. At the same time, the English centralizing tendencies either under the see of Rome, or, after the Reformation, Canterbury, changed the culture of the church in Britain. Whether Catholic or Protestant, the Welsh, Irish, and Scots, resisted this dominance. In Ireland and in the Scottish islands where Gaelic is still spoken, the Celtic traits of Christianity survived especially in the notion of God's presence in all things. In the nineteenth century, Alexander Carmichael gathered Gaelic prayers together in the treasure-trove *Carmina Gadelica*[18]. They had been passed down orally through centuries of generations. As with pagan Celtomania, renewed interest in Christian Celtic spirituality surfaced in that century.

Celtic Christianity today

Celtic Christianity is enjoying a huge revival today. George MacLeod's singular contribution put Celtic Christianity on the map for the British church, and especially young people. He restored Iona Abbey from 1938 onwards and established a community there, and in Glasgow. It was not a revival of the past, but a renewing of Celtic theology and spirituality in the present. So God's presence is felt in the urban landscape and in the events of our everyday lives and suffuses everything. The songs of John Bell and Graham Maule,[19] written in this spirit, are now established in British churches as part of standard hymnody. David Adam, who wrote many of his prayers[20] when he was vicar of Holy Island is equally popular. J. Philip Newell[21], Esther de Waal,[22] and many other spiritual writers could not satiate a market, such is the hunger for Celtic Christian spirituality in our times.

The appeal of Celtic Christianity to present day Christians is not hard to fathom. Even Christians more orthodox and patient than myself are wanting to join up the lines much more between their daily lives, creation, their sexuality, their emotional lives and their faith. This inter-connectedness between every living thing is of God. The gospel of Christ is seen as God's deep and abiding love for ourselves and all that lives on the earth, woven through by the Holy Spirit. Celtic Christian prayers express this.

My own story

This desire to connect the mystical, creative, emotionally literate, interior church and its public face when gathered for worship, had fuelled my own path towards becoming a priest in 2000. The weight of history in parish life proved too great for the fragility of this venture. I travelled on to another place that was not the centre-stage of parish ministry, and the lifelines that have always refreshed and renewed, remain. The poetically precise and emotionally road-worthy prayers of spiritual writers like Jim Cotter,[23] and Janet Morley,[24] have fed many like myself, and have now entered the mainstream. It is no coincidence that these prayers profoundly explore the relationship between faith and sexuality. Gratitude also to all the angel friends God has given to accompany me on the journey, to the communities that I have visited and stayed in, books (including certain parts of the Bible), poetry, other art forms like film, music and art, Nature herself, and all of these led by the Spirit who reveals and inspires. This prayer book is intended for personal use, and is written out of a need to express more nearly how the spiritual journey feels from the inside life as it is lived.

As a quester on the spiritual path, I have long felt a kinship with fellow travellers of whatever tradition. I would particularly like to thank my four sisters with whom I celebrate the wheel of the year. This often happens outside, which has been a lovely thing to discover. It is another source of these prayers. They come from both the Christian and Celtic traditions, and my hope is to allow the two traditions to dance together: to keep their bodies distinct but to discover the other as they move as one. For this is how the Spirit lives in me and how I have inhabited these traditions and it is my prayer for how we might live together, either on our inner journey or as a partaker of established religion.

How to use the book

The book is divided into months. Each month starts with an introduction to the seasonal themes. The introductions describe some changes that may be happening outside, and then describe the historical and current ways we celebrate the festivals that occur in the month. They end with Biblical and spiritual references that are embedded within the prayers, and can be looked up if so desired.

January – New Year, Epiphany, Twelfth Night

February - Brigid, Imbolc, Candlemas, Valentine, Shrove Tuesday, Ash
   Wednesday
March – Lent, Spring Equinox, St David, St Patrick, Mothering Sunday
April- Easter, Oestre, All Fools, St George
May – Beltane/May Day, Pentecost/Whitsun, Ascension, Rogationtide
June - Summer Solstice/Midsummer's Day, Corpus Christi, Father's Day
July – No festivals
August - Lammas, Lughnasadh,
September - Autumn Equinox, Harvest, St Michael and all Angels
October – Samhain, St Francis
November – All Souls, All Hallows, Bonfire Night, Remembrance Day,
   Thanksgiving, St Andrew
December - Advent, Christmas, Yule, Winter Solstice

The Celtic wheel is evenly spaced throughout the year. There are festivals
every six weeks. The Christian calendar is active between Advent at the end
of November and June, where Corpus Christi marks the last official festival.
It then moves into "ordinary time." In the prayers, ordinary seasonal moods
are celebrated, for example, "music" in July, "holiday" in August, "new" in
September. It is also an opportunity to celebrate the natural world. Trees,
rivers, the sea, mountains and hills, each have a day of prayers. Some themes
have evolved from the festivals, for example "crone," from Samhain in
October, "calling the directions," in June from solstice ceremonies,
"pilgrimage," in July, because it was the traditional month for pilgrimages.
Finally, the patron saints of the British Isles are included. St Francis has been
adopted as an honorary Celtic saint. St Brigid is hugely important in any
pantheon of deities or saints, and St Michael has been included because of
the current affection for angels.

These themes are taken up in the prayers that follow each introduction.
For each month, I have offered a week of prayers. The prayers are medita-
tional in style, and so you the reader must decide how they best suit your
current practice. At most, they could be used about four times each month as
there are a week of prayers per month. Because they unfold themes, it is
hoped they will yield different things on different weeks. They are topped
and tailed with morning or night sections, depending on when you are
praying. These are indicated by a moon or sun symbol. These are designed to
be guides only, and to be used creatively as they are helpful for each person.
One way to use the prayers is to use them on the particular day of the festi-

val, regardless of whether it is a Monday or whatever. The particularity of the prayers means that they do not replace meditation, or devotional reading, or intercessory prayer, but rather accompany those practices.

If all this is new, a quiet space is recommended for spending time with God. Most ideally, it should be a place where that is all that happens there, so you can return to it each morning or night and it is always there. If this is not possible, at least a place that does not become cluttered, and that you have to clear each time, is good. That way, your approach will be easier. It should be said that finding time to practice quiet does not come naturally to many.

When you have entered in, and opened the book, the sections for each day or night are divided thus:

On Rising/Resting – We greet God.
Praising – We thank God for who God is.
In Stillness – A time of quiet. This has been put here so that whatever mood we come to pray in, the words of the first two sections may centre our thoughts and focus us. However, depending on your practice, it may be preferable to still the mind and body first and then start to pray the words from the beginning. If you are used to meditating, this is the invitation to do so. If not, it is an invitation to sit comfortably, still and upright, to slow the breathing down and to try to bask in God's loving gaze, for however long feels right for you. Some spend five minutes, some spend half an hour. There are no rules. If it is a new practice, five minutes will feel like an age, so do not be too ambitious! Some like to empty the mind with mantras (repeated phrases). Some are content to be still and let thoughts and feelings "travel across" the mind, and gently notice them. It is a time of being, not doing, and you may feel nothing. It is a discipline and does not come easily. However, it can be a pause to become more attentive to ourselves and to the love of God, with, and within us.

Morning Invocation – This is the wake-up call for our bodies. We invoke the Spirit of God through each part of our body, mind and heart, as we arise.

Opening Out – This moves us from ourselves to others as we start our day. This section signals a looking beyond, to the wider world. It can be used to intercede for those places and events that are happening at the time. The guidance in the prayers is loose, but even so, the reader should follow their heart and pray for what concerns them. If it is your practice to keep a list of

11

"intercessions", this is the time to use it, or, in the "Night Shielding" section at night.

Thanksgiving – This is a night-time section. St Ignatius developed the "Examen," which was a tool to go over our day with God. More recently, it has been noted that if we counted three blessings each night as we lay down, it would contribute to our well-being. So, this is a space to say thanks for at least three things that we have received in the day. Often there are more. Sometimes, it feels hard to find three, but even the searching can be good.

Night Shielding – This night prayer is a common form in Celtic spirituality to seek protection from foe within and without. It is also a theme in the Christian office of Night Prayer to commit ourselves to God, and God's protection, until the morning, like a "tucking in". This section is a time to remember in prayer those whom we have met or who are on our minds that day. This section can incorporate the news that is troubling us and that we wish to offer before we sleep.

Blessing – We seek God's blessing as we set out this day or sleep this night.

Language Note: There is much difficulty with the word "God". It has unfortunately been appropriated as male, when God must surely be genderful if she/he is the creator of all things. I have sought to reclaim it as such. I have also not wanted to lose its usefulness as a universally recognized term. No other word is quite the same. So, "God" is used with this assumption when it appears in the prayers.

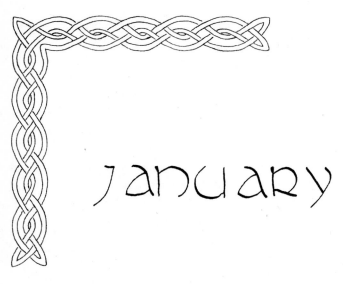

JANUARY

INTRODUCTION TO JANUARY

January begins with celebrations for the New Year, but outside, the natural world is bleak and can feel hard on the spirit. Evergreens are the only sign of life, which is why we brought them into our homes in December. By tradition, they are taken down again on Twelfth Night, January 6, along with the Christmas tree and other decorations. Days are short and cold and the land appears to be dead. It used to be that flowers bringing a little cheer did not appear until the end of the month. Snow is greeted with excitement as the landscape is suddenly transformed into a radiant magical place. It invites playfulness from children and adults. The wintering birds remain, like tits, finches, sparrows, blackbirds, thrushes, wrens and the much-loved robin. Wildfowl (ducks, geese and swans) can be seen feeding, flocking and roosting. It is also possible to spot owls, squirrels and foxes. The name of the game for creatures in January is survival. They tend to stay in groups more to find food and avoid predators, and make it through the lean months until the breeding season in Spring. Survival seems to be how many people see January too. The Christmas holiday is over; Spring seems a long way off, spirits are low and winter germs and bugs abound.

Before the month is underway though, its turn marks the beginning of the year, on January 1. This Introduction cannot be read separately from the Introduction to December, as the history of New Year and Christmas are so intertwined. Many of the customs span both months. It is a season of hope, of looking forward, and being thankful for another year of life to live and of reflecting on the year that has passed. It is a time to make resolutions to change things we feel would improve our lives. This is echoed in magazines, adverts, and television programmes. It is a time of transitions between old and new, of liminal moments, in-between places, the crack between the worlds. Spiritually, these sacred times are called "thin places," when ordinary time is suspended, and the sacred and earthly feel particularly seamless. It is therefore the time when rituals are plentiful, including "saining" rituals. These were for safe-guarding people and property against powers in the darkness, and for the year ahead.

First-footing and Hogmanays

First-footing was a custom practised in Scotland, England and Wales. Folks would go from house to house on New Year's Eve, and the first person over the threshold after midnight was believed to bring good luck. There would be a welcome of the door and blessings for the coming year and a celebration of hospitality. First-footers would bring a gift of wood, or a piece of coal, to put on the fire. It would be done in silence, and when the fire was stoked there would be cheers all round. They might also bring a mince-pie, bread or whisky, to put on the table. Sometimes they brought an evergreen branch or mistletoe to symbolize the spirit of growth.

New Year's gifts were commonplace until the nineteenth century and it is unclear why the tradition of exchanging gifts died out. In Scotland the gifts and blessings of New Year were called "hogmanays". In England and Scotland groups of children would go from door to door, bringing blessing and asking for a hogmanay. This would either be bread, a bannock, cheese or later, money. If given, they might walk sun-wise round the fire, singing something like:

"May God bless the dwelling,
each stone and beam and stave,
all food and drink and clothing.
May health of men always be here."[1]

If refused, they might curse the household and put a cairn of stones outside the door to ward off others. In Wales and the highlands of Scotland, blessings would also be splashed on houses by dipping sprigs of evergreen in spring water.

First-footing is still popular in Scotland today. The importance of Hogmanay there cannot be underestimated and it remains an important feast if not *the* important feast of the season, due to the history outlined in the Introduction to December. In times gone by, no job was left unfinished. The house was cleaned and beds changed. Debts were paid, borrowed items returned, and repairs done. The tone of the new was set before the New Year arrived.

Wassail and Twelfth Night

The English rite of hospitality and charity at New Year was the Wassail. This happened both on New Year's Eve and Twelfth Night. Wassail, which is from the old English for "be whole," or "your health," is an old drinking toast. A Wassail cup is an ornate bowl full of warmed, sweetened ale or cider spiced with nutmeg, and had roasted apples and pieces of toast floating in it. One form of Wassailing meant going from house to house, and donations were given as the cup was shared (see Introduction to December). It was also shared round a table in homes.

Wassailing also happened on Twelfth Night and was one of several saining rituals. The Twelve Days of Christmas end on January 6. The Wassail bowl was taken to the orchard and a toast was sung to the trees, or just one tree. The bowl was passed round and drunk from, and the rest poured over the roots of the trees, to ask for a good apple harvest later in the year. Songs would be sung like this one from Sussex and Surrey. The word "howling" refers to this custom.

"Stand fast root, bear well top.
Pray the God send us a howling good crop.
Every twig, apples big,
every bough, apples now."[2]

In Scotland, ritual fires were lit, as at Beltane, from burning juniper, and cattle were led in front of them for spiritual and literal purification. In England, men with lit torches ran round wheat fields. In the Western Isles they burnt animal skins. These fire and apple wassails were thought to bring health of crops and animals, and possibly derive from pre-Christian practices.

Epiphany

As the Twelve days of Christmas end, so Epiphany starts on January 6. This is the Christian festival that celebrates the visit of the Wise Men to the baby Jesus. January 6 was the Eastern date for Christmas, which is how the Twelve days came about. A rather lovely tradition which happened in Wales and neighbouring Herefordshire and Gloucestershire brought all the January customs together. The children going from door to door on New Year's Eve carried a symbol of blessing called the "calennig." It was three sticks made into a tripod daubed in flour and stuck with fruit, cereal and or nuts and herbs, signifying the gifts of the wise men: sweetness, wealth and immortality.

Epiphany is the story of the Wise Men, found in the gospel of Matthew 2.1-12. It tells of how they follow a star and travel across countries from the East to see what or who the star portends. They are philosophers, astrologers, or mystics. The star hangs over where Jesus lies. They offer him gifts of gold, frankincense and myrrh (symbolizing wealth of a King, holiness and myrrh was used in the preparation of dead bodies, foreshadowing his early death). These are dangerous times. King Herod wants to kill all the baby boys under two years old so that his kingship is not threatened. Pretending that he wants to visit the baby Jesus too, he asks the wise men to return to him to tell him where Jesus is. They are warned in a dream not to go back and return home by a different road.

There is an important church service on the night of January 6. The figures of the Wise Men are put beside the crib. There are Epiphany carols and a big gilded star is hung on the rood (crucifix on screen dividing choir from nave where congregation sits). The festival celebrates the gift of God to all people, not just to one nation. It also reminds us of our own journeys. This is especially appropriate for a January festival, when we reflect on the future.

Wren-boys, Mummers and Guisers

The season of charity and hospitality begun in December thus continues until Twelfth Night, and many of the midwinter customs provided money for poorer folks and bonded the community together. Apart from the customs mentioned, there were others. There was a strange custom focussed on the wren. It is the smallest bird, and was thought to make prophecy, so called the "magus bird", or the "druid-bird". On Twelfth Night, groups of youths called "wren-boys" would kill a wren and put it in a little bier, or hang several of them from holly boughs with ribbons, and ask for money. Later, they stopped killing them but still took them round in a little box with ribbons.

In Scotland there were guisers who dressed up in fabulous costumes and collected money. There were also mummers who performed ritual plays in pubs, and sometimes in homes. They used to be performed by working men to earn extra money in December, and until Plough Monday, as well as later in the year. A Father Christmas character would introduce a main story involving a fight with swords, and a doctor who revived the wounded one. The death and resurrection of the central character symbolized the death of the old year and birth of the new. This was the end of the official story but then the minor characters arrived and more amusement followed. Some were the same as the Morris dancers, for example, the Fool and the Bessy (a man dressed as a woman). There were also Beelzebub and Devil Doubt and St George, who would fight a Saracen, or a soldier called Slasher. The characters were essentially outcasts, devils, fools, quacks and bragging fighters. They enacted in a safe way, disrespect, pretend violence, and anti-social behaviour. Morris dancers and mummers still perform in some areas today.

17

Plough Monday

Plough Sunday was the first Sunday after Epiphany when priests blessed the ploughs. The next day, Plough Monday, was full of rowdy celebrations. Groups of men, called Plough boys, would dress up, or perform plays like the Mummers plays. They would go round with their plough for a donation which went towards a feast. If refused they might do damage to the property with the plough! The ploughing season thus began and continued until March. Nowadays, the return to work, around Twelfth Night for many, whilst no longer ritualized in the community, is a feature of people's lives at the beginning of January.

So January is a time of journeys, of crossing over boundaries into new places. It is a time of stars and dreams, and signs that hang between our prayerful perceptions and the reality of our daily lives. It is a season of reflection on the past and wise discerning for the future. It is a placing of trust, of following our longing and taking the first footstep from the known and familiar into unchartered territory. Epiphany means a "showing" or "appearance". We place our hope in the most bounteous Giver, who shines in this dark season. It continues the season of hospitality. The Epiphany story reminds us that God's love is revealed when people cross the threshold from known places towards each other. It is a season of gifts when we enjoy giving and celebrating. Once the official season is over though, it can also be a tough time when the dreariness of the season and the return to work and poor health can overwhelm. Spring can seem a long time coming.

MONDAY Thresholds

On Rising/Resting

Blessed be you, Turner of the nights and days,
moving from season to season, from dawn til dusk, til dawn again
☼ Give me hopefulness as I look to this new day still hooded in darkness.
☾ Give me thankfulness at this day's end.

Praising

God of promise,
Praise to you that your hope does not fade
or become tawdry as the baubles when the festivities are done.
Praise that your love cannot be put away in the box with the angels
for you came in the darkness, and reached out to us.
And when the return of routine is contemplated with relief and in weariness,
as at the bottom of a tall mountain,
praise for your promise of presence.

In Stillness

Be still in the silence and aware of the Love with and within.......

☼ Morning Invocation

Come O touchable God
and first-foot over the threshold of my heart.
Bring with you a coal to touch my lips
that I might speak in tongues of love.
A coal to touch my feet
that I might walk this day knowing you.
A coal to touch my hands
that their work might be blessed.
A coal to touch my groin
that my yearning might find meet embodiment.
A coal to touch my belly
that I might live from the depth of myself.
A coal to touch my heart
that I might open my door to another.
Spirit of new things, I welcome you,
as I set forth this day.

✿ Opening Out

Reaching-Out God you long for our company,
and made us to delight in the hospitality of one other.
May the lonely know the touch of good people,
not that contact may come as shock,
but that the bittersweet memory of tenderness
might rekindle hope and remind of your kindness.
I hold before you particularly this day

Enfold us in the peace of your presence.

☾ Thanksgiving

As I end this day in your safe-keeping
I count three blessings before my sleeping

☾ Night Shielding

Transforming Spirit
give me discernment as I lie down this night,
on the threshold between the old and the new.
Cover my marks with your mercy
that I may embrace the old things before I resolve to leave them behind.
Guard me on my journey and let me abandon myself to your grace
as I tread this year's road.
Be with all who fear what the next step might bring

In our waking visions and night-time dreams be the new familiar light
within.
Lead us freshly forward to the known of home.
Spirit go before me as I look to a new day.

Blessing

May the blessing of God the Holy Door-Keeper
be upon me in my new beginnings.
Guard all the doors through which I pass, and those that close before me.
Bless me with your homecoming welcome so I may share it with another
✿ however far I roam this day.
☾ as I return under lintel this night.

TUESDAY Stars and Signs

On Rising/Resting
Blessed be you, God of all, at home in heaven and earth.
The signs of your Showing are all around us.
☼ Holy Daystar dawning with us, I rise up with you this wintry morning
☾ Star-Scatterer across the darkness, shine on my sleeping this night

Praising
Bright Mystery,
your signs and clues are strewn across the Universe,
gleaming in the warp and weft of the ordinary.
When I perceive and follow the wavering glints
lead me to find your manifest presence
and glimpse your purpose and mine own.
Keep me pointing to the shining of your love
as I search for your handwriting in the stars.

In Stillness
Be still in the silence and aware of the Love with and within..........

☼ Morning Invocation
God of revelation who is hidden and shows,
reveal your skill in the work of my hands,
your direction in the way of my feet,
your wisdom in the secrets of my heart,
your compassion on all whom my eye alights,
your love in the thoughts of my mind,
your welcome in the words of my mouth,
your strength in my action this day.
Hide in the shadow of your wing
my lack of courage, my frustration and my pain.
Show to me their root as you repair my soul in mercy.
Veiled Spirit who covers and clarifies,
I welcome you now as I walk this new day.

☼ Opening Out
God whose evergreen love the chills cannot fade,

you made our hearts for stargazing and wonder.
Surprise me not only with your everyday epiphanies
but with those spectacular stellar moments
when I just know that this journey is the right place to be.
Be with all whose dreams have been trampled on
by hardship and circumstance.
I hold before you particularly this day

May they arise, shine and know their light has come.

☾ Thanksgiving
As I end this day in your safe-keeping
I count three blessings before my sleeping

☾ Night Shielding
May the strong Pole Star of your Spirit go ahead to guide me
as I take my rest this night.
Shine over the place where I lie down
and do not withdraw your presence
even when you are hidden from my sight.
Be with all those who feel your absence this night

Honour the path on which our seeking feet tread
Follow us with your safety and keep us from foe.
Spirit be my guide as I take my rest this night.

Blessing
O Divine Presence
Bless to me the lustre of your signs and wonders,
traces of our final home in land and sea and sky.
As you have made the mark of heaven in a human face,
may I see the imprint of your family likeness in every living thing
that your blessing might radiate
each day and each night,
until heaven and earth are One.

WEDNESDAY Gifts

On Rising/Resting
Blessed be you Giver of all good things
for giving me this new day, to be like no other,
this new year like none before.
✿ Generous, gentle One I rise up with you on this unique gift-day
☾ Generous, gentle One I rest with you trusting in the gift of this night

Praising
Original One
birthing all of life,
your bounty issues throughout the universe.
Praise to you for giving of yourself each moment of every day,
for your tricksterish delight in surprising me with your outrageous grace.
For catching me off guard and breaking open my stuck ways,
praise to you.

In Stillness
Be still in the silence and aware of the Love with and within.........

✿ Morning Invocation
Bringer of Gifts, fill me with gratitude this day:
Gratitude of heart that I might see the gifts of another.
Gratitude of mouth that I might sing their praises.
Gratitude of spirit that I might recognize the blessings you have brought me.
Gratitude of humour as I perceive the playfulness of your giving.
Gratitude of eyes that I might deeply draw on the wonders of your created world and know my part in its family.
Gratitude of open hands for all that you will place in them this day.
Gratitude of memory for my story which you have covered with tenderness and mercy.
Gratitude of feet for every step I take this day is as gift.

✿ Opening Out
O Giver of goodness,
not of my asking or choosing, not of my controlling or deal-brokering
does your love come.

Yet when it feels a long way off, and I lose the gift of receiving
I can fail to see the hand that cares.
Grow my heart to perceive your love in the gift of another.
Give me courage to show those who feel giftless and of no value their true
loveliness.
I remember this day particularly

Gift them with an awareness of your love,
a tiny flicker or an overwhelming knowing
that makes them smile this day.

☽ Thanksgiving

As I end this day in your safe-keeping
I count three blessings before my sleeping

☽ Night Shielding

Loving Creator, you made us infinitely special.
As I lie down this night under the varied stars,
melt the envy I sometimes feel for others.
Let me trust your grace in my own becoming
and the timing as you unfold your gift.
Abundant Spirit may I see the gift of yourself
in every stranger and friend that I have met this day

May I learn to rejoice in the uniqueness of each different soul
and our stories known only to you,
as I lie down this night with thanksgiving

Blessing

May the God of Surprises who delights in giving,
meet me in those unlooked for moments
where I am taken aback by the plenty of your love.
✿ Bless this gift of a new day to me
and my questing to your generous heart.
☽ Bless this gift of night-time peace to me
and my questing to your generous heart.

THURSDAY Wholeness

On Rising/Resting
Blessed be you O God of our wassail,
who bids us be whole with shared cup of good cheer,
✡ may I drink deeply in communion with you this morning.
☽ may I drink deeply this night with thanksgiving.

Praising
Uncontainable Love,
praise to you for you cannot be held by one tribe,
but made for all.
Reveal your warm blessing to each one of us in this cold month,
and stir our hearts to see that we are more alike than different,
and that in embracing our difference,
we are made whole.
Praise to you.

In Stillness
Be still in the silence and aware of the Love with and within........

✡ Morning Invocation
Holy Reconciler,
marrying our darkness and light,
bringing sunlight to the short dark days, come wind or rain,
cleanse me with your healing grace as I set out this day.
Sprinkle healing on my roots that the wounds of my story
may be the source of my wholeness;
sprinkle healing on my head that I might be protected this day from all that
would harm;
sprinkle healing on my heart that I might see with compassion not judgment;
sprinkle healing on my words that I might be balm and not a grating presence;
sprinkle healing on my body that I might have wellbeing in health and in
diminishment;
sprinkle healing on my path that I might see for the next step
and trust that that is enough as I go forth with you this day.

✿ Opening Out

Radical Spirit
who casts aside dull winter rags,
and dances through convention in her spangled dress,
strengthen all those who stand up for those who cannot stand;
who are willing to be the lone voice crying for the voiceless;
who dare to leave the comfort of their lifestyles
for those who have no comfort to leave.
May your dance in them sparkle with prophetic courage.
I remember particularly this day

You who walked the road of costly love,
keep inspiring us to do the same.

☾ Thanksgiving

As I end this day in your safe-keeping
I count three blessings before my sleeping

☾ Night Shielding

Holder of all that is divided and broken,
as I lie down this night
shelter me as I try to hold close
all that I would reject within myself
so that I do not reject it in another unawares.
Be with all this night who have suffered prejudice
when those who refuse to look inside, attack their fears outside.

May each of us discover the healing embrace of welcome
within, with each other, and from you dear God.
Hold all that is broken this night as I lie down to sleep.

Blessing

✿ Bless me this day as I walk out under the dome of a shared sky,
☾ Bless me this night as I lie down under the starry dome of a shared sky,
cradled and nourished by you from whom all nations come,
for I cannot be whole except as all creation is blessed,
in earth and sea and sky
this day, this night and always.

FRIDAY Journeys

On Rising/Resting
Blessed be you, Keeper of our past,
Guider of our stories, Holder of our secrets.
✿ Keepsie cherisher I rise up with you this day
☾ Keepsie cherisher I rest with you this night

Praising
Shielder of Intimacies,
praise to you
for our familiar is more precious to you than it is to ourselves.
What we turn away from, wincing with shame,
you look on with tenderness.
But honourer of home and history,
you also call us forward to leave home
and journey into unchartered lands,
sometimes on the haziest of portents.

In Stillness
Be still in the silence and aware of the Love with and within.......

✿ Morning Invocation
Embodied God,
on the ladder between the home of heaven and earth's dwelling place,
the crack between the worlds,
a baby journeyed,
belonging to both.
Come embodied love to my hands that my touch might soothe;
to my ears that I might receive words of kindness;
to my belly that I might have the courage to go beyond;
to my journey that I might be aware of a purpose;
to my feet that I might always treasure the earth that supports me;
to my heart that I might live for more than myself.
Come embodied love caught between heaven and earth,
at home in both,
walk with me in my travelling this day.

☼ **Opening Out**

Pilgrim God who had nowhere to rest your head,
be with those without home who know no comfort,
and those who are not at home inside their own skin,
for whom the indoor fairy-lit season reminds of wounds,
of unrecaptured past times or times never felt.
I hold before you particularly this day

Offer us fireside moments of place or presence
where we feel the sweet glimmer of a home within.

☾ **Thanksgiving**

As I end this day in your safe-keeping
I count three blessings before my sleeping

☾ **Night Shielding**

As I lie down this night,
Spirit Weaver go before me to be my guide,
and with the gentlest fingers
untangle the old and the unfinished and weave their ends into the next step
as directions change
and the cloth feels new and strange.
Be with all who hang on in fear this night

May we know that the texture of our journey
is shot through with your mercy
Weaving Spirit, fold me in as I take my rest this night.

Blessing

May the God who hangs her star over unexpected places,
lure us to the place we need to be,
where new things must happen,
and we have to return home by another way.
☼ Bless me this day as I let go……..
let go.
☾ Bless me this night as I let go…….
let go……….
let go into your peace.

SATURDAY Wisdom

On Rising/Resting
Blessed be you Accompanier on the spiral of my way,
who drew circles on the face of the deep,
with Wisdom delightful playing beside you, around and hidden.
☼ Be nearer than my winter breath, as I rise up with you this day.
☾ Be nearer than the unlit darkness, as I take my rest with you this night.

Praising
Praise to you sparkling Mystery,
luminous yet invisible.
You absorb my downcast trudging,
and ordinary numbness,
when the cheer of spring seems a long-time coming.
Midst the dark morns and evenings and barrenness of ground,
you pierce the gloom as you refract glimmers of your unfathomable love,
radiant in the crisp invitation of dawn
and comforting in the dank of dusk at day's done.

In Stillness
Be still in the silence and aware of the Love with and within.......

☼ Morning Invocation
Like a bare black leafless tree against a moonlit sky,
your stark hope is more distinct than the mantle of the easy green spring.
Define your peculiar wintry beauty in my eyes that I might see the less
obvious signs of your love;
in my arms that I might bear those for whom this season is too harsh.
Define your wintry beauty in my legs that I may walk with trust through
darkness and light alike;
in my relaxed muscles that I might rest in the hearthy indoors, aflame with
your quiet presence;
in my groin that as I unwrap my warmly layers I might offer my hidden
affection in sweetness.
Define your wintry beauty in me as I go forth with you this day.

☼ Opening Out

Invisible God who guides with unseen hand,
leaving shadowy clues that can only be found
with the vision of a listening heart.
Be with those who cannot see beyond what they can touch,
cannot trust beyond what they can acquire
and whose hunger for wealth and power can never be fully fed.
I hold before you any of us who need your wise ways this day

Meet us with circumstance or person
that help us towards the path of true wisdom.

☾ Thanksgiving

As I end this day in your safe-keeping
I count three blessings before my sleeping

☾ Night Shielding

☼ Sophia, Source of all Wisdom,
as I lie down this quiet night, keep deep within me
an open place that I might not foreclose your wise ways
with my own limited knowing.
Be my True North and guard my faith as patterns constellate,
for though I cannot show them to another
I believe them to be the sign to move forward.
Be with all who are seeking at this time

And should we misread the traces, honour the desire to take the loving path,
for it is the desire and not the road itself , that is marked by your love,
Mark me with your love as I close my eyes this night.

Blessing

Still Place at the centre of this world's story traffic
be my Lode-Star, my direction, my way through.
Keep me steady as I travel from place to place.
☼ Bless the discerning in my journey
as I go from the safety of now to the unknown of this day.
☾ Bless the discerning in my journey
as I lay my head down in safety, trusting for the unknown tomorrow.

SUNDAY Little

On Rising/Resting
Blessed be you, more constant than the robin with breast so red,
your colour undiminished, stay with me til season's end.
✿ Constant and faithful One, I rise up with you this day.
☾ Constant and faithful One, I rest with you this night.

Praising
Praise to you.
You do not desert us for sunnier climes,
or better times or for folks more loving.
But through the dying season,
when bulbs are hid and colour scarce,
and the job of survival seems all,
you sing out your presence among us,
small and scarlet and there.

In Stillness
Be still in the silence and aware of the Love with and within.........

✿ **Morning Invocation**
Spirit of all, beyond me and within me,
in the big bleakness of winter,
and the smooth flawlessness of the glossy image,
promising new wealth and health and happiness,
come to my ears and whisper that my littleness is loved;
come to my heart that my little love is enough;
come to my head that my mind might not be overwhelmed,
come to my feet that today's steps are all that is required;
come to my eyes that I might notice the little things;
come to my tears that I might find you in the ordinary.
Come to me as I set forth in the big world this day,
Spirit of all, beyond me and within me.

✿ **Opening Out**
Creator of the tallest tree, the widest sky,
the deepest ocean, the highest mountain,

you gurgle and grasp in a baby,
miniature of nail and toe
needing the care of another.
Hear the silent cry of all who feel childlike
and small and pocket-size.
I remember particularly this day

May we know that in recognizing our fragility
we are blessed by the vast expanse of heaven.

☾ Thanksgiving

As I end this day in your safe-keeping
I count three blessings before my sleeping

☾ Night Shielding

Beloved God, your infinite care is shown in even a hazelnut,
for you love and keep all that you have made.
As I lie down this night may I remember that in
the littlest baby,
the tiniest star,
the smallest bulb,
the diminutive wren,
lies the seed of love that overturns the universe.
You raise the little ones and bring the powerful down to their true size.
Be with each I have met this day

Shelter us in the palm of your hand,
and may I trust that all will be well
as I come to rest in you, Beloved God, this night.

Blessing

Bless to me my germ of faith.
Bless to me my shortness of vision.
Bless to me my vulnerability of heart.
Bless to me my trembling of courage
and at this day's start/end cover me with your grace,
for blessing is of gift and not of might.

FEBRUARY

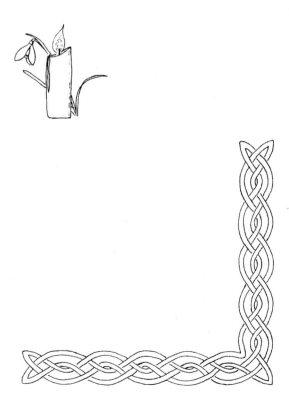

INTRODUCTION TO FEBRUARY

For many February is the bleakest month so it maybe no coincidence that it is packed with festivals. It is the last month of winter and the earth is just beginning to re-awaken. It is not so spring-like that it brightens the spirits, but snowdrops and crocuses appear at the bottom of trees reminding us that it is beginning and spring will happen. Depending on the severity of the winter, there may seem little else to see until the end of short February. However, if it is mild, daffodils and catkins arrive as March approaches and the beginning of the mating season can be spotted by the appearance of frogspawn in ponds and pools. Badgers, who do not strictly hibernate, but sleep long and stay underground during cold days, are active producing cubs in February. To see an adult would be a rare delight but it would be impossible to see the new-borns as they do not emerge from their setts until April onwards. In February then, things remain fairly hidden.

Easter is a movable feast that can never occur before March 21, or later than April 25. Ash Wednesday is forty six days before Easter Sunday and most commonly occurs in February. The prayers are therefore divided thus: Shrove Tuesday and Ash Wednesday can be found in the February prayers, the March prayers will have a Lenten theme, and Easter is prayed in the April prayers. However, depending on when Easter falls, it may be preferable to start using the March prayers before March 1, as Lent gets underway. Consequently the April ones could be started on the Sunday before Easter called Palm Sunday which is the beginning of Holy Week. This may be before April 1, and then whatever the date of Easter, returning to the May prayers on May 1.

Brigid and Imbolc (pronounced "Im-bolk" or "Ee-mulk")

On February 2, it is Brigid's day, Candlemas and Imbolc. The different strands of this day and its eve the night before, have woven together in a way that is now hard to separate. Brigid (or Bride or Brigit or Bridget) has been particularly loved in Ireland in both her forms, as goddess and as St Brigid the Christian saint. As goddess, she is the maiden aspect of the triple goddess: maid/virgin, mother and crone. The triple goddess is an archetype and energy that gives women their godliness and God her womanliness. Each aspect is celebrated in different seasons. In this season, which honours both Brigid and Mary, it is as if the opening of spring celebrates womanhood, and was celebrated particularly by women and girls, especially in Ireland.

Brigid is the Keeper of the Sacred Fire and Sacred Waters. In her saint incarnation, it is told that the church at Kildare was built on the site of a pagan temple where a sacred flame was kept alight. Brigid's nuns kept the fire burning there for another thousand years. Brigid who was born in AD 453, was feisty and generous, and her father, who despaired of her giving away his wealth, arranged for her to be married. She refused, and when she was taking the veil, it is said that an old bishop was so in awe of a ring of fire that appeared above her head, that he consecrated her as a bishop by mistake. She started an educational order of men and women. People came for healing, and her well, in Kildare, is kept as a healing place. She is associated with many things in both her guises: with learning, poetry, prophesy, healing, metal working, and friend to animals, birds and people. She is often pictured with a white cow and has associations with milk. The word Imbolc means milk or ewe's milk, which was thought to come in at this time. She was said to be the wet-nurse or mid-wife of Christ, and Imbolc is often thought of as mid-wifing the year. As provider of plenty, Brigid is also known for her green mantle spread out across Ireland. Everything given to Bridgid's hands seemed to grow. It is maybe this combining of Mother with Maid that earned her the name "Mary of the Gaels".

People in several areas and especially Ireland celebrated her by making Brigid's crosses of rushes. In the original story of the saint, she is said to have come to the bedside of a dying Celtic king and have made a cross from rushes on the floor to tell the story of the gospel. So people would make these crosses and hang them. They would also lay ribbons, like pieces of Brigid's cloak, on the windowsill, for when Brigid was meant to visit and bless on Brigid's eve. When they caught the morning dew of Brigid's Day it was said to have curative powers. These cloths were used for healing all year. Some folks made a "Brideag," which was a doll made of corn. It was often the girls and women who did this and they would lay her in a crib and welcome her with, "Bride's bed is ready, let Bride come in." In Christian places they might also add: "Preserve the house for the Trinity is welcome."

Candlemas

Another woman is also celebrated at this opening of spring. Candlemas is the feast of the Purification. The story is told in Luke 2.22-38. Mary and Joseph go with the baby Jesus to the Temple to perform the ceremony of purification. It was done forty days after the birth, which is why it is kept on February 2. Sadly, childbirth was seen to make a woman unclean, and this continued in the Christian tradition, in a ceremony called "the Churching of Women," well into the end of the last century. It is still held occasionally today. Women were not meant to receive visitors in the home directly after child-birth. Their first outing was meant to be to church for this ceremony, hence the name. The woman was then deemed clean.

This is unlike the mother aspect of the triple goddess where childbirth and the birth-giver are celebrated. The maiden aspect is also differently perceived. In the Christian tradition, sex and sin have long been associated and so virginity is seen as purity and in some way morally virtuous. For Mary to be both virgin and mother is perfect for the Christian tradition because in this way Jesus is not conceived "in sin". The maiden aspect of the goddess is seen much more in terms of ripeness and as a woman's fullness before becoming mother, which is not perceived to be unclean. The connection between childbirth and the natural world is not something that puts women lower than men, as has often been regarded, but is a cause for celebration. It is, in all senses of the word, natural.

The festival is called Candlemas because in the same story, the old prophet Simeon, full of the Holy Spirit, takes the baby Jesus in his arms and utters the words of the Nunc Dimittis, often spoken in funerals today:

"Lord, now let your servant depart in peace,
for mine eyes have seen your salvation
which you have prepared in the presence of all peoples,
a light for revelation to the Gentiles...."

- Luke 2.29-32a

So Candlemas is about Jesus being the light to all peoples. It was probably taken up as a popular festival to celebrate the returning of the light in dark February. There is a candlelit procession in church. In times gone by, people would bring their candles to church to be blessed for the year. This was believed to make the devil fly away, and they were to be taken home and could be later placed in the hands of the dying or used in storm or sickness.

At this same time, Simeon says to Mary "a sword shall pierce your own soul too." This extraordinary prophecy portends the events of the crucifixion where Mary stands at the foot of the cross on which her son has been so savagely killed. So here, in the midst of the occasion of Mary's requirement to be purified from the natural processes, the mess, blood and pain of giving birth, an old man can see what messy, bloody, painful times are ahead for a woman loving from the depths of her mother-heart.

Even in pre-Christian thought, there was a notion of purification or spring- cleaning at this time of year, as a fresh start to the activities of spring proper. As Candlemas waned in popularity in churches, it moved to homes, and candles were sometimes lit and set on sills. That too soon disappeared and the vernal equinox became a more popular time to celebrate the arrival of the springtime. However, Candlemas is celebrated in churches commonly now.

St Valentine's Day

Exactly in the middle of the month is St Valentine's day when cards are exchanged either anonymously or to partners celebrating romantic love. There were three St Valentines, and one was martyred on February 14 AD 269. There is a story that goes around that one wrote a farewell letter to his jailer's daughter, who had become his friend, and signed it "from your Valentine". However, there seems no real connection between the saint and the feast of lovers.

Shrove Tuesday and Carnival

February is the most common time for the Christian festivals of Shrove Tuesday and Ash Wednesday, the beginning of Lent. It can also fall in early March. Shrove Tuesday or Mardi Gras which means "fat Tuesday" is carnival time, carnival meaning "goodbye to meat". The last stocks of meat, eggs and cheese were eaten up before the fast of Lent, which began on Ash Wednesday. Being the winter, stocks were often low anyway and so carnival was good to release emotion. It's as if, before the discipline and order of Lent, the untamed pageantry of our unconscious souls must be let loose. Carnival costumes often contained opposites like dressing up as our shadow-selves, or the part we do not reveal. This will be explored more fully in April with All Fools, another feast of misrule. Both Lent and carnival are about looking at the un-named, which wells up within us. At carnival we let it go into the streets for a day, with feasting and play and relaxed rules, and during Lent we bring it before the loving gaze of God. Lent carnivals are more to be found in Catholic, warmer countries now.

Many households keep the tradition of eating pancakes on Shrove Tuesday. In times gone by, there were sports and pancake races and going from door to door, begging for pancakes. To shrive means "to absolve sins" and people were encouraged to go to confession so that they went into Lent with clear consciences. Once the fast of Lent arrived, people could not marry or make love. Lent occurring in spring as daylight lengthened, has always meant that both joy and abstinence have been associated at this time of year.

Ash Wednesday and Lent

The day after Shrove Tuesday is Ash Wednesday, when people traditionally go to church, as some still do today. They receive a cross on their foreheads made from the ashes of last year's palm crosses, with the words, "remember that you are dust and to dust you shall return." It remembers the time in the gospels when Jesus went into the wilderness for forty days and nights and was tempted by the Devil, directly before the three years of his public ministry. This story can be found in Matthew 4.1-11, Mark 1.12-13 and Luke 4.1-13. Ash Wednesday opens the forty days of Lent when people traditionally forego some pleasure, originally to identify with the self-discipline of Christ. He came face to face with himself. Through Lenten self-examination, we are asked to do the same during Lent and so face our own mortality. The ashes remind us that death is the great equaliser: the proud and humble stand together. As if from the dormancy of winter, both spring and our hearts are awakened to the life of God, which we came from, on which we depend, and to whom we shall return.

So the themes of February are manifold and paradoxical. We are still in the darkness, still waiting on rumours and promises of light. There is the strength of generativity in the maiden aspect of the year, seen in both Mary and Brigid. Simeon hails the arrival of the light, which we welcome after so many dark months. He also foretells the pain and darkness that comes with loving. Love itself is celebrated. Lent begins with exuberance but then drops down into the sobriety of forty days and nights of self-examination as the green emerges. It is a month of preparation for that which is to come, a month that looks forward, with hope, to the birth of Spring, but for now things remain hidden.

MONDAY Return of the Light

On Rising/Resting
Blessed be you Light of Life,
source of the sacred flame within each of us,
light which the darkness cannot put out.
☼ I rise up with you this day.
☾ I rest with you this night.

Praising
Praise to you for the crisp sunshine that lengthens our days
and bids the bulbs peep through.
Draw us closer to the warmth of your love,
as we long to emerge from the dark winter casing,
but fear the exposure to your watchful eye.
For the dark is no darkness to you,
the night as clear as the day.
Praise to you for seeing and still loving.

In Stillness
Be still in the silence and aware of the Love with and within..........

☼ Morning Invocation
Lovesmith divine,
may your fiery love purify my life with your compassion
as I set out this day.
Purify my deeds that I might act for more than myself;
purify my words that I might speak with integrity;
purify my heart that I might know your presence more;
purify my perceptions that I might distinguish between the
impurity of self-centredness and the dirt-honest job of being true to myself.
Smithy my soul in the workshop of this world
that when I pass through the fire I will not be burned,
but tempered to forge a way more loving,
by your transformation at work in me this day.

☼ Opening Out
Living One,

whose love finds us in the wintriest of times,
encircle with kindly glow those who cower in the corner
of their own misery, warm and familiar,
afraid of the brightness of change and letting go.
I remember this day particularly

Give us hope to dare to begin uncurling,
and courage to trust,
that we may be dazzled only by the light of your love,
unchanging with the season.

☾ Thanksgiving

As I end this day in your safe-keeping
I count three blessings before my sleeping

☾ Night Shielding

Spirit of peace
As I lie down this night under the mystical moon,
in this season still more dark than light,
cover me with your safety.
Let me undrape myself of the day now gone.
Help me unfold the images that remain, so I may lay them down,
and let me unfurl in the dreamy night-time,
and the letting fall of my prayer,
in the sweet repose of your eternal presence.
Cover all who need your peace this night

Spirit of peace, keep us close through thick of night
and bring us safe to morning light.

Blessing

Beloved One who gives me life and tends my growth,
keep my face turned toward the light.
As your countenance shines upon me
warm me with your blessing and draw me onwards,
☼ as I set out this day.
☾ as I rest in your comfort this night.

TUESDAY Carnival

On Rising/Resting
Blessed be you outrageous One
who turns our thinking inside-out,
rampant with grace, glorious in colour,
☼ I rise up with you this day.
☾ I rest with you into this night.

Praising
Praise to you wide awake God
who is unafraid of our shadow.
You parade in us all that we fear to show.
You party in us all that is undiscovered.
You show in us all that is unshowable
in the costumed pageant and gay procession
of all that you love at our wild and untamed centre.
Praise you for loving us more than we love ourselves.

In Stillness
Be still in the silence and aware of the Love with and within...........

☼ Morning Invocation
Maker of the living,
maker of people with bodies,
be in my enjoyment of eating as I share a table with another;
be in my enjoyment of clothes so I may delight in self-expression;
be in my enjoyment of touching that I might celebrate another's body with my fingertip;
be in my enjoyment of ritual that I might worship and find meaning;
be in my enjoyment of you that I might be filled with wonder.
Be in my enjoyment of this day as I live it down to my roots,
maker of the living,
maker of people with bodies.

☼ Opening Out
Living One present in the feast and fast of our lives,

thank you that with you, there is no waste,
no left-over strands of our stories,
that cannot be taken into the banquet of heaven.
Be with all those who feel their true colours
are uniquely toxic

May we know that the safety of your acceptance
is far broader than the danger that we feel.

☾ Thanksgiving

As I end this day in your safe-keeping
I count three blessings before my sleeping

☾ Night Shielding

Spirit in the holy solitude,
As I lie down this night,
meet me as the last melodies fade away.
The people of my day have gone home.
The carnival is over.
The harlequin trails his pipes
into the moonlit horizon,
leaving only your silence deep and still.
Protect me in my aloneness this night,
and all whom you have given to me this day

Spirit in the holy solitude,
meet me as I lie down this night.

Blessing

You are Rhythm-maker pulsing through the whole circus of creation
and Stillness at the centre.
You see behind our masks and cannot disguise your love.
✿ May your blessing be upon me as I set out this day.
☾ May your blessing be upon me as I take my rest this night

WEDNESDAY Ashes

☼ On Rising/Resting

Blessed be you Wilderness God
Pared down to the emptiness to meet yourself.
○ Christ of the desert, strengthen me as I set forth this day.
☾ Christ of the desert, strengthen me as I lie down this night.

Praising

Praise to you who knows our struggles.
Led by the Spirit before your life's work began,
you wrestled with your demons.
Accompanied only by wild beasts and angels,
you could not be beguiled.
Praise you

In Stillness

Be still in the silence and aware of the Love with and within...........

☼ Morning Invocation

Tempted in your own body, you cherish my body,
for you wove me secretly in the depths of the earth
and knit me together in my mother's womb.
You know my rising up and my sitting down and have searched out my path.
Walk with me as I continue on it this day.
Be merciful on the experience told by my scars and lined face.
Be tender with my inner wounds that show and hide themselves in my health.
Make my inward eye compassionate as I examine my heart.
Grace me with humility for it is only by your gift that I have life.
I know that I am dust and to dust I shall return, no different from any other.
Yet will you hold me in the withering of my flesh-life,
for it carries my story and bears the life that only I can live.
Help me to honour my body and soul and walk this day as if it were special.

☼ Opening Out

Holy Spirit of integrity
You are who you are and know no deceit.
Bear my shame and give me courage

when all that I love is the other side of the line,
and alone, I face foe and self, with no escape.
Be with all those who wrestle this day especially

May we know that our limp from the fight
is a blessing, a holy legacy
from seeing you face to face and surviving.

☾ Thanksgiving
As I end this day in your safe-keeping
I count three blessings before my sleeping

☾ Night Shielding
Guiding Spirit,
keep me as I lie down this night.
Be with each of us when we follow you in good faith
and find ourselves in desert places starved of goodness and comfort.
Bring courage to all I remember at this time

Protect us within and without, from creatures of the long dark night.
Send your angels to guard that we may wake in the morning
saying "Surely God was in this place and I did not know it."

Blessing
May the blessing of God,
from whom I came and to whom I shall return,
be upon me as I take each step of this sacred journey.
Remain with me this day and every day
Until you lead me into your peace dear God.

THURSDAY Joy of partner-love

On Rising/Resting
Blessed be you Intimate God.
You long for us with an unimaginable desire
☼ and I, restless for connection, rise up with you this day.
☾ and I, longing for connection, rest with you this night.

Praising
Praise to you O Love-Maker, Fire-Worker.
You made us to crave the company of another
when a thousand technicolour stars shoot in every cell of our bodies.
Praise to you O Story-Sharer.
Your faithfulness is more heartening
than old couples laughing at the same time,
or carrying bags for each other down the street.
Praise to you for making the world turn on love.

In Stillness
Be still in the silence and aware of the Love with and within............

☼ Morning Invocation
O Constant One,
you never desert me through my seasons of love.
Warm the loneliness of my solitary flesh
should I yearn for the touch of a journey-companion.
Contain me should I be in love
and ground me as my value is weighed in the delicious risk.
Be the easy knowing of another's smile should my love be long-trodden
seeing all and loving anyway.
Hold me should I feel the twisting pain of love lost,
searing and blearing across the lens of this bleak day,
starting out again like half a person.
O Constant One you never desert me,
give me grace to love well this day.

☼ Opening Out
Lonely God who aches for us,

and mourns when we turn away,
be with those who suffer rejection this day,
those who long for the lover that will never return,
and those who searched for, but never found one to share the world with

Earth the heat of our desire in your love this day.
Absorb the nothing doing, no-one else, no-where to put it, energy
that throws itself against an empty sky and yearns for boundary.

☾ Thanksgiving
As I end this day in your safe-keeping
I count three blessings before my sleeping

☾ Night Shielding
✿ Capricious Spirit
who blows where you will.
Your recklessness in the partnering dance
reminds me that love is gift and there is no protection.
Yet still I must take the risk
for I am born hungry and open to wounding.
Be with all those who need your comfort this night

Capricious Spirit, show us your mercy.
Give me rest as I close my eyes this night.

Blessing
God of all love,
who folds into yourself all my pain,
bless to me your way of love each day and each night.
Bless to me the height, length, breadth and depth of your love
that I can never be separated from and will be all I know at my end.

FRIDAY Brigid

On Rising/Resting
Blessed be you Divine Presence,
Provider of plenty, earthed in wisdom and courage.
☼ Come to me with open hand and open heart as I wake up this morning.
☾ Come to me with open hand and open heart as I lie down this night.

Praising
Praise to you O Caring one,
nurturing, generous and milky kind,
yet defiant as the snowdrop in a cold climate,
feisty, pure and natural
with your white singular unbroken focus,
Maid-Mother to us all,
praise to you.

In Stillness
Be still in the silence and aware of the Love with and within............

☼ Morning Invocation
Healing Spirit,
midwife of my newness and growth,
tend the fresh shoots of my emerging as I set foot this day.
Heal my birthing soul when I pass through ring of fire and broken waters
on my journey through this world.
Fuse my backbone mettle with your courage
as I stand firm against all that is unjust.
Craft my words that they might meld heart and mind
and mend with fiery precision.
Befriend my creaturely ways that I might be friend to all your creatures who
share our precious planet.
Create in me a prophetic eye that I might see the new thing that you are doing
this day and have vision for tomorrow.
Healing Spirit, be with me as I walk this new day.

☼ Opening Out
I lament with you this day

the poisioning of the rivers, the cutting down of forests,
the culling and cruelty towards animals,
the irreverent use of creation's resources,
the unthinkable treatment of children and the vulnerable.
I lay before you my own dishonouring
of the family of your making, to which I belong

Before you my God I say that I am sorry.
Forgive me and help me to cherish and care for all that you have given us
and on which we depend.

☾ Thanksgiving

As I end this day in your safe-keeping
I count three blessings before my sleeping

☾ Night Shielding

Spirit of greening,
spread your mantle over me as I lie down this night.
As a mother could not forget her young,
come by with your blessing on me and all whom you have given this day.

Bring healing with the morning dew
and nourish us with creamy instinctive goodness
that I may grow stronger in you, my Creator, with each passing day.

Blessing

Bless the ancient bark and the early blossomed branches.
Bless the purple-sheathed crocus beneath.
Bless the birds that sing to us in this wintermost season.
Bless the creatures that the eye cannot see.
Bless the peoples and tribe of every nation.
Bless the sun, moon and planets beyond our circle.
Bless the seas, skies and land of our home planet
   ✿ as I set foot on the shared earth this day,
   ☾ as I take my rest under the same sky this night,
for you have the whole universe in your hand.

SATURDAY Hope

On Rising/Resting
Blessed be you O Living One,
for here, in this place, you are present with me now.
✿ Though the dark is cold and uninviting, I wake in your love this day.
☾ Though the dark is cold and uninviting, I lie down in your love this night.

Praising
Collected in quiet I come to you.
My twilight spirit enters slowly.
In the stillness,
in the silence,
you look on me and love
and say it is enough.
To be here,
at this moment,
is enough.

In Stillness
Be still in the silence and aware of the Love with and within.........

✿ Morning Invocation
Re-awakener of the earth,
by bright celandine and charm of catkin,
your promise is there to be seen, this day,
reminding me that your Spirit is always generating.
Even in the desertscape days when I cannot feel the juice of your presence,
be the inhale and exhale of my breath,
the rhythm of the present moment.
Be in the sole of my foot and palm of my hand as I touch the world today.
Midst the off-colour drudge and drear,
the virus and infection,
be the care that creates the world and renews in apparent barrenness.
For I know that buds will burst from their hard shell,
and spring will follow winter,
and so may I know your unseen hand, in the fact of this day as I set forth.

☼ Opening Out

O Divine Presence,
as the last dregs of winter pall and weary,
be with all those who are only just keeping their faith alive,
those whose hope has run dry,
and those who have fallen into despair

Give them tangible signs to believe again in things invisible.
And when all seems grey and our spirits are parched,
may we find droplets that lead to the source
of your thirst quenching love.

☾ Thanksgiving

As I end this day in your safe-keeping
I count three blessings before my sleeping

☾ Night Shielding

Spirit of comfort, seal this day to its rest.
Cradle me this night and at my days' end.
Unclothe me of my worries,
Unburden me of my regrets,
Unencumber me now, for I am weary.
Let me lay down my troubles
and lay before you those whom I have met this day

Enfold them into your safe-keeping.
Night has fallen now.
What is done is done.
Let it be.
Spirit of comfort, bless to me my sleep this night.

Blessing

May your blessing be upon me,
in frailty and uncertainty,
in dullness and dormancy.
Cast me not away from your presence
and create in me a hopeful heart even in the most ordinary of days,
for your love brings new life out of death.

SUNDAY Candlemas

On Rising/Resting
Blessed be you, long awaited One,
light that scatters the darkness of the world.
✿ Lighten my path as I rise up this day.
☾ Lighten my path as I lie down this night.

Praising
Praise to you O Hope-bringer,
dream of newness, alive and before me now,
dawning into my ordinariness and routine,
the prophetic moment
when I see and understand what my life might be about,
and I take it into my arms,
and hold it close to myself,
and say "praise to you".

In Stillness
Be still in the silence and aware of the Love with and within.............

✿ Morning Invocation
Substance of our faith, lit in recognition,
reveal yourself to me this day.
Stop my feet in their daily tracks
that I might not miss today in some vague hope of tomorrow.
Unfold my prayer to wisdom
that I might discern love's purpose in the events of this day.
Open my eyes to see your presence in another human life.
Deepen my mystical eye that I might know those revelatory moments.
Unclasp my hands from their holding on
and teach me to let go into your peace.
Substance of our faith, reveal yourself to me
and teach me to let go into your peace, as I set forth this day.

✿ Opening Out
O Living One,
you do not hover above me undefiled

but enter the world that is charged with the mess and pain of living.
Be with all those known to me this day whose loved ones are suffering,
as they watch and wait,
helpless in the non-negotiable contract of love

Even as their hearts are pierced,
may your Spirit bear their grief and hold them in their sorrow.

☾ Thanksgiving

As I end this day in your safe-keeping
I count three blessings before my sleeping

☾ Night Shielding

Spirit who leads me to my heart's desire,
content me as I rest this night.
For when my body returns to dust
and my life to the love from which it came,
let me depart in peace as I depart this day,
knowing that I have beheld you.
Be with all whom you have given to me this day

Spirit content us as we take our rest
and let me wake, morning by morning, changed from knowing you.

Blessing

As the old brown face etched with experience,
encountered the baby new plumpness, the ancient of days,
may your face shine upon me and give me your blessing.
✿ Grant that I would live my life loving well as I would this day,
☾ Grant that I would live my life loving well as I have spent this day,
until I rest in the light of your countenance at journey's end.

MARCH

INTRODUCTION TO MARCH

Easter can be on any Sunday between March 21 and April 25. As it is therefore more likely to fall in April, Easter is described in the Introduction to April and the Easter prayers are in April. If it is in March in the year you are using this book, please start the April prayers on Palm Sunday.

"March comes in like a lion and goes out like a lamb", it is said traditionally in our isles. It comes in with the darkness left over from February but after the spring or vernal equinox on March 21, the light feels as if it truly is returning. The weather in March is unpredictable. It can be sunny and warm, windy, rainy with early April showers and snow can appear. March is traditionally associated with winds, hence the adage: "March winds, April showers, bring forth May flowers".

In Scotland, there is the variation "March comes in with adders' heads and goes out with peacock tails" drawing attention to the awakening adder and the mating ritual of the peacock. March sees a much more evident re-emerging of mammals from hibernation. It is the mating season for many creatures. Lambing starts, and other animals and insects begin to give birth. The famed, but not often seen, "mad March" hares appear to box in their mating ritual. The first butterflies can be spotted. The first migrant birds return from their travels to the sun. Birdsong can be heard in much fuller voice and the mating call which we know as the dawn chorus, at dawn and dusk, once again brightens our waking and resting spirits. Flowers continue to emerge. Much-loved daffodils spring up in abundance. Pussy willow, catkins, forsythia, blackthorn (sloe) and other blossom appear on the trees. Violets and primroses break through at our feet. The earth is waking up.

Spring Equinox

The spring equinox, on March 21, thought of as the first day of spring, matches the autumn equinox on the other side of the wheel and is the time when the day and night are of equal length. Before electric lighting, households could go to bed at dark and wake in the light for the first time. In some homes, there was a ritual where the maid would hand over a candle to the mistress, symbolic of the light that had lit the home in the evenings since the autumn equinox. Spring is visualized as a maiden because of the associations with fertility. The Pagan tradition celebrates her union with the young ardent man as nature springs to life.

In most years, Lent will extend through much of March. Lent which means spring, may well have derived from the word "lengthen". Everything is increasing but stocks after winter were low in agrarian communities. For some, ploughing began and fields were sown. In our culture, spring planting begins. So this period of growth, preparing and hard work fitted with the idea of abstinence during Lent. As noted earlier, fighting and sexual intercourse were prohibited in older times. This is no longer the case even for those who keep Lent. Other customs survive. To this day, churches that observe the sacramental aspects of Christianity veil the statues, often with purple, which is the colour of Lent, during the last week of Lent and Holy Week. No cut flowers are displayed in churches during Lent. Today it is interesting to note that non-religious people often still give up something in Lent and eat pancakes on Shrove Tuesday. Christians try to practise a deeper spiritual awareness during the five weeks of Lent.

Lent

If the gift of the Celtic tradition is its breadth of spirituality, seeing God and spirit in all created things, the gift of mystical Christianity is its depth. This is seen no more clearly than in the inner pilgrimage that Christians undertake throughout Lent, which mostly dominates March. To the outside eye, Lent is a time of giving up luxuries and exercising self-discipline. With the eye of faith it is a focussed and time-limited journey of spiritual "spring-cleaning," where the pilgrim turns to God and allows God to look on all that s/he surveys within. This is evoked in the beautiful Psalm 51 recited on Ash Wednesday:

"Have mercy on me, O God,
according to your steadfast love;
according to your abundant mercy
blot out my transgressions.
Wash me thoroughly from my iniquity......
You desire truth in my inward being
Therefore teach me wisdom in my secret heart.
Purge me with hyssop and I shall be clean.......
Create in me a clean heart, O God,
And put a new and right spirit within me,
Do not cast me away from your presence,
And do not take your holy spirit from me.........
A broken and contrite heart, O God you will not despise."

This "truth in our inward being" is balanced by the knowledge that the climax of Holy Week and Easter, at the end of Lent, turns us outward to the reality of our world and of God's action in it. So our self-exploration is always in the context of the world and of our God. Of course, this searching for God and allowing God to search us does not end on Easter Day, but particular times of intensity can be helpful, as few can maintain that all the year round.

Saint David and Saint Patrick

In March we celebrate two of our favourite Celtic saints, David and Patrick. Both are honoured even to this day. Both Patrick and David were renowned for their missions converting the pagans to Christianity. Of David, the patron saint of Wales, whose day falls on March 1, facts are scarce. He is famous for saying "do the little things." He lived a frugal and simple life and is sometimes called "the Water Drinker" because he drank so much of it. He would also stand in a cold lake reciting Scripture as a self-imposed penance. He died in AD 589. Patrick, also born in Wales, but the patron saint of Ireland, is celebrated on March 17, the day he died in AD 461. Brought up a pagan he converted to Christianity. He travelled throughout Ireland, establishing monasteries, schools and churches across the country.

Much Irish folklore surrounds St. Patrick's Day. One traditional symbol of the day is the shamrock. This stems from a more likely Irish tale that tells how Patrick used the three-leafed shamrock to explain the Trinity: how the Father, the Son, and the Holy Spirit could all exist as separate elements of the same entity. His followers adopted the custom of wearing a shamrock on his feast day. Even now, his lorica, or breast plate, remains one of the best-loved prayers in the English language:

"I bind unto myself the name,
the strong name of the Trinity,
the Three in One and One in Three.
I arise today
through God's strength to pilot me,
God's eye to look before me,
God's wisdom to guide me,
God's way to lie before me,
God's shield to protect me…….."

Lady Day and Mothering Sunday

On March 25, there is a festival which has traditionally been called Lady Day. It is the day when the church remembers the Annunciation of the angel to Mary. It is nine months before Christmas and recalls the accepting by an ordinary girl of the revelation of God in her life, when she was told she would give birth to Jesus. Not unrelated, is Mothering Sunday around this time. This may have originated from people in village churches flocking to their mother church or cathedral. It is also linked to a later time, when children were sent away from home to work. On the middle Sunday of Lent, sometimes known as Refreshment Sunday, because the Lenten discipline was relaxed on that day, they came home to see their mothers bringing with them a simnel cake. These sometimes had little marzipan eggs on the top representing the number of weeks that the child had been away from home. Flowers were also given and posies are still given out in churches today.

So the themes of March are about the Lenten interior journey as the earth re-awakens. Our spiritual lives can never be separated from the way we live. Just as there is balance in dark and light at the equinox, there is balance in our outer and inner lives. In the Christian mystical tradition, the desert mothers and fathers of the fourth century, knew that the longer time alone in their cell or in the desert, like the desert of the Lenten journey, the more they would face both their inner demons and their difficulties in community. Patrick and David both had a robust and simple spirituality wonderfully grounded in the stuff of life. Our inner lives are played out in the complex and messy world of our outer lives just like the task of mothering which we reflect on towards the end of the month.

MONDAY Balance

On Rising/Resting
Blessed be you Boundary-Crosser,
for breaking through the hard surfaces
for coming in the quiet like the birdsong,
on the edge of night and day.
✿ I wake into this day with you.
☾ I lie down to sleep resting in you.

Praising
Praise to you O God of Joy,
reclaiming the colourless places
with daffodil humour, playful and bold.
Praise to you O Forever One,
for being there
even before the blossom appears.
Praise to you

In Stillness
Be still in the silence and aware of the Love with and within........

✿ Morning Invocation
O Sacred Balance, poised at true,
in this season when night and day are equal,
by moonlight and sunlight,
come with your holy searchlight
as I survey the different calls on my life.
Be in my discernment of time as I go between world and home today.
Help me to discover my need
for busyness and rest,
for solitude and togetherness,
for self and other.
Be the deep well within me
fluidly moving between discipline and mercy,
that I might live in the ebb and flow of your rhythms
knowing that there is a time for all things.
Make me steady in my day as I set forth this morning.

✿ Opening Out

Peace-giver,
who delights in the uniqueness of every different life,
help us to find the sure contentment
of right relations with ourselves,
with each other and with you dear God.
Give wisdom and support to those who struggle to balance their lives

May we make the changes we need
and release us from the guilt that prevents us breaking through
the hard surfaces of our previous choices.

☾ Thanksgiving

As I end this day in your safe-keeping
I count three blessings before my sleeping

☾ Night Shielding

Still-point at the centre,
draw all my day's work into yourself.
Take from me all my doing,
and all that cannot be changed now,
so I may lay it down, and let go into your calm.
Give peace to all the burdened whom I have met this day

Still-point at the centre, help us to rest in you.
Let me sleep trustfully in your care, as I lie down this night.

Blessing

Ever-creating Maker,
budding newness on old trees.
Bless to me my growth in you.
Bless those in such change at this time,
that past and future are out of kilter
and equilibrium is not for now.
Bless to each of us a strength at core,
that holds in darkness and light because it returns to you.

TUESDAY No short cuts

On Rising/Resting
Blessed be you Innermost God, outside,
in the wide-open wilderness with no walls.
☼ Walk with me in my poverty this day.
☾ Cover me as I take my rest this night.

Praising
Praise to you who knows our harsh times,
when the universe withdraws its friendliness,
and we are thrown back on our own resources.
For whether we feel your absence or presence
there can be no pretence.
Praise to you who bears our "how long?"

In Stillness
Be still in the silence and aware of the Love with and within……..

☼ Morning Invocation
Deep down and darkly down, there you are,
there in the core where the world turns,
here in my marrow where no-one sees.
May I feel your touch in my flesh,
especially when I seem to have no skin.
May I feel your strength in my muscle,
especially when I seem to have no fight.
May I feel you down to my bones,
when I can come no other way.
Go beyond my bones when all has run dry.
May you remain there at the seat of my deepest desire,
present when I have forgotten my passion.
Be my comfort and my stay as I move through the world this day.

☼ Opening Out
O Vulnerable One who hears our silent cry,
be with each person this day who is wandering their own lonely desert.
Encircle with your love

those who know there are no short-cuts,
who cannot go round but must go through

Thank you that we do not get to the garden,
until we have travelled through this featureless barren terrain.
For this is not a detour for the unlucky,
but the touching bottom of being alive,
where we must reckon with what is.

☾ Thanksgiving
As I end this day in your safe-keeping
I count three blessings before my sleeping

☾ Night Shielding
Courageous Spirit,
who leads us past the threshold where we dare not tread,
contain me as I lie down this black night.
Protect me as I am taken to places
where I must push out the limits of my soul
to make a bigger space.
Be with all on my mind at this time

Forge new courage in us that will never leave
because we have met our foe.
Spirit contain me as I lie down this night.

Blessing
When all seems hollow bless me.
When all seems broken bless me.
When you seem like a mirage bless me.
When I know you are not there bless me.
When I do not care if you are, bless me.
Take my unkempt face in your hands,
smudged and grimy from the road
and stroke your blessing into my features,
for you will never turn away a broken spirit.

WEDNESDAY Do the Little Things

On Rising/Resting
Blessed be you, O Simple One
whose heart is with the little ones,
with the voiceless and marginal,
in the tiny honest violet.
✿ Help me keep it simple this day.
☾ I lie down in the peace of your simplicity this night.

Praising
Praise to you O Living One,
who does not hold on to power,
but gives it to us to choose.
Help us to pay attention to every little thing we do,
that even a cup of water given,
or jar of pussy-willow set on table,
will sing of your care for us.

In Stillness
Be still in the silence and aware of the Love with and within............

✿ Morning Invocation
Ordinary God bringing heaven in the detail,
by weather forecast and pip,
by kettle boil,
by sound of washing on,
by pattern of seat on bus,
by lingering a moment with colleague,
by reflection of self in charity shop window,
by kind word said at check-out,
by smile at unexpected mail,
by over-cooked ready-meal,
by mild amusement in flicker of tv screen,
by pleasing smell of new soap,
your living presence is with us
as we do the little things we do this day.

☼ Opening Out

By writing in the sand,
by morning walk of solitude,
by welcome of children,
by receiving the gifts of women without causing shame,
by breakfast on the beach for friends,
your great love is shown in the small ways among us.
Be with all those who feel they have nothing to give

Give each of us the grace to attend to the little things.
And may I be big enough to allow another's presence
to anoint my brokenness this day.

☾ Thanksgiving

As I end this day in your safe-keeping
I count three blessings before my sleeping

☾ Night Shielding

Spirit of Holiness, make your mark in me daily,
for when I lay me down to die
they will know me not by the big things
I never did to change the world.
It will be my belongings, my quirks
and one-off acts of foolishness that will make them weep.
Be with all those I love this night

Spirit let us be unafraid to make our mark in ordinary,
little by little, for Love's sake, as I take my rest this night.

Blessing

May the blessing of our day-in, day-out God be upon me.
Grant me a little love, a little shelter, a little bread.
Teach me to so honour what you have given,
that I need not hold on to it,
but give it away trusting that your faithfulness will provide again
morning by morning.

THURSDAY Spring Clean

On Rising/Resting
Blessed be you O Springtime God,
re-awakening our senses to your freshness
between sunrise and sunset.
✿ I wake up to your creation this morning.
☾ I go to sleep in your peace this night.

Praising
Praise to you who shines
in the corners we would rather hide,
and reveals the dusty webs
of moments and feelings we have spun together,
and tried to leave behind,
fragile and neglected.
Praise to you for knowing
when we are ready to look.

In Stillness
Be still in the silence and aware of the Love with and within.........

✿ Morning Invocation
Lure of all our longing
draw us on our inner pilgrimage.
As the soil on land is ploughed and sowed,
prepare the ground of my being to do the soul-work.
Prepare my feet to walk the untrodden paths.
Prepare my hands to receive the unexpected.
Prepare my face to withstand whatever the weather.
Prepare my shoulders to offer strength to fellow-traveller.
Prepare my desire to sift my dreams.
Prepare my resolve to shift the shapes that I put in the way.
Prepare my discernment to see what is no longer needed.
Prepare my back to relax as you carry my load.
Walk beside me and lure me deeper into you as I set out this day.

✿ Opening Out

Great Sower of the seeds of love,
make my prayer receptive
that they might bed deep in my weakness
lest I hurt another.
Be with all this day who are victims
of those who refuse to look
as they scatter their seeds of destruction

Be with those blind to their damage because they were victims too.
Reveal the web of moments and feelings
they have spun together, left behind and met on another soul.
Have mercy on each one of us this day.

☾ Thanksgiving

As I end this day in your safe-keeping
I count three blessings before my sleeping

☾ Night Shielding

Spirit who cleans my heart,
Help me put my house in order this spring
as I rest from my outward journey tonight.
Though my homestead will always be in need of repair,
may it become simply furnished and loved
because it is your dwelling place.
Protect all whom I have met this day.

Give us your peace as we lie down this night.

Blessing

Lure of all our longing,
as I travel another step closer,
make me ready for your homecoming embrace
when I enter your sanctuary
footsore and hungry for the supper you have already waiting.
✿ Bless me on my way as I follow my journey's course this day.
☾ Bless me on my way as I take my rest this night.

FRIDAY Lorica of Early Spring

On Rising/Resting
Blessed be you my Shelter and Safety
✿ I arise this day
☾ I lie down this night
with amulet of love deep within
and talisman of truth as my strength

Praising
Praise to you who charms away my fears
by never abandoning me on my path.
You hold back the branches for me
and make my way clear.
You catch me when I stumble
and show me the wonders of your creation.
Praise to you.

In Stillness
Be still in the silence and aware of the Love with and within..........

✿ Morning Invocation
I gather to myself this day,
the care of nesting bird with grass in beak,
the playfulness of boxing hare,
the encased promise of bud on tree,
the gladness of blossom as it bursts free,
the hope of brightening sun after grey,
the mystery of moon that sanctifies by night,
the balance of equinox within and without,
the joy of dawn chorus that wakens with light,
the freshness of scent on shrub and bough,
the fecundity of frogspawn, in stream and pond,
the confidence of daffodils jubilant abound,
the wind of your Spirit blowing over the hills,
the trust in your providence that creates and renews,
I gather to myself this day.

✡ Opening Out

Protecting Spirit I invoke you
as I step forth in the world this day
and offer you whatever falls across my trail.
Be with each person whose journey's surprises
causes sorrow at this time

May we arise in the strength of your faithful presence
however faltering our foot.

☾ Thanksgiving

As I end this day in your safe-keeping
I count three blessings before my sleeping

☾ Night Shielding

I gather to myself this night
The containing of God to hold the broken,
God's ear to listen to my story,
God's smile at my head-down folly,
God's wing to shelter when I come home,
God's joy to see me however far I've roamed,
God's hand to wipe my tear from eye,
God's dream of peace as I lie down.
The angels of heaven to be my guard
I gather to myself your own.

Blessing

✡ I lift up my eyes to the newness of this day and ask for
Blessing of God to keep my life
Blessing of God to keep me from harm
Blessing as I pass across doorstep
Blessing as I return under lintel
☾ I close my eyes in the oldness of your love this night
and ask for your blessing to keep me til mine end.

SATURDAY Living the Questions

On Rising/Resting
Blessed be you Action of love in stillness
and Contemplative heart amidst activity.
✿ May my action this day be for love's purpose.
☾ May I contemplate your love in the silence of this night.

Praising
Praise to you O Desert God,
who knows that alone, I meet my struggle with others
and in the messiness of my peopled days
I cannot escape the stark ways I have failed to mend my singular life.
Praise to you O Desert God
for holding up a mirror to my inward and outward ways
and never leaving me to face myself alone.

In Stillness
Be still in the silence and aware of the Love with and within.......

✿ Morning Invocation
As I set forth this Lenten day wrestling with conflicts within,
Inspirit my flesh with your courage, that I might live the questions,
flesh that inhabits,
flesh that touches,
flesh that makes and creates,
flesh that is mucked in with others,
flesh that is unwell,
flesh that is graced with good health,
flesh that is active,
flesh that stays still,
flesh that stores my body-memory,
flesh that could tell the story so far.
Help me to love my flesh with all its contradictions
and know that it is only by living that I make my mistakes
and only by grappling with my mistakes that I discover how to live.
Give me wisdom as I tussle with the stuff of life this day.

✡ Opening Out

O Divine One, whose sole purpose is love,
tune my attention to a simple mindfulness
and let the distractions fall away,
that I might walk this day with thankfulness for every step.
Be with each of us when we become overwhelmed
by our own making or because of our situation
or we cannot tell the difference.

Give us faith that the unfolding of your love each day
is the goal of the journey.

☾ Thanksgiving

As I end this day in your safe-keeping
I count three blessings before my sleeping

☾ Night Shielding

O Sacred Mystery,
let me surrender my need to know this night.
Gratitude when I trust you enough to have no answers.
Gratitude when I allow the work to teach the work
and not seek the end before I have started.
Be with all who are on my mind as I take my rest this night

Give us the grace to feel that however far-off our dreams,
today it was good to be alive.
Sacred Mystery enfold me in this present moment
as I close my eyes to sleep this night.

Blessing

May the blessing of God be upon my head
with warm "well-done. I delight in you."
As I continue on my quest,
may I not be haunted by my unlived life
but blessed by you, the goodness of other people
and your world, that takes my breath away,
and shows me my place in the universe.

SUNDAY Mothering

On Rising/Resting
Blessed be you Mother-Labourer of all,
brooding and opening yourself to suffering,
as when the chaos-waters broke,
and you birthed all creation from nothing.
✪ I rise with you this day my Maker.
☾ I rest with you this night my Maker.

Praising
Praise to you O Sacred Source,
your generativity rises and falls with every wave
as the life-stream pours out with watery rhythm.
From ocean pulse and on and on you love each of us into being,
and carry us into the swim of all who went before
and into the river that will flow with our children
and our children's children
and will return to the Source.

In Stillness
Be still in the silence and aware of the Love with and within........

✪ Morning Invocation
Bearer of all, bent over the world,
Toiling and tending, watching and weeping,
surround me by your Spirit, as I was once held,
in the dark waters of another's body.
Once carried and bathed, rocked and dandled
be with me as I walk this day's road like a grown-up.
Cherish my specialness as I make my way in the crowd.
Be the natural love grounding my body
because I am made in the image of you.
Be the tender gaze that sees all I do
and cannot stop loving even when I need to learn.
Be as a lioness, protectress, still but ready
for when my untamed wandering would meet with harm.
I set out in the memory and desire of your care this day.

✿ Opening Out

Mother of all, you see the heart
of those who long to come running with posies
and feel the security of a womb-grown love.
Listen to the unheard cry of those
whose mothers could not be there for them
and those whose mothers leave loving print on all they do
but who now rest in the eternal arms

In the pain of missing what never has been or can be no longer,
give us mercy to let them go into your fathomless abiding love.

☾ Thanksgiving

As I end this day in your safe-keeping
I count three blessings before my sleeping

☾ Night Shielding

As I lie down this and every night,
may I discover your Mother-blessings
in the circle of friends that surround me.
May they hold me when I need protection
and give me space at centre to fly.
Be with all those precious to me this night

Deepen our healing down root and into wing
in each of those you have given me to grow with.

Blessing

May Mother God above me
bless me with a child-like trust, simple and true.
May Grandmother Spirit smiling within me
bless me with an old wise love that has put away childish grasp.
May Mother Earth beneath me
bless me with awe and wonder at her gifts around me
✿ as if seeing with the eyes of a child this day.
☾ as I lie down with the faith of a child this night.

APRIL

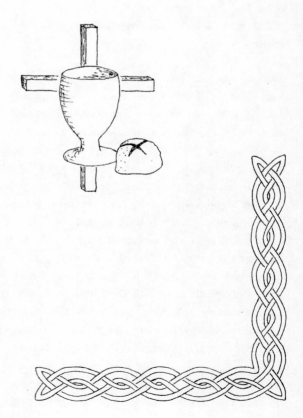

INTRODUCTION TO APRIL

The spring more evidently gets underway in glorious April. British Summer Time means longer light evenings. April showers are often broken with sunshine. Insects and mammals emerge. Badgers, hedgehogs and moles, or their activity, can be spotted. The ponds and streams are teeming with tadpoles and also newts, stickleback and minnows. All kinds of flowers begin to bloom including cowslips and primroses, and at the end of the month the bluebells carpet the woods. The resident birds are caring for their first brood of the year. The migrant ones return from Africa, like the swallows, house martins, swifts and the willow-warblers and chiff-chaffs. Most famously in April, the cuckoo returns and people claim how early they have heard the first cuckoo in spring. It is not usually much before April 25. The cuckoo is also associated with being foolish because it lays its eggs in other birds' nests and the young cuckoo evicts the other eggs from their own nest. April Fool's Day is celebrated on the first of the month. The natural world heralds the Christian festival of Easter as Christ's rising from the dead is remembered, and new life is celebrated.

Spring and Oestre

Easter can fall in late March, though it is commonly in April, up until April 25. This is because since the eighth century in the British Isles, it was decided that Easter should be on the Sunday after the first full moon following the Vernal Equinox (March 21). The word Easter is not a Christian word but the Christian festival was overlaid on a much older rite of spring. Easter is named after Oestre, the goddess of light and spring. She was a Germanic dawn deity and the Anglo-Saxon phrase "estor-monath" means season of opening and new beginnings. Oestre is sometimes pictured with a willow basket of eggs. Long before eggs were associated with the Christian festival of Easter, eggs were seen as a symbol of new life and were exchanged. Oestre's symbol is a hare, which perhaps evolved into the much-loved Easter bunny. Hot-cross buns, traditionally eaten on Good Friday, originally represented the moon and its four quarters. In Scotland particularly, the moon was venerated in April but the early Christians re-interpreted it as the cross. April was another time for fertility rituals and asking the gods for good harvests.

Easter

Like the pre-Christian festival, the Christian festival of Easter is associated with delight, relief and optimism. Eggs would be dyed in bright colours and rolled down hills. There were numerous sports and fairs in the Easter holidays. In Ireland and Scotland, people gathered on the hills at dawn because the morning sun danced for joy at the resurrection of Christ. Christians still celebrate Easter atop of hills as the dawn breaks on Easter morning. It is also a tradition for people to wear new clothes. Undoubtedly this was in a spirit of celebration but it may have had a more religious origin. Easter was the traditional time for people to be baptized. In the early church it was adults that were baptized. They would be fully immersed in the waters of the baptistry in the church. They would walk in naked, and be dressed in new white robes as they emerged from the water in the first light of dawn on Easter morning. This symbolized being cleansed and clothed in Christ. Baptisms and renewal of baptismal vows still take place in the Easter Vigil today (see below).

Easter is the supreme festival for the Christian. It starts on Palm Sunday, the Sunday before Easter, and opens Holy Week. The drama of the first Easter is played out in the services on Maundy Thursday, Good Friday and Easter Sunday. Seen without faith, it is the story of a good and innocent man being unfairly tried by the state, tortured and killed. History is strewn with the early deaths of people whose lives shone a light that the darkness of the world chose to put out. For a Christian, this radical price of love is the central message of Christianity. However, Christ's rising from the dead would be part of the story as well. Even for those who find that nature is their "text" or Book of Life, rather than the Bible, the cycle of birth-death-re-birth is the pre-dominant metaphor for their spirituality.

The Christian story is that God forgives us by Christ dying on the cross and rising to new life and so opening up a new relationship between ourselves and God. However, it depends on what tradition within Christianity a believer would understand this. Certainly, all would hold that God in Christ, meets us in the most wretched of circumstances. It is one of the most extraordinary and profound things about being human that people hang on to some kind of faith amidst terrible times, enabling them to get through it and be changed by it. This is why the events remembered in Holy Week and Easter also have a universal quality. All human life is there – betrayal, denial, grief, injustice, suffering, love and forgiveness. All of it could just as easily happen now as then.

The story is recorded in all four Gospels: Matthew 21 and 26 onwards, Mark 11 and 14 onwards, Luke 19 and 22 onwards, John 12 onwards. This introduction is one of the longest in order to describe the events of Easter for those who are not aware of them. However, much of the impact of the story is in the detail, and reading one of the gospel accounts, which would last as long as a mug of tea, may serve better than the following potted version. After telling the story, some of the rituals are also described. In the Christian tradition there are the more sacramental churches and more word-based churches. The sacramental ones for example, Eastern Orthodox, Roman Catholic and "high" Anglican churches are those who express their faith more through rituals and symbols. The word-based ones, including the Non-conformist churches like Methodist, United Reformed, Presbyterian, Baptist, Evangelical, Pentecostal, and "low" Anglican churches, express their faith more through expounding the Bible. In the sacramental churches, Holy Week is a true spectacle, and what can be seen today is either little changed or revived from the early established church.

Palm Sunday

Holy Week starts on Palm Sunday. This is the day when Jesus weeps over Jerusalem and then enters it on a donkey. A donkey showed that he came not as a warrior on a charger but as a person of peace on a lowly animal. He is greeted by the crowd, who wave palm branches. They hail him as being of God and shout "hosanna." Only weeks later, they will be baying for his blood with shouts of "crucify him." This day is kept in some churches with an outside procession where people carry big palm leaves and sing hymns, sometimes there is even a donkey. This is the service where palm crosses are distributed.

The famous story is recorded in some of the gospels that it was when Jesus got to the Temple in Jerusalem that he overturned the money-changers' tables. He drove them out, and those selling cattle, sheep and doves with the words " my house shall be called a house of prayer but you have made it a den of thieves." This dramatic story shows Jesus to be angry and is remembered in Holy Week.

Maundy Thursday

The next main service is on Maundy Thursday. The word "maundy" could refer to the maunds or baskets in which gifts were given to the poor. This was traditional on Maundy Thursday and is still represented by the Queen giving her Maundy money out to pensioners to this day. In Britain, this tradition of giving to the poor is said to have originated with St. Augustine in AD 597 and has been performed by the monarch since the days of Edward II. Up until the eighteenth century they also used to wash the feet of the recipients as Christ did at the Last Supper. As well as the leader serving, there was more general almsgiving on this day as well. The other meaning of maundy is from mandatum, which means commandment. After Jesus had washed the disciples' feet, he gave them a new commandment that they should love one another.

Jesus went to Jerusalem for the Jewish festival of Passover. On Maundy Thursday, we remember that after the Passover meal, his last supper with his male friends, he takes the bread and wine and shares it among them in a ritual that they do not understand. He says that it is like his body which is to be broken and his blood which is to be shed and asks them to remember him whenever they eat these staples of bread and wine. The Church later takes this on in the service called Holy Communion or the Eucharist.

Jesus then takes a towel and bowl and washes their feet. The humility of this act is heightened by the poignancy of his knowing he would no longer be with them before the night was out. He declares that one of them will betray him. Peter protests that it will not be him and Jesus says that he will deny him three times before the morning comes. Judas, still intent on his actions and caught in the web of deceit he has spun himself, "goes out. And it was night" (John 13.30).

In church this is remembered by a ceremony of washing feet, and reserving the Sacrament (which means putting some bread and wine in the tabernacle, a tiny cupboard, after communion). There then follows a simple but powerful ceremony called the Stripping of the Altar. The congregation remain seated whilst the clergy remove all the decorations, linen or candles from the chancel (area where the altar is). It is done in silence and with low-lighting until the chancel is bare. It takes about five minutes. The congregation stay to "keep watch" and leave in silence and alone.

Good Friday

Good Friday, which used to be called "Long Friday", is probably taken from the German for "God's Friday" and it is the day that Jesus dies on the Cross. Later on the Thursday evening, Jesus and his other disciples go out to the Garden of Gethsemane. He asks them to watch and pray with him because he knows that he will be captured. They fall asleep which Luke compassionately describes as "because of grief" (22.45). In one of the most moving parts of the story, Jesus is left alone with his God facing his fears: "if you are willing, remove this cup from me; yet not my will but yours be done" (Luke 22.42) "the spirit is willing but the flesh is weak" (Mark 14.38). It is then that Judas and the soldiers arrive with lanterns and torches. Judas kisses Jesus to indicate to the soldiers which one he is. Peter tries to fight them off and follows Jesus as he is led away but when he is accused of being with Jesus, he denies this three times. When the cock crows at dawn, he realizes that Jesus was right and is filled with remorse. Likewise, Judas throws the thirty pieces of silver (his payment) at the chief priests' feet and goes to a tree and hangs himself.

Meanwhile, Jesus undergoes a series of unjust trials where he says very little. He is accused of treason because they say he calls himself the King of the Jews. The soldiers make a crown of thorns for him, beat him and mock him. Jesus then carries his cross through the streets of Jerusalem and up the hill to Golgotha. This journey is remembered in churches with the Stations of the Cross that can form part of Good Friday meditations. Jesus is crucified alongside two robbers on other crosses. It is said to have gone dark across the whole land between twelve and three o'clock when he was on the cross.

Throughout the four gospels, Jesus' "Seven Last Words" from the cross, are recorded. These are: "My God, my God why have you forsaken me?" (Matthew 27.46), "It is finished" (John 19.30), "I thirst" (John 19.28), "Woman behold your son", to Mary about John the disciple, (John 19.26-7), "Today you shall be with me in Paradise", to one of the crucified robbers, (Luke 23.43), "Into your hands I commend my spirit", (Luke 23.46) and "Father forgive them for they know not what they do" (Luke 23.34). These Seven Words can form part of the meditations in church.

Holy Saturday

This is one of the most under-rated days in the Christian calendar and is not marked by any service in church. Jesus' body is laid in a tomb, which is sealed with a huge stone rolled across. Pilate ordered soldiers to guard it, knowing that it may be stolen by Jesus' disciples. One of the ideas about what happens to Christ on Holy Saturday is called "the harrowing of hell." He goes to hell to meet the powers of evil and release the people there and so save them. There are beautiful icons depicting Christ reaching out across a chasm and pulling the people across to bring them into heaven. This is a stylized image to help explain what is in fact, the mystery of where Christ goes after his death but before resurrection, before that bridge has been constructed. Holy Saturday can be seen like those unthinkable moments when the planes hit the towers, when mothers ran back into Dunblane primary after hearing the shots or when high school children suddenly realized they were not witnessing a prank in Columbine High, when the toddler watches the stranger kill his mother in the park. It is utterly black, devoid of meaning. It is despair with no relief or comfort.

Easter Vigil and Resurrection

The first celebration of Easter is called the Easter Vigil and can be kept on the Saturday night or as dawn breaks on Easter morning. The Christian faith is based on the belief that Jesus rose from the dead. There are different resurrection appearances described in all four Gospels.

In Matthew 28 and Mark 16, there is the story of Mary Magdalene and other women coming to the tomb with spices to anoint Jesus' body. Angels appear in the empty tomb saying "He is not here. He is risen". Luke in chapter 24 adds "do you look for the living among the dead?" The women go and tell the disciples who do not believe them at first. Later, they are with Jesus on the mountain when he tells them to spread the good news to the whole of creation and "Remember I am with you always, to the end of the age" (Matthew 28.20)

Luke has the story of the Road to Emmaus which tells of two of Jesus' followers walking on the road with a third among them. As dusk falls, they say to the third man "Stay with us because it is almost evening and the day is now nearly over." The man comes home with them and when he breaks the bread, they recognize him. He disappears and they realize what they have seen saying, "Were not our hearts burning within us while he was talking to us on the road?" They go to Jerusalem to the upper room with the other eleven disciples to tell each other that they have seen Jesus. Then Jesus appears with them and says "Peace be with you." He tells them to touch his hands and feet and asks them for some food. They give him some broiled fish, which he eats with them. John, in chapter 20, adds that Thomas in particular, doubted. Jesus invites him to touch his wounds, which he does and as a result, believes.

John's version of the women at the tomb is different to the other Gospels. He records that only Mary Magdalene goes to the tomb. She stays by the tomb weeping. Jesus is behind her but she does not recognize him and assumes him to be the gardener. He asks her why she is weeping and when he calls her "Mary," she recognizes him. He tells her not to hold on to him and she runs to tell the good news.

John also gives us the story of the disciples going back to business as usual in their fishing boats on the sea at night. We imagine them trying to return to their daily routines in their grief, after the drama in Jerusalem. They catch nothing and at daybreak, Jesus appears on the beach. He tells them to cast their nets on the other side of the boat and it becomes full of fish. Jesus has lit a fire on the beach to cook the fish and calls to all of them to "Come and have breakfast."

The Easter Vigil, which can be held at dawn on Easter morning, is the most spectacular of the Christian rites. The people gather at the door of the church before dawn. The Easter fire (a bonfire at the church door) is lit, and the priests light the Easter candle and take it into the church. Everyone enters a darkened church and then lights little candles from the Easter candle. Then the haunting Easter Proclamation, or Exsultet, is sung. This is particularly beautiful if the light is by then coming in through the windows and the birds are singing along outside! The Exsultet proclaims the story of God with the repeated "This is the night" verses. It talks of this holy night which "dispels all evil, washes guilt away, restores lost innocence, brings mourners joy; casts out hatred, brings us peace, and humbles earthly pride. Night truly blessed when heaven is wedded to earth, and man [sic] is reconciled to God." It is all the hope and longing fulfilled after the despair of Holy Saturday. In the new light of this, baptisms take place and baptismal vows are renewed. Easter Day has arrived.

All Fools

Though Easter dominates, there are two other days that are marked in April. The first day in April is April Fool's or All Fool's Day. The origin of All Fools is not clear but a springtime festival honouring misrule and mayhem has ancient roots. Originally the Roman festival of the Saturnalia happened at the end of December (see Introduction to December). A prince of Saturnalia or Lord of Misrule was allowed to rule for the day and reign over misbehaviour. Across mediaeval Europe, this became the Feast of Fools where church rituals were parodied and a mock Pope elected. Before 1582, under the Julian calendar, April 1 was New Year's Day due to its proximity to the Vernal Equinox. Then the Gregorian calendar was introduced and January 1 was declared to be New Year's Day. It was resisted across the British Isles and particularly in France. England was the last to change its traditions, which it finally did in 1752. All Fool's is thought to have started because in France people played pranks on those who kept the old calendar and would not change. This has also been disputed. To this day, people deceive others for fun or send people on fruitless errands. The media has joined in with some cunning hoaxes. None of it is meant to cause harm.

Saint George

England's patron saint is honoured on April 23. St. George was in fact Palestinian. The story most associated with him is that a dragon that lived in a lake required a daily human sacrifice to feed upon. When it was to be the princess to be sacrificed, the King offered a large reward for anyone to kill the dragon. George came by on his white charger and killed the dragon with his lance. He then preached a magnificent sermon that converted the locals, and distributed the King's reward to the poor. There is a legend this might have happened in Uffington, Oxfordshire. Dragon Hill is said to be unable to grow grass at the top where the dragon's blood ran. It is unlikely, though, that George came to England. He was a high ranking officer in the Roman army, and was said to have been beheaded in Palestine in AD 303 when he refused to deny his faith.

With its fairy-tale-like story, and archetypal chivalry, this military saint became extremely popular in England in the wake of the Crusades, where there would be "ridings." These took the form of Mass, followed by a municipal dinner and processions led by the guilds, and headed by a model dragon. The Reformation dulled these festivities. In recent times, celebrating St George was felt to be too jingoistic after the second world war. England is on the cusp of remembering St George's day again in an attempt to claim more of a cultural heritage. Though the story of St George is beloved by children, he will always be associated more with military might than remembered for his spiritual attributes like David, Patrick and Andrew. Sadly, this maybe befits the patron saint of a country that has often sought to dominate other countries politically. His flag (the red cross on the white background) flown more commonly in England now than the Union Jack, still sits uneasily between national pride and bigotry.

So April is about the celebration of new life after death. It is also about power being turned up-side down. It is about courage and faith in the face of adversity, evil and suffering. For some the difficulties in our own journeys can find invisible meaning in the life, death and resurrection of Christ. Whilst outside, we observe visible echoes of hope in the re-birth of the natural world around us. Ultimately it is about how we can live in peace with God, with each other, with the earth and with ourselves.

MONDAY No Peace without Justice

On Rising/Resting

Blessed be you who comes in peace,
undazzled by the trappings of status,
but resplendent in plain integrity.
☼ May I be genuine as I wake up this day.
☾ May I be genuine as I offer this day to you.

Praising

Praise to you Honest Spirit,
who requires that we meet you in truth
and weeps over us when we do not see the depths of our deceit.
Call to my deep, O deep natural God
that I might come as I am
and allow you to reveal my masks.
Praise to you

In Stillness

Be still in the silence and aware of the Love with and within……..

☼ Morning Invocation

O Divine Peacemaker,
you know the rising of passion at all that is not just.
You know that peace comes, not sweet-faced and false, but with a sword.
Come with your sword of justice and cut away all that beguiles me
and keeps me from seeing the truth.
Cut away the layers I create so I can avoid relating.
Cut away my shame when it blinds me to another's power to humiliate
and does not belong to me.
Cut away the anxieties that prevent me from looking towards the world.
Cut away all the tasks I invent to shore up kin and kind,
so I may remember my unknown family, who will go without today.
Cut away the complexity of my daily doing so I may love simply.
O Divine One bring me your peace as I set forth this day

☼ Opening Out

Giver of just anger,

be the right fire in my protest at the powerful,
who set up their stall on the holy ground of people's lives
and disregard their sanctity.
Be with all those this day who have given what is precious
into the hands of those who do not value their worth.

Give us eyes to see what is scandalous
and courage to reclaim all that is hallowed,
to know its true value and stand sure.

☾ Thanksgiving
As I end this day in your safe-keeping
I count three blessings before my sleeping

☾ Night Shielding
O Spirit of peace,
let me lay my action down
and rest in you this night.
Give me the wisdom to discern between passion and arrogance
but let me not be too sensible.
I leave the burden of the wrongness of this world
in your care, which I name before you now

Bring your justice to all this night,
for there can be no peace whilst even one suffers.
As my prayers rise to you, give me the rest of sleep at this day's end.

Blessing
May the blessing of God be upon me,
you who fashioned and formed me.
You love all that you have made
and never forget or forsake.
Grant me the grace to do justice,
love kindness and walk humbly with you, my God.

TUESDAY Here be Dragons

On Rising/Resting

Blessed be you Rough Guide,
who cannot be nailed down to ordinance,
and whose Spirit cannot be contained by religion's Law,
☼ give me wisdom to follow the heart this day.
☾ give me wisdom to reflect by heart this day as I lie down this night.

Praising

Praise to you Living Presence,
who created our instincts to draw close,
who knows we need maps when we start out
and as a way of coming home to you.
Praise to you for the gift of faith when I must leave my familiar
and abandon my old map,
in order to find my true direction home.

In Stillness

Be still in the silence and aware of the Love with and within.......

☼ Morning Invocation

O Great Spirit, who knows the routes of all,
walk the unknown path with me this day.
Past the maps edge, where all the landmarks cease, here be dragons:
Give me courage to meet them.
Embolden my vision that I might deeply see.
Embolden my steps where I fear to tread.
Strengthen my resolve when overwhelming threatens.
Equip my soul when I face them head-on,
that my love may know because it has dared.
Fill me with compassion to befriend all that frightens.
Inspirit my faith that through brave adventure,
I may trust you more as I set out beyond the signs.
Stoke the fire in my belly that I might live my life passionately
and see things more off-road as I continue my journey this day.

✿ Opening Out

Fool-Hero who leaves all
to search for the pearl of great price,
be with each of us at those cross-roads places, where X marks the spot,
and we must dig hard for the hidden treasure of the heart.
Be with those I remember before you this morning

May we come to cherish our experience
that no rust or moth consume or thieves steal,
until heaven takes all our story and enfolds in love.

☾ Thanksgiving

As I end this day in your safe-keeping
I count three blessings before my sleeping

☾ Night Shielding

O Holy Shepherd,
keep me as I settle down this night.
There is no place that we can go
that is outside the reach of your care.
Guard us when we set out like new lambs,
unsteady on long legs,
though sure pleasure by tail's flick at suckle.
Be with each person I know who feels lost at this time.

Search for them and keep them from harm's way.
May we all be found by you wherever we may be.
Lead me to stillness as I lie down this night.

Blessing

May the courage of God go with me
as I leave the fold of my security.
May the guidance of God be my pilot
when my old map no longer works.
May the love of God keep me
when I feel danger of foe within and without.
And may the Spirit of God lead my heart
all my journey through until I reach the home of heaven.

WEDNESDAY The Fool

On Rising/Resting
Blessed be you Trickster God,
your naughty Spirit takes me where I would rather not go.
Give me enough rope for my own sweet way to lead me to your wisdom
☼ as I set forth this day.
☾ as I lie down this night.

Praising
Praise to you Holy Fool,
Your wisdom is foolishness to the sleek.
Your folly is wise to those who let love rule
and do not count the cost.
For the folly of love,
praise to you O Truth-telling One.

In Stillness
Be still in the silence and aware of the Love with and within.........

☼ Morning Invocation
Master and Mistress of Up-side-down,
jangle and dance your way around me as I set out this day.
Make wayward my straight-path feet that I might not walk narrow.
Tickle my stiff shoulders with your feather rattle
that I might not die a martyr.
Whisper stories of mischievousness to my grim face
that I might spend this day more playful.
Cough and splutter whilst I dazzle them with my self-importance.
Melt the arrogance in my chest
that I might laugh from my belly with another.
Warm the cold hidden place where my fear lies
that I might dare to visit it and smile with you,
and speak from it with timbre true.
Spirit of Up-side-down be at play in me this day.

☼ Opening Out
Sacred Jester in the court of life,

your outlaw words and misfit deeds still draw and repulse in their power.
As you disturb the comfortable and smug,
comfort with your healing touch all those known to me
who are disturbed and troubled in spirit this day

May your love be as a spring in the desert,
a well of wisdom from which they drink,
whilst the proud walk away empty
blind to their need and your gift.

☾ Thanksgiving

As I end this day in your safe-keeping
I count three blessings before my sleeping

☾ Night Shielding

Spirit of fool's knowing,
as I lie down this night under lunar light,
beam with wisdom and open my inner eye
so I may see in the dark.
For when leaders misrule
the child-like hearts sees their nakedness.
Be with me, and those known to me,
in our own craziness

Shine softly on our flaws and show us they are holy
because you have needed to work more love in them,
as I rest in you this night.

Blessing

May the blessing of a Child give me honesty in a grown-up world.
May the blessing of the Trickster give me cunning in a glamorous world.
May the blessing of the Christ give me compassion in a harsh world.
May the mirror of the Holy Fool show me wisdom in a distorted world.
And may the delight of God give me abundant laughter
in a world that doesn't suffer fools
✻ as I rise up with you this day.
☾ as I rest with you this night.

THURSDAY Betrayal

On Rising/Resting

Blessed be you Divine Friend,
who eats with us and meets us in the daily round,
who weeps when we weep and rejoices at our rejoicing.
☼ Let me not forget your faithfulness to me this day.
☾ Let me not forget your faithfulness to me this night.

Praising

Praise to you Friendship Giver,
for showing what love is,
for coming to our table and bringing us supper,
with the kiss of death hanging darkly over you.
As you tenderly wash each travelling foot,
in the lastness of it all,
in the job of love to be poured out, come what may,
praise to you.

In Stillness

Be still in the silence and aware of the Love with and within……..

☼ Morning Invocation

O Constant One, the Sacred and Domestic of my days,
Make me more faithful as I walk this day with you.
Wash my feet before I set out and show me how to serve.
Place bread in my hands this morning for I need food for the journey.
Share your cup of liberation that I may share forgiveness.
Keep me open to truthfulness and give me courage to speak it,
but should I fail and betray another or myself, show me a way back.
May the mercy I recieve make me more merciful,
the understanding I am shown, help me understand.
Keep my sleepy eyes awake to the injustice that happens right beside me.
Remember me through my day, even when I do not remember you.
O Constant One, keep faith with me as I set forth today.

☼ Opening Out

Come walk with me this day,

you who trod the unforgiving earth,
and went with willing feet at soldiers' hands
as love was betrayed.
And it was night.
Be with those with booted feet
who will run into ordinary houses to kill this day.
And those with smart shoes who walk the corridors of power
ordering the killing, especially in

May the cock-crow conscience dawn in their hearts
as they see what their hands have done.
Walk with each of us the barefoot ways of peace.

☾ Thanksgiving

As I end this day in your safe-keeping
I count three blessings before my sleeping

☾ Night Shielding

Watchful Spirit who stays awake
and guards us through the night.
Protect those we betray when we deny the worst in ourselves
and misuse our power.
Or when we deny the best in ourselves
and fearfully bury our power for love.
Be with all those who have been betrayed by another

Be the gentle balm on the shock of their hurt and anger.
Assure them when they set out on the hard road of trusting again.
Spirit, guard them in their wakefulness and give to all of us rest this night.

Blessing

May the blessing of your friendship be upon me
so I may be a true friend to you, to myself,
to those I know and the ways of justice.
✿ Give me your loyal blessing as I set out in the world this day
☾ Give me your loyal blessing as I lie down in the world this night.

FRIDAY Desolation

On Rising/Resting
Blessed be you Lonely God,
who knows our aloneness when the mid-day sun hides black
and the weeping rainy thunder cracks.
☼ Shelter me as I face the world this day.
☾ Shelter me as I cover my body this night.

Praising
Praise to you Forsaken One,
for huddling with me,
in the smooth-walled corner of abandonment.
Praise to you for suffering with me the roofless grief
for the loved ones lost too soon.
For knowing my pain, praise to you.

In Stillness
Be still in the silence and aware of the Love with and within..........

☼ Morning Invocation
God who holds the whole world in your hands,
hear my lamentation as I rise this day.
Hold me when I am weak and lost as you hold the world's lostness.
Hold me in my anxiety and those who wait with worry pacing the floor.
Hold me when I hear the news I dread and those who stare blankly at the wall.
Hold those who weep and the dry-eyed who are numb.
Hold me when I feel unsafe, and those who fear inside their own home.
Hold me when I try to kill my pain, and those who live to fix theirs each day.
Hold me when I doubt and those who've lost their faith in goodness.
Hold those of us marginalized by a centre we never defined.
Hold us when our value is unseen or maligned.
Hold us when our dreams get trampled on or never came true.
Hold all the lonely hearts and hurting souls in this strange cold world I pray.
Hold each and every one of us as we make it through this day.

☼ Opening Out
O Love Divine,

do not go silent in those times and places
where relief does not come with the morning.
Be with those bloated with hunger too weak to fend.
Be with those re-building to survive the damage untold
by wind, earth, fire or flood
Be with those whose lives have been strewn apart
by terrorists and war-mongers

Though you may go silent on our questions,
do not go absent with your love.
Keep aflame the hope of the broken and the peacemakers
as they struggle against the darkness this day.

☾ Thanksgiving

As I end this day in your safe-keeping
I count three blessings before my sleeping

☾ Night Shielding

Thirsty God,
I came from the womb thirsting
for the succour of a loving one.
Remember me as you thirst for a world more loving.
As I let the darkness of this long lonely night enfold me,
I lay down all the things in my heart that separate me.
Be with those who have felt isolated this day

Give us good people on our journeys who will take us in,
whose shelter connects us to your love this night.

Blessing

The blessing of God on my strife within.
The blessing of God on the conflict without.
The blessing of God on the patterns that chain.
The blessing of God on the chains that bind us all.
And at this day's start/end God's protection for our world.

SATURDAY This is the Night

On Rising/Resting
Blessed be you Gone Ahead God,
who went to the nightmare landscape
shutting the doors behind you, that we might not have to go.
☼ Protect me as I rise up this day.
☾ Protect me as I lie down this night.

Praising
Praise to you O Hope bringer.
For even and all the terror we have seen with single eye,
there is no black place without chink or peep or crack,
without seam of escape, or silver vein or glimmer,
because there is no place that you have not visited
with your light of way-through.
Praise to you.

In Stillness
Be still in the silence and aware of the Love with and within..........

☼ Morning Invocation
Life-Giving One, I lay down before you this day
the dark night of this world
where I long for redemption and a brand new day.
I yearn for a dawn, a dawn most blessed,
when every child has protection and is cherished;
every fist opened, every caress for giving not taking;
every word for kindness, every tear for joy.
every clenched heart that hits out, be melted;
every mouth fed, every head sheltered;
where weapons would be beaten once-for-all into plough-shares;
where difference could be celebrated
as the walls of dogma and division come down;
where broken relationships may be restored;
and unspoken family members hold each other in long embrace.
Give us faith to believe in hope as we set out this day.

☼ Opening Out
O Hope Bringer, bring the new dawn,
a dawn where the cure might be found;
when the rivers run clean once more, the trees cared for;
where not speed and comfort and appearance,
but the skies and the soil matter more;
the creatures in every variety range freely and receive no cruelty from us;
where men and women could enjoy the other without fear.
My especial prayers this day for

Come and make your home with us this holy day
that we might glimpse the oneness of heaven and earth.

☾ Thanksgiving
As I end this day in your safe-keeping
I count three blessings before my sleeping

☾ Night Shielding
O Spirit of presence,
toll your bell in me in and in each one of us
who shares this lonesome night.
Cover with your wing the little ones, in illness and ill times
who stare into the dark with sleepless eye

Send them your angels and carry their prayers
in the downy mystery of your hope.
Break our soul's weariness with sleep's refreshment,
before the first-light comes and feather on the breeze
reminds of your company through long night past.

Blessing
May the shiny light of God's own face,
and the gazy love and the Daystar grace
rise over the hill in the morning,
keep us from the endless night,
and shed in us a hope that will never go down
til heaven's peace on earth has come.

SUNDAY Joy

On Rising/Resting

Blessed be you risen with the sun,
for arriving soft-foot in the garden unawares,
and surprising us with friendly news
that hope has sprung, the dead season's gone.
✿ Let me rise with a joyful heart this day.
☾ Let me lie down with a joyful heart at this day's end.

Praising

Praise to you O Holy Gardener
for what was sowed in tears is now reaped in joy.
By forsythia and primrose, you break out in newness.
By swallow and swift, your happy return.
Praise to you

In Stillness

Be still in the silence and aware of the Love with and within...........

✿ Morning Invocation

Living One,
I go to look where I last found you but that is now stony and dead,
for you who lead me forward to new life are always one step ahead.
As I leave the old and step out in the new this day,
bring new life to my fingers that I might
touch the signs of your life among us and have faith.
Bring new life as I eat my breakfast that I might know you
in the breaking of my daily bread.
Bring new life to the work of my hands this day
that I might trust the abundance of your gift.
Bring new life when you interrupt my old ways and name me
that I might recognize your calling me on.
Bring new life to my eyes that I might see you beside me
as I walk my road this day

✿ Opening Out

God of the first Garden,

all the goodness of this earth comes from your hand
and into our hands you have committed this goodness.
Be with all the risk-takers this day who have the sassiness
to reach out beyond what is required in love or questing.

Give us wisdom to know when to ignore the "do not touch" signs
because to not take action would be the way of death
and when to obey them because by forgoing our need today,
we receive news of goodness for tomorrow.

☾ Thanksgiving
As I end this day in your safe-keeping
I count three blessings before my sleeping

☾ Night Shielding
Spirit of peace,
as I lie down this night,
do not bring me only happiness
for happiness is fleet of foot and sure to depart.
Bring me your joy grown from the same root as suffering.
Spirit of peace be with all those tonight
who have known the pain of division

Give us faith to trust that the joy of
forgiveness and reconciliation is possible.
Spirit of peace grant me rest as I lie down this night.

Blessing
May God of the Easter garden bless in every season of the heart.
May God of the mountainside bless in time set apart.
May God of the beach bless whether tides ebb or tides flow.
May God of the upper room bless my doubt that I may know
afresh the deep love of God that is stronger than death.
✿ May it rise within me as I set forth this day.
☾ May it fall softly within me as I rest in you this night.

may

INTRODUCTION TO MAY

"For we are up, as soon as it is day-o,
for to fetch the summer home,
the summer and the May-o,
for summer is a-coming in
and winter is a-gone."[3]

May 1 is full of festivities and remains a public holiday. It is easy to find a May Day procession in the rural areas of Britain, and in many areas, with morris dancers too. Although May is the peak of spring, being the mid-point between the vernal equinox and the summer solstice, May Day's celebrations traditionally mark the first day of summer. By May, whatever the weather, the "merry month" is here and spring has definitely sprung. Evenings and mornings are lighter. By and large, it is warmer. Sometimes we get the first hot days in May. The birdsong is like a natural sacred choir. Plants and wild flowers, including weeds, are blooming and bringing their colour to brown gardens and fields and woodlands. The bluebells, which may have started in April, bedeck the floors of woods making them magical places. It is thought to be a "thin time" when the fairy folk are out and about, sometimes making mischief. Some of the invocations and rituals for the year's growth and fruitfulness were to deter witches, fairies and spirits.

May is a time when gardeners are busy, planting and sowing for later months. On May Day, people would make up garlands, often with yellow flowers like cowslips, primroses, and buttercups, to welcome the sun for the summer. The birds are in the middle of their breeding season and some, like blue-tits, can be spotted flying to their nests with food for their open-mouthed babes. Nightingales can be heard. The migrants continue to return, including the house martins, back to their mud nests under the eaves. Dragonflies and insects can be seen especially around ponds and streams. All over, the rebirth of life for the year begins and is welcome after the dying part of the cycle. Creatures are active and the mating season is underway. May is the time to celebrate fertility, sexual union, and life itself.

Beltane

The power of the life force in nature after the long dark winter time is celebrated by communities in various ways. Where there is little evidence for some of the Celtic seasons, there is a first century Irish text which describes

Beltane in Ireland and suggests there was a fire festival around May 1. It was the beginning of the summer pastoral season. Two fires were lit, and cattle and sheep were driven through them for protection, on their way to the summer pastures. There is documented evidence for fire rituals in the British Isles in the eighteenth and nineteenth centuries too. Beltane is a cross quarter festival and marks the coming of summer and life. It is opposite to Samhain on October 31 which opens the winter season and is about death. Beltane means bright or goodly fire. It possibly derived from the worship of Belenos, the pagan sun god. Druids and their successors lit fires, sometimes made of nine sacred trees, high on the hills, to bring the power of the sun down to earth. To this day there is the annual procession up Carlton Hill in Edinburgh.

The tradition of 'jumping the fire' derives from a notion of purifying and protection for the summer months. Men, and when the flames were lower, women and young people, jumped the fire three times to ask for good fortune on pregnancies, crops, travels, future partners. Some would walk round them sun-wise three times. Some would say prayers whilst doing this. Children were carried across the smouldering ashes. The ashes were then scattered on the crops in the fields or taken home to start new fires in their hearths. In contemporary rituals, people might leave something they wish to shed from the winter, and seek blessing on an intention for the summer, as they jump.

May was the time when the livestock would be taken up to the summer pastures or mountains, called the "shielings." There would be a happy procession there of families with the animals, and everyone would greet each other after being indoors in the dark months. This need in our spirits to greet the lengthening sunlight is ritualized in all the Maytime celebrations as they evolved over time and in different areas. The variations will not be detailed here but there are common themes.

May Day

May is not only the name of a month but a noun and a verb. To go "a-maying," referred to the custom of young men and women going to the woods on midnight before May Day, to the sound of drums and cowhorns. They would break down branches and decorate them with flowers. They would collect flowers and make garlands. They would also pair up and return with their clothes and hair a little rumpled! The hawthorn or May tree is the traditional tree of May, and its boughs and flowers would be gathered. It is associated with love and sexuality. (Before the calendars changed in 1752, May Day would have fallen around May 13 or 14 so the little white hawthorn flowers would have been in full bloom). At dawn, they would return, singing May carols and scatter flowers on thresholds such as doorsteps and windows, for protection and blessing. This was called "bringing in the May." Mayers would thus bring summer to the village and celebrate it's coming with song, dance and ritual. They would process in the May procession and children used to go "garlanding", meaning to sell the garlands. The "May" is also the name given to a large wicker construction carried in the procession. It was shaped like a bell, covered in violets, cowslips, wallflowers, oxlips and other May flowers. Today, some people still decorate the May bush or bough with ribbons and garlands to welcome summer and ward off evil spirits.

The May Queen and the Green Man

The main characters in the procession are well-known. The May Queen was originally a representation of the goddess of spring. The Roman festival Floralia, from April 27-May 3 was the festival of the flower goddess Flora. May is named after Maia, the goddess of increase. In the Roman Catholic church, there is a tradition of crowning statues of Mary with flowers on May 1. The May Queen was a young girl in the village and she was Queen from sundown on the eve of Beltane until sunset on Beltane. She had a crown and throne of flowers and ribbons and watched over the festivities. Originally there was a Lord of the May but he has not survived the tradition. A further twist to the celebrations, especially in Wales and the Isle of Man, was that the King of Summer would battle with the King of Winter for the May Queen's hand.

Another character was a man dressed in a wicker frame covered in greenery called Jack-in-the Green. He represented spring, and danced throughout. He is also associated with the Green Man, an archetype familiar to us and seen as either a face or a whole body made of leaves and twigs. Less familiar is the "Obby-Oss" meaning hobby-horse, who is still paraded in the Padstow procession in Cornwall. He is a spectacular, frightening creature, half-man, half-horse in black, red and white. He cavorts and dances rhythmically to the drums and music of the Mayers all dressed in white. The Oss ritually dies while the song of summer fades and then surges back as the Oss is reborn after winter's death.

Mummers and Morris

The procession also featured mummers (see Introduction to January) as well as the musicians and dancers. These were masked characters who had a close relationship with morris dancers. In both, the character of the Fool appears, especially on May Day. In the morris he carries a bladder on a stick and hits the other dancers and the people with it, standing as he does, between both. Another character was the Betsy, who was a man dressed as a woman. Morris dancers have survived many different phases across the different regions and it is not easy to say when they started. Some dance with sticks, some swords. In Lancashire they have blackened faces. Although predominantly a male dance troupe, there are also women morris dancers. All wear bells round their legs that jingle when they dance, and they wear white with coloured ribbons. Sir James Frazer[4] declared them to originate as an ancient folk rite to induce fertility. They have certainly been a long established part of the English way to celebrate the re-birth of spring, and make their first appearance of the year on May 1 in country fairs across England. The rhythm of the dance was thought to drive away demons and rouse the earth spirit and the crops.

The May Pole

Another familiar May tradition is the May pole, still seen in village greens and in schools. They used to be permanent and made of pine, larch, elm, birch or ash. They were painted with bright colours and decorated with flowers, herbs and green boughs. Handkerchiefs, flags or ribbons streamed from it. It is of course a phallic symbol planted as if down into the earth's womb. Dancing round it was a mating rite, an invocation of fertility, so the Puritans banned it in 1644. It re-appeared during the Restoration though. It has survived until today, though the dances round it are much more sedate and tend to be by children. The original dances were with adults and were wilder affairs that ended in a banquet.

Dew and Holy Wells

Fire was not the only element honoured for the coming of summer. Water was also important in May. The May Day dew was thought to have special properties. Most commonly, the girls who bathed in it were thought to have beautiful complexions. People would also walk barefoot in it, roll in it, and men who washed their hands in it were thought to become good at tying knots and making nets. Mothers would wrap their sick children in clothes soaked in it. It was thought to be healing and bring blessing. Several of the May Day customs involved sprinkling people from holy wells or other sacred sources of water. Parents would take their children to such places like St Madron's well in Cornwall, walk them sun-wise around it, dip them three times in the water, and a piece of their clothing would be taken and ripped and hung on a tree, called a "clootie," as an invocation for their healing. At Beltane, the element of the fire from the sky or Upper-world and the water from the sea or Under-world are important together as their power unites on Earth in a sacred marriage, resulting in the fertility of every living thing.

The custom of well dressing still happens today, for the most-part, in Derbyshire. It's origins are pre-Christian, indeed the early Christians tried to ban the custom but were unsuccessful. Well dressing is a picture on a board set above a well made from flower petals and other natural materials. They take hours to make and some villagers dress their wells in secret on the night before May Day, and some let others watch to see how it is done. The well dressing season lasts until late September and the wells are opened with a blessing by church and civic dignitaries.

The Greenwood Marriage

For some who keep Beltane now, the Greenwood marriage is celebrated between the horned god and the fertile goddess. Horns have always been seen as phallic energy, and the horned god is seen as the wild and instinctive man of the forest. The goddess is equally instinctive and free about her womanly sexuality. Through their union, she becomes grain-mother and gives birth to the fertility of the land. Christianity, which has been deeply suspicious of sexuality, has pictured the devil as a horned god and so conflated evil with the liveliness of male sexuality. Female sexuality has similarly, been notoriously feared in the church, as indicated in the veneration of a virgin mother, so a blatant celebration of sexuality or understanding it as part of our sacred nature has been repressed and forbidden. Thus the roots of its darkness and danger as well as its joy remain unexplored. This is not to advocate the ritual sex that might happen as part of marking Beltane, but is to cheer on making love outside to celebrate the onset of summer! Interestingly, both the church's attitude to gender and the pagan view are strongly delineated in the male and female archetypes, and the revolution that is occurring in Western culture around issues of gender and sexuality has only just begun to be addressed by both.

So the theme of Beltane is the union of energies, male and female, the mystical and physical, rational and instinctive, fire and water, active and receptive. It is about allowing the extremes to exist and through their union, transformation occurring. It is a celebration of the rising sap, the fruitfulness, the fecundity of all living things, all in a process of becoming. However, there is an awareness of the precariousness too. Summer still might not bring all it promises.

Ascension and Rogationtide

Ascension is on the fortieth day after Easter and so always falls on a Thursday. Rogation Day falls on the Monday to Wednesday before Ascension day. This was originally a pre-Christian festival. The word comes from the Latin 'rogare', meaning to ask, and these were the days when God's or the gods' blessing was asked on the crops, planted a few weeks earlier.There was the custom of "beating the bounds." People would perambulate the boundaries of land in the times before maps. They would pause as they passed certain trees, walls and hedges that denoted the extent of the boundary to exclaim, pray and ritually 'beat' particular landmarks with sticks. These sticks or wands were often made of willow and the bark removed called "stripping the willow." The Church took this on to mark the parish boundaries. The priest would lead the people in a procession with banners depicting saints and there would be food and drink. Some of the landmarks would be named like "the Gospel Oak" or "Amen Corner." This popular pre-Christian and Christian festival is still celebrated today in some areas. Modern pagan groups have also taken up beating the bounds.

The Ascension of Christ is described in Acts 1.6-11. It describes a cloud taking Jesus from the sight of the disciples, thus ending his physical time on earth. Two men in white appear and say to them "why do you stand there looking into the sky?" Most churches hold a service on this day.

Whitsun or Pentecost

In the Christian calendar, the church has its own fire festival, Pentecost! Pentecost is the Jewish festival of Shavuot which was originally the spring grain harvest festival and later the celebration of Moses receiving the ten commandments on Mount Sinai. All the followers of Jesus were gathered together for it when the Holy Spirit appeared in tongues of flame as an outpouring on all human flesh. It is therefore said to be the birthday of the Church. It is literally the gift of the Spirit/Ghost of Christ in people once his body was no longer on earth. The original word for Spirit was inanimate and means breath or wind, either in Hebrew or Greek, and is female. However, she has also been there from the beginning. The Bible records her hovering over the waters of the world at the dawn of Creation (Genesis 1.2).

Eastertide lasts fifty days, therefore the earliest date for Pentecost is May 10 and the latest is June 13. Since the eleventh century in Britain, Pentecost

has been called Whitsun. It may have been so named because it was a time
for baptisms and so refers to the white robes worn. In the north of England,
and most particularly Manchester, there were Whit Walks, which were processions of Sunday School children dressed in white, followed by their parents and other members of their church, and preceded by a band. The liturgical colour for Pentecost is red, and it is always a joyful festival celebrating the
fiery power of the Spirit sweeping through the church. It lacks the physical
and sexual dimension of the spirit of Beltane. However, expression of spiritual ecstasy is encouraged in more Pentecostal or "Spirit-filled" churches.
The Biblical symbols of the Spirit are wind, dove, water, cloud, dew, fire and
breath. In the Celtic church, the wild goose was the symbol of the Spirit.

Pentecost is described in the second chapter of Acts. All the disciples and
other followers of Jesus were sat in one room when a powerful wind came
and tongues of fire separated and rested on the heads of each of them. They
were all filled with the Holy Spirit and could talk in languages not their own.
Others understood the languages that they spoke to be their native tongues
and were amazed. Some thought they were drunk. Peter stands up and makes
a speech:

It is I the Lord who speaks –
I will pour out my spirit on all humankind.
Your sons and daughters will prophesy
Your young people shall see visions,
Your old ones shall dream dreams.
On my slaves, men and women
I will pour out my spirit.
I will display portents in heaven above
And signs on earth below......." - Acts 2.17-19

Thus Peter describes the activity of the Holy Spirit as prophetic, visionary,
compassionate, powerful and for all, until the end of time.

So the new life manifest in May is celebrated by both the Celtic calendar
and the Church calendar in thankfulness for the colour, energy, the renewed
beauty of the earth and the joys of spiritual and sexual fruitfulness. It is about
hope and becoming and putting our faith in the Life-Giver who is both seen
and unseen. It is about gratitude for the Spirit of God who pulses between and
within us, connecting all living things to our Creator and entrusting her/him
with the precariousness of it all. The way of the Spirit though is not just exu-

berant and joyful. She dances a radical path of justice and freedom that cannot be an easy route in a world that is neither just nor free. So she preceded and continues the flow from the hard journey travelled by the life, death and re-birth of the Christ.

MONDAY Returning

On Rising/Resting

Blessed be you Source of All.

In your greenly greeting you return to the earth.

☼ Your beauty cheers and renews as I rise up this morning

☾ Your beauty cheers and renews as I lie down to rest at this day's end

Praising

Praise to you O Spirit of Life.

Your green-fingered abundance and brilliance of colour

in blade and petal and shoot and leaf,

sprung in us again when all seemed gone.

By invisible hand your faithful nurture

grows visible sweet-smelling loveliness,

your outrageous declaration of hope, year after year.

Praise to you

In Stillness

Be still in the silence and aware of the Love with and within............

☼ Morning Invocation

Pulse of all life

beat through all I am and all I do this day.

Beat through my feet that I might walk in awareness of the earth.

Beat through my thighs that I might go the extra mile for fellow-traveller.

Beat through my groin that I might cherish the darkness and joy

that stirs there.

Beat through my hands that I might touch with awe all you have created.

Beat through my heart that I might better know the connectedness

of every living thing.

Beat through my body that I might respect what I take for granted.

Pulse of all life, beat through your world and myself as part of it,

as I set forth this morning.

☼ Opening Out

You who are risen with newness,

be with all those who feel old this day.
Those with weary bodies, tired spirits,
those who feel stuck in ancient patterns that never seem to shift

Help us to trust the cycle of your healing,
spiralling like the rings of a tree, coming to the same place
but deeper and different this year round.
Age in us a stability in the freshness of your mercy
appearing anyway, morning by morning.

☾ Thanksgiving

As I end this day in your safe-keeping
I count three blessings before my sleeping

☾ Night Shielding

Quickening Spirit,
You have given to me my breath this day.
Gratitude for all the life I have been part of
gratitude for my body, mind and spirit;
gratitude for each person I was given;
gratitude for each creature;
gratitude for this tiny piece of your living planet;
that came into my sights this day;
Be with all who need the connection of prayer this night

As we lie down in the Oneness of all your creation
grant us rest and peace this night.

Blessing

Bless to me your quickening and fill me with your life-giving Spirit.
Bless to me your fecundity and fill me with the creativity of your Spirit.
Bless to me your manifesting and fill me with the love your Spirit shows.
Bless to me your returning and fill me with faith in your renewing Spirit
✿ as I rise in the life of the world this day.
☾ as I rest in your generosity this night.

TUESDAY Fire and Water

On Rising/Resting
Blessed be you Living Waters,
springing from under the ground and in the depths of ourselves,
healing and quenching and giving life.
☼ Rise up in me this day.
☾ Flow still and deep this night.

Praising
Praise to you, Whitsun Fire,
leaping and sweeping through this unjust world,
purifying and protesting, with passionate Spirit,
warming like the fiery orb above,
rising on each and every one of us,
alighting with tongue of flame, whispering "you are not alone",
desiring life in all its fullness for the whole earth.

In Stillness
Be still in the silence and aware of the Love with and within.........

☼ Morning Invocation
Sustainer of Life,
By sun and rain you send down your goodness on the fertile earth.
As I bathe my face in the morning dew of my early communion with you,
may my countenance glow with your blessing.
Purify my loving intention with the goodly fire of your Spirit this day.
Bless my body with warmth and water that I may know good health.
May I be thankful for my food and drink this day
that fuel me as I work and play, that keep me while I rest at night.
When my body is alert with love or exercise,
my thanks for the heat and sweat of being alive.
And at the time of my death,
my body cooled and juiceless, my breath expired,
no more need of sun and rain or heat and flow of body's rhythm,
but returned to the Source of Love, aflame yet poured out and running over.
Anoint me with that love as I set forth this day.

☼ Opening Out
Giver of Sun and Rain,
I offer to you all those in less temperate places
who are in danger of perishing by heat or flood or drought.
Warm our apathy by the blaze of your justice
that we might share the good things your hand has provided.
For all in need of food and water, shelter and dignity this day

Sear us with compassion for each under the sun, made by your same love,
depending on your providence and protection, come rain or shine.

☾ Thanksgiving
As I end this day in your safe-keeping
I count three blessings before my sleeping

☾ Night Shielding
Hidden Source,
as I go down this night to the river to pray
to the subterranean stream, where my day-worn soul is refreshed,
let me drink of your life there.
Its depths are unknown
and the journey must be made in solitude and stillness.
May others know its quenching who are burdened by this day

Like an old clootie reminds by holy waters,
I remember your grace from prayers gone by.
So I entrust our healing to you through the hours of this dark night.

Blessing
By blessed union of fire and water, gratitude for life on the earth.
By blessed union of man and woman, gratitude for the children on the earth.
By blessed union of the creatures around, gratitude for their continuation.
By blessed union of your Spirit and all the living things on the earth,
gratitude for showing forth your Sacred Life,
☼ as I walk out under the fire of the shiny golden sun this day.
☾ as I lie down by the waters under silver wafer moon this night.

WEDNESDAY Love Song

On Rising/Resting

Blessed be you my Beloved,
for you sought me and found me sitting under the lilac tree.
And I, unknown even to myself, was joyfully met by you.
☼ Search for me and know me as your own this day.
☾ Search for me and know me as your own this night.

Praising

Praise to you my Fair One,
for calling me to arise and come away
to the mystical meadow where we can be alone
and I can enter your life and you can enter mine.
For now the winter is past, the rain is over and gone.
the flowers appear on the earth; the time of singing has come.

In Stillness

Be still in the silence and aware of the Love with and within............

☼ Morning Invocation

Sweet Presence let me hear your voice and see your face this day.
Scatter your petals across the doors and sills of my soul
that the fragrance of your loveliness may be the welcome for another.
Grow a sturdy faithfulness in my heart
that my love might not evaporate with the morning dew.
Take my hand and lead me through the wending and winding of this day.
Cup my feet with your healing hands before I trust them to this day's path.
Hold my face whilst I gaze at you and embolden my thighs
as I step out in the strength of your seeing me and knowing me.
Let your presence linger in my awareness this day by your Spirit,
that my work may carry the freshness of this encounter with you.
My Beloved, I delight in your friendship as I rise with the morning light.

☼ Opening Out

Spirit of God radiate in me this day as a new-found love.
For all who believe they have never tasted your love;

for all who have never felt the contentment of your peace;
for all who have never been met in the deepest places;
for all who are not aware of being held by you;
or who have never been in awe at your beauty on the earth

May we know that even when we search elsewhere,
you are with us, desiring us to awaken to your presence.

☽ Thanksgiving

As I end this day in your safe-keeping
I count three blessings before my sleeping

☽ Night Shielding

Lover of my soul,
as I lie down this night
in the serenity of your companionship,
I come bringing this particular May day home.
And with it, all those in need of cherishing,
who do not know the deep-down love
that adores the uniqueness of their gifts and flaws
and sees the secrets of their hearts

Better even than the finest mate or sultriest union,
your love for us is never spent.
And I rest in the balm of its contentment this night.

Blessing

As a child is crowned with cowslips and honeysuckle,
garland me with the beauty of your Spirit.
As a lover longs for the arrival of a beloved one,
bless me with the questing of your Spirit.
As a partner unlocks the gate to my enclosed garden
bless me with the intimacy of your Spirit.
✿ I set forth this day in the truth that I am loved.
☽ I lie down this night in the truth that I am loved.

THURSDAY Transformation

On Rising/Resting

Blessed be you O Living One.
The world is shot through with your radiance,
reviving the earth, changing lives.
May I be aware that this day/night is charged with the splendour of heaven

Praising

Praise to you Spirit of transformation.
As the rising sun lengthens each day
and shines on the land with life-giving ray,
your sacred alchemy turns all my offering that is base metal
into the gold of fruitful living and nearer love.
Praise to you til the sun goes down
and you turn this day to night
and night to morning.

In Stillness

Be still in the silence and aware of the Love with and within...........

✿ Morning Invocation

Life-force of God, you make the sap to rise,
the swelling of bud to burst the sheath.
May I let the fruits of your Spirit grow in me this day.
Spirit of love abide in my ears as I listen to stories different to mine own.
Spirit of joy beam in my eyes as I meet the gaze of another.
Spirit of peace breathe through my attitude.
Spirit of kindness blow through the words I speak.
Spirit of patience breeze across my frustration before I say or act.
Spirit of faithfulness guard me when I'm tempted to stray.
Spirit of generosity spill over in all I think or do or say.
Spirit of gentleness be fragrant in all my dealings with the world.
Spirit of self-control do not limit, but channel the abundance of your fruits
as I partake in your transforming ways blowing through this day.

✿ Opening Out

Vivid God maker of variety and vitality,

no two of us alike, rich in mysterious complexity,
yet sharing our need for mercy.
Come to the unique garden of my soul
and give me discernment between wildness and weed.
Be with each one this day who feels their weeds
are more abundant than their beauty

Walk with us and help us to remove,
at the right time, and with your sensitive touch
all that blocks our potency and growth for tomorrow.

☾ Thanksgiving
As I end this day in your safe-keeping
I count three blessings before my sleeping

☾ Night Shielding
Spirit of God,
surround me this quiet night.
I offer you all the fears that come with change;
the changes in the world that make it strange to me;
the changes in my work and community that I have not chosen;
the changes in my family and friends that mean I must adjust;
the winds of change in my life that have blown me in a different direction

O Spirit as I lie down this night,
help me to trust your changing me unawares;
your gentle beckon when I want to return to the known,
for the bloom cannot show lest the bud break open.

Blessing
Constant One, ever-creating,
bless me in times of settledness;
bless me in times of change.
And in the moments of each breath in, breath out day,
bless my becoming in your Spirit
and faith to follow where she leads this day/night.

FRIDAY Divine Image

Awakening/Resting

Blessed be you in whose image we are made.
Male and female and genderful
you see that it is good
☼ as I wake to the world a woman/man this morning.
☾ as I lie down to sleep a woman/man this night.

Praising

Praise to you O Complete One,
for enjoying difference and union;
for you generate and nurture; you dare to risk and you hold safe.
For creating men with strength and gentleness,
for creating women with strength and gentleness,
for the love on which your world turns,
praise to you

In Stillness

Be still in the silence and aware of the Love with and within............

☼ Morning Invocation

Creator God, maker of all our bodies,
maker of who I am, which I cannot know except my body,
flow creamily through my body this day with ease and thanksgiving.
Flow through my eyes when I feast on another's body that gives me delight.
Flow through my fingers when I touch acquaintance or friend.
Flow through my arms when I embrace well-met fellow or well-loved one.
Flow through the base of myself that connection may not be difficult.
Flow through my systems and bless me with health and liveliness.
Flow through all that disables my body, that in my weakness I may learn compassion.
Flow through my gender, when the thrill of attraction orientates me towards another.
May my orientation be in you this day, who made me uniquely in my body.

☼ Opening Out

Divine Origin, you blessed us in your image.

In the delicious flesh of man and woman you made us.
Forgive us that we cannot cherish our own
without denying another.
Forgive us for failing to perceive with awe
the salving strangeness of another.
Heal each of us who have been wounded by difference

Have mercy on our wounds and those we inflict on others
we believe to be different.
Teach us to be deeply human that we may know our likeness
to each other and to your image.

☾ Thanksgiving
As I end this day in your safe-keeping
I count three blessings before my sleeping

☾ Night Shielding
Holy One, whole and complete,
hide us in your mercy at this day's end.
Help us mend the struggles and fears of our sexuality.
Be with all this night who have been numbed
from feeling the joy of intimacy with another.

May your healing cover all our memories and shame
and restore our connection between body and soul.
I trust myself to your care and my body to sleep as I lie down this night.

Blessing
Midwife of the soul, you have known me from even before
"it's a boy/girl" shaped my sojourn on this earth.
Bless the family I began in, that formed the habit of my relating.
Bless the company of lovers past, bless the loves that have eluded me.
Bless my partnering and the space between us.
Bless my solitude and the intimacy known only to you.
Bless my part in the common wealth of your image made flesh
as I learn to enjoy who I am this day/night.

SATURDAY Breath of Life

On Rising/Resting
Blessed be you Breath of Life
You gave me life, you will take it away
Blessed be you, my God for invisibly sustaining me
as my chest rises and falls this morning/night.

Praising
Praise to you Gentle Breeze of the Spirit
For you blow where you will.
I hear the sound of you but
know not where you come from
or where you go.
Let me be aware of your presence
as you breathe across my life this day,
though I can never grasp you.

In Stillness
Be still in the silence and aware of the Love with and within.........

✿ Morning Invocation
Living Presence, I come here this morning looking up at the sky
longing to see you and have my soul earthed in security.
Embody yourself in all the life around me this day.
May I recognize your loving hand as the events of today unfurl.
May I be aware of you in the unlooked-for moments with another.
May I worship in the magic cathedral of the blue-bell wood.
May my spirit soar with the song of willow-warbler and chiff-chaff.
May my body feel alive with love as your Spirit resides in me.
May I trust your compassion in the struggles that I find around me.
May I trust your compassion in the struggles that I find within me,
for though you cannot hold my body with your body, you hold my life
in yours.
Earth me securely in your love as I set forth this day.

✿ Opening Out
Inspirer of the Universe

By your breath of life which infuses all living things,
as I inhale the spirit of the people I meet, may I exhale your love.
As I inhale the news of today, may I exhale prayer like incense rising.
As I inhale rumours of war, may I exhale supplications for peace.
As I inhale the air which the leaves of the trees give to me,
may I exhale care for all that bears leaves.
As I inhale the same air of the creatures around me
may I exhale freedom from all that causes suffering.

Inspirer of the Universe,
by your grace, may we breathe your loving purpose this day.

☾ Thanksgiving

As I end this day in your safe-keeping
I count three blessings before my sleeping

☾ Night Shielding

Spirit of God,
your kindly gusts have blown over me this day.
As my movement dies down in the stillness of this night,
may I feel your care nearer to me than my own breath,
for I am known more to you than I know myself,
loved more than even the dearest love that I have received.
Protect all who need your silent care this night

Spirit of God, assure us of your presence
as we lie down tonight in your peace,
and rise in your company in the morning.

Blessing

May the breath of God be near me
May the Spirit of God encircle me
May the love of God breathe through me
✿ May God bring blessings on the wind of this new day.
☾ May the deep peace of God enfold me as I lie down this night.

SUNDAY Native Tongue

On Rising/Resting

Blessed be you Spirit of God.
You speak in every different tongue
through the vitality of our language and custom.
Yet you share with us the common parlance of the heart.
☼ Show me the One Love across every tribe and neighbourhood
as I rise up this morning.
☾ Show me the One Love across every tribe and neighbourhood
as I take my rest this night.

Praising

Praise to you Word of Life,
who speaks from the depths of the silence
to the deep of me, in my mother tongue,
not in sentences or commands but in Spirit,
reaching to the bottom of my soul
before I think straight or arrange what I mean.
Like when I was held at the beginning and there were no words.

In Stillness

Be still in the silence and aware of the Love with and within............

☼ Morning Invocation

Source of all, I come from you
and of my native self do I give to you this day.
Talk to me in accents that I can understand
especially when my reception seems dim.
Be the clear listening in my ears when other folks get lost in translation.
Be in my heart that I might see beyond what is said aloud.
Be in the hidden parts of my body when I offer them in love
that I might use my touch to express how I feel.
Be the action in my hands and feet this day that I might not be all words.
Be the sense in my reading of print or image or screen
that I might not be beguiled.
Be the words in my mouth that I might speak with integrity.
Be the word in my flesh trusting as I set forth this day.

☼ Opening Out

Writer of the Story of all,
as I survey the field of my life this day,
let me read you in the Book of Creation.
Yet further still, beyond my line of vision, your presence is in my story
for your love is unmapped and knows no bounds.
Be with all this day who are surveying the boundaries of their lives
discerning what must stay and what must go.

Holy Spirit show us when to tend and deepen what you have already given
and when to push out and extend our horizons further.
Bless me with spaciousness so I may receive you this day.

☾ Thanksgiving

As I end this day in your safe-keeping
I count three blessings before my sleeping

☾ Night Shielding

Prophetic Spirit,
whisper to me as I lie down this night.
Come with your comfort as I visit my dreams
which rise from the wordless place beyond memory.
Let me into your dreams and visions.
Give me language to tell them.
For you look upon a world of silent struggle,
obscured by well-spoken babel-spun words

Comforter Spirit, lead us from our own fears and our fears for our world,
that we might lie down with hope this night, for a new tomorrow.

Blessing

As the rain and sun come down from the heavens making the earth to grow,
so may your word not return to you empty,
but embed itself in the soil of my silence.
May I discover what makes for peace, whatever my language,
and know your blessing this day/night, on which our peace depends.

JUNE

INTRODUCTION TO JUNE

Flaming June is never guaranteed, of course, in the British Isles, but it is common to have hot days in June. Nature could not be more abundant or ripe. Solar energy is at its strongest. It is the month with the longest evenings and the morning light arriving long before most people's working day starts. This is because the summer solstice, which happens around June 21 and mirrors the winter solstice on December 21, is the shortest night and longest day. The sun has reached its northernmost point in the celestial sphere, furthest from the earth. As the earth continues its journey, the sun wanes until it is at the southernmost point on the shortest day at the winter solstice. It is around these days that it appears to stand still. The moon in June was thought to be a special one because of its proximity to the solstice. When the solstice coincides with a full moon it seems particularly spectacular.

The birds that started breeding may be producing more than one brood. As they fatten and grow their feathers which can only take a few weeks, they prepare to fledge. They fly off, one after another from their beautifully crafted nests. Birds can carry empty eggshells to another place to deter predators and sometimes, we can spot them on the ground if they are dropped. On the British coastline it is the best time to see seabirds as they breed – terns, gulls, cormorants, shags, guillemots to name but a few and the much loved puffins, delightful in colour and design with their amusing gait. Below on the rocks, the peaceful seals and their pups can be seen as they rest and watch us, unafraid, with their big dark eyes.

June sees an increase in the amount of insects. Though not always welcomed, their industry contributes to our food cycle. However, in previous times, they brought disease with them and that was also a threat to the food cycle and to the health of people. Ladybirds, butterflies, bees and beetles remain tiny little airborne creatures of wonder none the less. Also flying about at dusk, from the trees and across the sky, fleeting and as obscure as the dusk itself, are bats.

The wild flowers and garden flowers are too many to mention. In June the abundance and brilliance of the flowers are at their peak and make the heart sing. To name but a few are fox-gloves, daisies, orchids, elderflower, clover, meadowsweet, lavender, love-in-the-mist, poppies and still Britain's favourite flower and England's symbol, the rose. It is the month for another quintessential English plant – the strawberry. Flowers play a significant part in the midsummer and Christian rituals of June. As well as fruit and flowers, herbs are ready to be plucked and used and their healing properties thought to be at their most efficacious. Those most associated with midsummer are St John's wort, vervain/verbena, yarrow, lemon balm, mugwort and elderflower. They were and still are used for healing and protection, in medicines and tea, hung over doors or barns or made into sachets and put in the bed or in clothing. They were also used as dyes, flavouring, cosmetics and skin lotions.

The trees are in full strength and thick with green at Midsummer. In Celtic the Oak is called "Duir," which means doorway, and it is seen as the tree standing at the doorway to the second half of the year. Mistletoe is traditionally gathered on Midsummer's Eve.

Midsummer and Summer Solstice (sometimes called Litha)

The solstice can fall on June 20-23. The Christian feast of St John the Baptist is on June 24 which overlaid the traditional Midsummer's Day. Celtic people believed the day started from dusk the night before, not dawn as we do now. So Midsummer's Eve was on 23 June and also a night for festivities. The Midsummer revelries were therefore a several-stranded affair. It was a sun festival. There were, as at Beltane, Midsummer fires across the British Isles. In Ireland, they were more important than the Beltane fires and continue to this day. The Midsummer fires were in part to celebrate the longest day and to entreat the sun not to go back into darkness. They were also invocations to swell the fruit and ripen the grain. Similar rituals pertained as at Beltane with the fires, like jumping the flames, taking animals through, walking sun-wise round them. It was done for the same reason: protection of people and live-stock, especially from the seasonal danger of insect-borne disease.

In England, from the thirteenth century onwards, people hung out lamps. Houses were decorated with roses and other flowers. Churches were decorated with fennel and birch. There were torchlight processions and pageants with morris dancers, giants, a dragon and mummers. The Cornish Midsummer bonfire tradition was revived in the 1920s. Today a chain of fires is still lit from hill to hill. There are spiral dances with names such as "Threading the Needle" and "Snail Creep" and a Lady of the Flowers who brings a huge sheaf of herbs and flowers tied in ribbons and throws it on the fire. Herbs and flowers were ritually tossed into the flames of Midsummer fires. Often the fires would be lit on the windward side of a field so the smoke would blow over the crops for protection. Many people would take a lighted brand and carry it back to the house without a flame falling, for blessing on that house. In Ireland on St John's Eve, there were salmon community dinners. Across

Britain there were sheep-shearing feasts with suppers and singing. In Wales and the West country they bound straw to cartwheels, lit them and rolled them down the hill to celebrate the journey of the sun. The wheel is the symbol of the sun across many cultures.

Pre-dating all of this we have the mysterious Stonehenge and the Callanish Stones on the isle of Lewis in Scotland which are the finest examples of our many stone circles. Callanish is designed with a stone avenue and then stones like the four directions, and a central stone called "the Shining One." These stone circles are aligned to the sunrise and sunset at the solstice. Pagans today have reclaimed these stone-circles for ritual practises. In modern rituals, either the larger public ones or smaller private ones, the directions are invoked – North, South, East, West and a fifth, Spirit. They have corresponding elements – fire in the South, water in the West, earth in the North, air in the East and Spirit is in the Centre. Spirit is also believed to be around the edge too. It is everywhere within and without, and is both immanence (all around) and transcendence (beyond), and said to give birth to the four. Spirit is the Oneness connecting the directions and therefore all within the four corners of the earth. Calling the directions has roots in matriarchal cultures and indigenous traditions.

Midsummer is another "thin" time, and Shakespeare's "Midsummer Night's Dream" will ensure it remains in our national consciousness, even though our culture is far less open to the world of mythic and spiritual consciousness than it once was. Ireland leads in keeping it alive on a national scale. The faerie folk who were said to live in hills as well as the domestic ones like hobs or brownies went by all kinds of names: "grogans and gruagachs, spriggans and spunkies, boggles and bogies and bugaboos"[5]. They were thought to be out and about, playing and being mischievous. At Midsummer there was a notion of being taken to "the Summerlands", an earthly paradise where it is eternally summer. It could be entered through a faerie ring. Much of the protection sought ritually by the fires is also protection from evil spirits, bad faeries and witches too.

St. John the Baptist day fell naturally on Midsummer's Day, which was no doubt convenient for the church at the time, who would not be able to quell the Midsummer celebrations. John, who was the son of Elizabeth, whom Mary visited when she was pregnant, was Jesus' cousin and six months older than Jesus so his birthday was six months before Christmas Day. Traditionally in church they would recite the Benedicite. This is a tiny extract of the beautiful canticle, all of which can be found in the Morning Prayer section of any official Anglican prayer book:

"O all ye Works of the Lord, bless ye the Lord: praise and magnify him forever.

O ye Angels of the Lord, bless ye the Lord: praise him and magnify him forever.........

O ye Waters that be above the Firmament, bless ye the Lord: praise him and magnify him forever.....

O ye Winter and Summer, bless ye the Lord: praise him and magnify him forever

O ye Dews and Frosts, bless ye the Lord: praise him and magnify him forever........."

The Benedicite continues and implores most living things to bless the Lord. It is a canticle that remains popular today. It is similar to the Canticle of the Creatures/Brother Sun by St. Francis of Assisi.

St. Francis is an Italian Catholic saint, but he is like an honorary Celtic saint because he lived the three "P"s of Celtic spirituality. He found God's presence in the natural world, his writing is exquisitely poetic and his pilgrimage with God was undoubted. He wrote the Canticle around 1225, just eighteen months before his death. A version of it became the hymn "All Creatures of our God and King". This is a tiny fraction of the original:

"........May Thou be praised, my Lord, with all Thy creatures
especially mister brother sun,
of whom is the day, and Thou enlightens us through him.
And he is beautiful and radiant with a great splendour,
of Thee, Most High, does he convey the meaning.
May Thou be praised, my Lord, for sister moon and the stars
in heaven Thou has made them clear and precious and beautiful."

Corpus Christi

Corpus Christi is latin for 'the Body of Christ' and is celebrated ten days after Whitsun so is always on a Thursday. It is the Thursday after Trinity Sunday which celebrates God as three persons in Creator, Redeemer (Father) and Sustainer (Holy Spirit.) As Whitsun honours the coming of the Holy Spirit at Pentecost, after the Ascension of Jesus, Corpus Christi is another festival where Christians honour how Jesus can be experienced now. It is the thanksgiving for the gift of Holy Communion. Communion is one of two central sacraments (the other is Baptism). A sacrament is an outward sign of an inner reality. In this case, the bread and wine are believed to be a way that Christians "take in" Christ's body and blood. Corpus Christi ends the Easter Cycle of festivals and also ends the six months of festivals in the Church. Officially, the liturgical year does not start again until Advent in December. Certainly for the next few months it is "ordinary time" and the liturgical colour is green.

These days, Corpus Christi is a lesser festival and only kept in sacramental churches (see Introduction to April). However from the thirteenth century onwards it was a huge procession led by clergy, holding up a "monstrance." This is a tall silver object, it's top shaped like a sun and containing the large round priest's wafer, the body of Christ. Pageants were performed by trade and craft guilds telling Bible stories, sometimes on carts wheeled round to different parts in the town. Each guild took a different part of the story that was appropriate to their trade, and added funny stories or characters to the Gospel. So the nail-makers did the Crucifixion, the shepherds were the shepherds in the Nativity and the bakers did the Last Supper which was the relevant story for Corpus Christi. In Wakefield, York, Coventry and Chester these became the Miracle, Mystery and Morality plays which are still performed and popular today.

Across Europe a tradition that continues today in the Catholic countries, are the flower carpets at Corpus Christi. At the beginning of the procession "Lads of the Lord" scatter flowers and rose petals as they process. In Italy, at the "Infiorata" flower festival and in Spain they make spectacular flower carpets across the whole of a main street in natural and coloured sand and flowers. They must be swept away that day but are incredible to see. In Switzerland beech foliage and flowers are gathered and made into wreaths and garlands and fastened to houses. On window ledges, they put flowers, mosses and little sculptures and altars. In Britain, Arundel Cathedral has a flower carpet in the nave for Corpus Christi. Less grandly, some churches still scatter rose petals as they process down the aisle.

Father's Day

Although Father's Day is, what is often referred to as a Hallmark festival, or a product of card manufacturers wishing to make money, it has been taken up in Britain with enthusiasm and is kept by many now. The current younger generation may not even be aware that once, there was only Mother's Day and will no doubt, pass the "tradition" on. This seems appropriate with roles of parenting less polarized than they once were.

So June is about celebrating nature in Midsummer, at the peak of its lushness. It is about being outside more in the long evenings and celebrating the longest day, knowing it is a transitional point. From the end of June onwards, the days shorten, though the holiday season is not yet fully upon us. It is about the end of festival activity in the churches and getting on with the ordinary business of living and finding God in our lives, in the religious sacraments and in the Created sacraments all around that are radiant with God's love. Flowers are one such outward sign of God's grace and generosity though their simplicity may seem more straightforward than our inner journeys sometimes feel. For some there is an awareness of needing to be fed by God at community tables in bread and wine, in the company of others. For others, a need to be outside, maybe on a hill, to call in the directions and to feel connected to Spirit who connects us all. For others still, the need is for both.

MONDAY Benedicite

On Rising/Resting

Blessed be you Source of Life.

Let all your Works praise you.

☼ From the rising of the sun to its setting, let me praise you this day.

☾ From the setting of the sun until it rises again, let me rest praising you.

Praising

O you Sun and daylight long, bless your Maker.

O you Moon and Stars in short night-time praise.

O you Planets that circle the Sun bless your Maker.

O you Earth where I belong praise.

O you Continents and Countries bless your Maker.

O you Place where I live praise.

In Stillness

Be still in the silence and aware of the Love with and within.............

☼ Morning Invocation

As I arise from sleep this morning,

O you Body of mine bless your Maker,

O you Eyes that open to the world praise.

O you Birds that sing the morning in, bless your Maker.

O you running Water and food for belly praise.

O you Flowers and Trees that I see on my way, bless your Maker.

O you Babes in arms and Little Ones of fat bow limb praise.

O you Children with backpacks going to school bless your Maker.

O you Men in suits and hard-hats, all manner of men, praise.

O you Women in cars and on foot, bless your Maker.

O you Older folk, strong and slowed, praise.

O you Home where I may rest and return bless your Maker.

O you Days and Nights that we are given praise.

O you Birth at beginning and Death at mine end, bless your Maker.

O you Maker of this day before me, I give you my praise.

☼ Opening Out

Give thanks O Fire of greeting Sun.
Let me give thanks as I set forth this day.
Praise you invisible Air that gives me life and breath.
Give thanks O stable Earth on which I tread.
Praise you O Water that bathes and quenches.
Give thanks all Creatures in our care.
Praise you O Fellows this day I'll meet.
I offer you praise for those who need my prayer

Maker of all, give us the gift of grace
that we may honour you in all times and places.

☾ Thanksgiving

As I end this day in your safe-keeping
I count three blessings before my sleeping

☾ Night Shielding

Give thanks O Moon with wisdom's milky shine
under which I lie down this night.
Praise you sparkling Stars and dusky Bats flitting across the sky.
Give thanks O Sea whose tides keep rolling.
Praise you Land that rests til morning.
Give thanks O Darkness and all those waking now in the Light.
Be with those known to me this night
who are weary, lonesome, and struggling

Spirit of God bless us to our rest, renew to us our faith
that we may meet you with thankfulness as the new day dawns.

Blessing

O you Angels bless your Maker, O you Heavens praise God too,
O you Old and Young, you Proud and Humble-hearted, stand together.
Give me song to bless my Maker, all my journey this world through.
☼ For at this day's beginning as at my beginning on your blessing I depend.
☾ For at this day's end as at my life's ending I give you my praise.

TUESDAY Fledging

On Rising/Resting

Blessed are you, Warm-winged Provider.
How lovely nests my soul in your dwelling place
where I can rest and be nourished.
☼ Collect me in stillness before I set forth this day.
☾ Collect me in stillness as I lie down this night.

Praising

Praise to you, Ever-present One,
singer on the Wind all around
reminding me of your nearness.
Praise to you, Wild Goose,
flying through the sky above,
reminding me how far can be our horizons.
Praise to you, Holy Dove,
reminding me of your gentleness,
when you come in peace assuring overhead
"This is my Beloved in whom my soul delights"

In Stillness

Be still in the silence and aware of the Love with and within............

☼ Morning Invocation

Celestial Spirit who soars with me,
when earth-bound and awkward and crumpled,
I stop on the edge and learn that it is not easy taking flight.
Strengthen the wings of my heart when I want to draw back and stay.
Strengthen the wings of my feet when I take my first faltering leap.
Be the Wind under my wings when I am unsure and fear to fall.
Be the Wind under my wings when you inspire me to more.
Be the vision in my eyes as you guide me to what I need to see.
Be the homing in my belly sensing when to rest and return to still.
Be the knowledge of flying in my bones that has danced with angels
and will never lose the mark of heaven in my wings.
Be with me as I set out into this day.

☼ Opening Out

Broad-winged One,
the sound of playground children stirs times long gone,
when our curious fledgling whys and wherefores
could jump off and land in secure places.
Be with all this day who are wrestling with questions
of choice and choicelessness
and those who have taken the risk but still do not know

May your dwelling be our safety wherever we touch down.
May it be the taste of our final roosting place
when all will be answered and enfolded in your peace.

☾ Thanksgiving

As I end this day in your safe-keeping
I count three blessings before my sleeping

☾ Night Shielding

Spirit who broods over all,
as I lie down this night,
remember those times when I flew and fluttered and could not settle.
Remember when I flew too near the sun and got burnt.
Remember when I glided with the wind and life was good.
Remember all known to me who rest this night with broken wing

Hover over our chaos and changing times.
Shelter us close until you have created new things from our deep
and we can fly again.
Shelter me under your Holy Wing, as I take my rest this night.

Blessing

Precious Spirit,
you bore us with restless wings.
Our feet are made of clay but our souls were made to fly.
Bless my dusty dreams with God's own dream.
Bless all my days and nights with the peace of angels
until at the last, I rise with them, fully fledged and free.

WEDNESDAY Calling the Directions

On Rising/Resting

Blessed be you Spirit at centre,
Source that birthed all four corners of the earth.
Bless the Wind that brought me to an awareness of you.
✿ Be at my centre and beyond the edge of the world this day.
☾ Be at my centre and beyond the edge of the world as I lie down to sleep.

Praising

Praise to you Divine Presence.
You laid the foundations of the earth
when the morning stars sang together.
You burst the seas from its womb
and made the land to stop its proud waves.
You called forth the first fireball thirteen billion years ago.
May the flame of prayer kindle in each corner of my home
that this place might be sacred for encountering you.

In Stillness

Be still in the silence and aware of the Love with and within………..

✿ Morning Invocation

Living One, you forged the elements of my bodily being;
you know the workings of my soul; you made the four winds to blow.
I arise this day amidst their directions, rooted in your One Spirit.
Come air in the East where the sun rises each morning and breathe through my thinking this day.
Come fire in the South under the midsummer sun, enflame my love with your compassion.
Come earth in the North, ground me with stable faith and be my rock and stronghold this day.
Come water in the West flow through my feelings and intuition that I might deeply know your presence.
Come Spirit at Centre connecting all that there is.
Come to my heart and let me see you in all things this day.

✿ Opening Out

Great Spirit of Love,
how awesome your breathing over the first waters,
the circling moon and the wheel of fire in the first skies.
And here on earth after time passed, you created us part of all the wonder.
You made us a little lower than the angels with the imprint of heaven.
Be with each one this day who feels lower than life itself
and isolated from the company you have set us amongst.

May we notice little bits of birdsong, little flowers on stem,
the touch of little children, little grasps of holy hem,
little fragments of good fortune, little kindnesses from gentle souls,
that reconnect us to the height, width breadth and depth
of your great love for us this day.

☾ Thanksgiving

As I end this day in your safe-keeping
I count three blessings before my sleeping

☾ Night Shielding

Spirit at Centre bring your peace within as I lie down this night.
When I look to the star-lit skies, I feel sadness
because we have not cherished the work of your hands.
As forests, waters, land and skies are ravaged for our greed
and blood is shed upon the ground,
I confess my sorrow when I break the circle of life

Have mercy on us and all that we have not honoured.
See my need for newness of heart, strengthen my resolve,
and give me peace as I close my eyes this night.

Blessing

Creator of all, how precious is your handiwork in all the earth.
May the blessings of North, South, East and West be upon me.
Bless the road I have come from and the one I am bound.
✿ Give me true direction on my journey as I set forth this day.
☾ Give me true direction on my journey this deep dark night.

THURSDAY Corpus Christi

On Rising/Resting

Blessed be you our brother Jesus,

who calls us one and all, to community suppers in our neighbourhood,

for the feast of life prepared by God.

✪ Give me this day my daily bread.

☾ May I lie down this night fed and met by you.

Praising

Praise to you Divine Host,

for your gracious invitation

to all who hunger and thirst and know their need of you.

Praise you for the bread made for the whole of the world,

with grain sourced in the earth and kneaded by hands of men and women.

Praise you for the wine, fruit of vines grown in the dusty soil

crushed by the feet of men and women, barrelled and bottled for all.

By your Spirit they become our holy food.

Praise to you.

In Stillness

Be still in the silence and aware of the Love with and within.........

✪ Morning Invocation

I gather to myself the Welcome of God, as I arise this day,

drawing me to meet and share at one table

with all who have gone before and the whole company of heaven:

"Come fetch the flour, yeast and water.

Make the dough to rise and the oven baked smell to fill the air.

Come bring the pitchers brimming with wine to glug into cup.

Place on the table's plastic cloth, laid with loving hand,

for a feast under the shady bough of the Tree of Life.

The plates are unmatched for none of you are both the same.

There is plenty for all.

For at this table all can be refreshed and find mercy.

Come you weary and heavy laden, for here there is rest.

Come into my story and sit down at the place that I have prepared for you.

Come and celebrate the life that can be shared this day

and taste the hope that one day, peace and justice will finally come."

☼ Opening Out

O Living One, poured out and broken
be with all the other innocent ones this day
who have had their bodies violated
and those whose blood has been needlessly spilt.
Hear the cry of those who mourn
and those who hunger and thirst for just ways.

May you who Entered-in and knows the world's darkness, give us hope
for that day when all will sit down, one with another, in peace.

☾ Thanksgiving

As I end this day in your safe-keeping
I count three blessings before my sleeping

☾ Night Shielding

O Hallowed One with body torn by division,
come to me this night.
Comfort me when I feel excluded from the banquet.
Give me insight to see when I too, overlook the stranger.
Enlarge by your Spirit, those who guard their table fiercely
and refuse entry to the unchosen ones.

Have mercy on the brokenness we bring to the table.
May we know that all are named as guests of honour
whose company you request.
Bring your healing to all that divides as I lie down this night.

Blessing

Generous God, may the blessing of your presence be upon me
at the ordinary tables and at the holy tables.
And at my life's end, grant me the blessing of your welcome table
where I might sup and rest in your house forever.
☼ For all the tables I will sit at this day, be the unseen guest.
☾ For your blessing at all my tables today, I give thanks this night.

FRIDAY Ordinary Time

On Rising/Resting

Blessed be you Loving One you see my sleeping and waking.
You know my inside self when I am going from one thing to another.
☼ Accompany me as I spend this day in special and ordinary.
☾ May I rest in you at this day's end that was both special and ordinary.

Praising

Praise to you Maker of the Summerland,
who sends the sunshine, bringing ease and light.
Praise for the outside days with doors and windows open,
neighbours' music, children playing, racquet thwacking,
when the birds sing out the pleasure of ordinary all through the day.
You bring your balm as well, to those for whom the sun changes nothing
their struggles undiminished by windless warmth.
For loving all under the sun
praise to you.

In Stillness

Be still in the silence and aware of the Love with and within...........

☼ Morning Invocation

Holy Fold-Keeper and Wanderer-with-us,
wander beside me on my journey this day.
Sacred is your tending and caring for me every day of my life.
Sacred your delight at my frolicking in the world when it was new.
Sacred your walk with me when care became no longer free
and I found myself up mountainside on the dry steep exposed tracks.
Sacred your company through meadow of plenty, by streams of comfort.
Sacred your seeking and shepherding when I got caught in thicket
lost to myself, to my natural ways, and to you.
Dip me in your healing love and cleanse me from all that binds.
Shear me of the layers I have grown to protect myself and no longer need.
Keep me safe when the wolf is at the gate.
Bring me home on your shoulder rejoicing wherever I roam this day,
and at my days' end lead me to the sheiling of deep peace.

☼ Opening Out

Beloved of my days,
you come in the urine-smelling one on bus who sits beside me,
the one in my work-place with whom I cannot relate.
You teach me patience when unforeseen nuisance
changes the pattern of my plans.
You give me dignity when I am slandered by bully or rudeness or gossip.
Be with me in the daily troubles of my day

Give me grace to shift perspective, be creative
and find you unexpectedly in the ruffling of my spirits,
in the everyday workings of your limitless love.

☾ Thanksgiving

As I end this day in your safe-keeping
I count three blessings before my sleeping

☾ Night Shielding

Spirit in all things
you see with fine detail each moment of my day.
You see the speck of insect that crawls across my table.
You have noticed the nuances of my mood
and the brushes of the world against my soul today.
You have paid more attention to me than I have to you dear God
and for that I am thankful.
As I lie down to sleep, I ask your open-eyed care on

Sustain and protect us this night and make us ready to greet you
as another new day dawns full of tiny opportunities to love.

Blessing

The blessings of God in ordinary time be upon me.
Blessings when I take a bath or take the bin out.
Blessings when I am doing nothing in particular.
Blessings on the little things that catch my eye.
Blessings on the quirkiness of the thoughts that belong to me
  ☼ that you alone know and love this day.
  ☾ that you alone know and love as I fall asleep and dream this night.

SATURDAY Canticle of Midsummer

On Rising/Resting
Blessed be you Creator of All Life.
I see your splendour in the sheen of sun on water,
your lustre on the earth, your sheer transparency in the air.
✿ Light the texture of my life with your glory this day.
☾ Keep alight the lamp of your glory within as I take my rest this night.

Praising
All praise and honour and blessing to you
for shining forth your love in all your creatures.
Praised be you for Mother Earth,
nourishing with her goodness, enlivening my senses.
Luscious flesh of fruit to taste, delight of eye at petal's palette,
sound of midsummer breeze through tree's fat leaves,
tissues of memory in smell of freshly mown grass,
touch of ground on newly browned skin.
Praised be you for Sister Senses to perceive you.

In Stillness
Be still in the silence and aware of the Love with and within.............

✿ Morning Invocation
Praised be you through Brother Sun for coming round the corner of the short
night and lighting the morning this day
Praised be you through my Friend Body,
greeting you as the universe unfolds afresh
Praised be you through gracious Sister flowers in the gardens and meadows,
Sisters Lavender, Poppy, Fox-glove and Rose;
Praise through their healing Brothers Mugwort Lemon Balm and Elderflower.
Through the fulsome Brother trees and great trusty Brother Oak.
Praised be you through the food you provide in allotment and fields
Through Brother Beans, Lettuce, Brothers Asparagus and Aubergine
Through Strawberry and her Sister Berries; Sister Peach and Sister Cherry
Praised be you through all Creatures and specially Companions in our home;
Brother Dog who lies with sleepy eye by stove, Sister Cat all folded in,
for they show me how to uncomplicate my love and live in the moment.

135

May I live in the moment of your abundant love in the day that lies before me.

✪ Opening Out
Praised be you through Fellow Brother and Sister that we meet today
especially those tender ones who suffer at this time;
those who feel disconnected, out of harmony, out of sorts,
in their body, from their loved ones, in the troubles that beset

Praised be you through Fellow Feeling and Sister Grace.
May they know your care through the Family of Spirit
that we are part of this day.

☾ Thanksgiving
As I end this day in your safe-keeping
I count three blessings before my sleeping

☾ Night Shielding
Praised be you through Holy Sister Moon-shine
and her Sister Stars glimmering above me,
as I meditate in the intuitive dark,
listening for the secrets of your sacred purpose.
I recollect with you, the story of my day
and remember those who have stayed in mind's eye now

May we know your care as surely as you illumine the sky this night.
And when, at the end,
I lie upon my bed and recall the story of my life,
may I praise you through Sister Death
for following me with mercy this day and all my days.

Blessing
May the blessing of the Creator from whom we all come,
radiate through all that is above, beneath and around me
and shed kind beam on all my Kindred Creatures
✪ as I walk another mile with them in the company of Brother Day.
☾ as we rest together under cloak of Sister Night.

SUNDAY Fathering

On Rising/Resting
Blessed be you Source of Divine Fatherliness,
for trusting my travelling, yet keeping me as the apple of your eye
whatever troubles fall across my path.
☼ Smile on me as I set out this day.
☾ Smile on me as I take my rest this night.

Praising
Praise to you, O you with strong arm,
ready to protect and shield.
You lead me into the distance of this big world
and show me its wonders until I can walk with certain stride.
You do not withhold your presence from me
but love me with humour and compassion.
Praise to you

In Stillness
Be still in the silence and aware of the Love with and within................

☼ Morning Invocation
Father of our prodigal ways,
your generous spirit longs for our freedom.
Be the wisdom in my decisions as I choose how to spend this day.
May the wildness of my desires make me creative in my hands and heart.
Protect me from squandering my wildness,
until my hands are empty and my heart desperate.
Be the no-waste love when my wandering seems fruitless,
for with you nothing is futile and you see beyond the day.
Be my homing Spirit within that I might not become lost to myself.
Be the courage I need to turn around when I have been foolish.
And be the Father who sees me when I am still far off,
who does not wait til I get to the door but runs to meet me
with warm open arms, falling on my neck wet with tears.
Generous Father, be the homecoming of my story
in this day, and at my journey's end.

✪ Opening Out
Father of all you see the heart
of those who long to win approval and blessing
and be the pride and joy of a father's love.
Listen to the unheard cry of those
whose fathers could not be there for them,
and those whose fathers leave loving print on all they do,
but who now rest in the eternal arms

In the pain of missing what never has been or can be no longer,
give us mercy to let go into the wideness of your abiding love.

☾ Thanksgiving
As I end this day in your safe-keeping
I count three blessings before my sleeping

☾ Night Shielding
As I lie down this and every night
may I discover your Father-blessings
in the affirmation and encouragement of the friends that surround me.
Teach us to cheer every person we meet from the side-line,
for their pain is unknown to us and they may be untutored in love

Cover each of us as we lie down this night
in the faithfulness of your Fatherly care.

Blessing
May Father God above me
bless me with a child-like trust simple and true.
May Grandfather Spirit within me
bless me with an old wise love that earths and chuckles
and does not cease exploring.
May the Generative Presence around me
bless me with awe and wonder at the force of life in this world
  ✪ as if seeing with the eyes of a child this day.
  ☾ as I lie down with the faith of a child this night.

138

JULY

INTRODUCTION TO JULY

July is the only month in the calendar that has neither a Christian festival or a Celtic one. Lughnasadh/Lammas can start on July 31st but these prayers will reflect it on August 2nd to balance with its sister festival on another Cross Quarter, Imbolc on February 2nd. All the Cross Quarter festivals, Imbolc, Beltane, Lughnasadh and Samhain, can fall between the 31st and 2nd of the two months that they straddle. In this book, July and August will be used to celebrate aspects of the natural world that are with us always and not particularly seasonal, for example, sea, forest and mountains. We will also look at some seasonal themes, for example, holidays and music festivals.

Like June, July is one of our warmer months. It is still predominantly light. Vegetation remains lush and in colour and creatures are still out and about and to be seen. It lacks the fresh newness of May and June, and many plants are going over, though others are just coming into season. July brings the unique smell of firm-skinned juicy red tomatoes on the vine, ready to pick, and also one of our favourite fruits, the raspberry. The broods of birds have grown and flown. Some start new broods but many do not, and a few even begin their summer migration. Some of our most colourful insects are in abundance: bees, butterflies, moths and dragonflies. Dragonflies are so-called because the nymph looks quite frightening. They live for two years underwater and then only last a few weeks as we see them, and the smaller damselflies, above the water. Their shape and shimmering blue-green colour entrancing us and inspiring many a jewellery maker. Whilst moths do not get a good press and butterflies delight, they can both be exquisite and, like our flowers, have names that must have been thought up by early poets. Moths have such names as ruby tiger, white ermine, dark-bordered beauty, nut-tree tussock, peach blossom, and burnished brass. Butterflies are called red admiral, painted lady, clouded yellow, chalkhill blue, purple emperor and speckled wood. Wasps are not welcome and seem ever-prevalent, especially around our outdoor meals in July, but their nests are a wonder of design, as are the more famous bees' honeycombs. Bees appeal more because their stripey jerkinned rotund bodies seem almost furry and strokable and because honey-bees give us such sweet nectar, delivered straight from flower via natural factory to human hand.

The Dog Days of Summer

July 15 is St Swithun's Day and it has long been said that whatever the weather, be it rain or shine, on that day will be the same for forty days thereafter. Would that British weather were that consistent. We are a nation of weather-watchers because our climate is so unpredictable and come July expectations are running high. There is nothing more beautiful or, as Shakespeare commented, more temperate than a summer's day in Britain. Everyone is beginning to think about holidays because we have all been trained in school and July is the end of the academic year. For agricultural workers though, July and August signal hard work because harvest is beginning. Even so, the sun brings us outside and our thoughts turn to rest and leisure. The uncertainty of the weather in Britain has a new unpredictability factor. Despite warnings, we have continued to damage the ozone layer with our activities, and so our weather is not only up and down, but can be extreme now. The sun can burn with a ferocity that we are only just beginning to prepare ourselves and our environment for. We call the longed-for sunny days (blessed by a sun that does not harm in our imagination), "dog days." We think of balmy heat and inactivity as dog days which last from July 3rd to August the 11th. This is because the brightest star in the night sky, Sirius, or the Dog Star, rises and it was believed that its heat augmented the sun to give warmer weather.

Holidays

Most people know that the word "holiday" derives from Holy Days. As a nation we have had our official rest periods, in both Christian and pre-Christian times around religious festivals. This has been true until only the last few years where in some areas of Britain, the school holiday will no longer revolve around Easter. No doubt this is the beginning of a growing trend. However, because the Christian festivals were overlaid on the pre-Christian ones and their rituals and rites were seasonally focussed, it is hard to imagine a time when we will not have rest periods at midwinter, Easter and the summer. Both our seasons of activity and our body rhythms seem to need to rest at least around those times. We live in a predominantly work-focussed culture in the West, though this is being challenged slowly. Some people are wanting to change the life-work balance in favour of life, and finding side-ways moves, or completely new changes in direction, more satisfying. However, in years gone by, rest was seen as part of the healthy balance with work, and it is an indispensable part of the Christian life. In the story of Creation (found in Genesis chapters one and two), God rested on the seventh day. This is called the Sabbath. The notion of Sabbath is the sacred idea of setting regular time aside to relax, to be, rather than do, to be with people who are precious to us, and to be alone. For some this is about being with God and for others, it is about attending to our souls, when routine and activity have stopped. Though as old as the hills, it is a radical way to live in our culture and cuts against burn-out and running on empty. For many people it is so crucial to their soul's survival that they keep sacred space on a daily, weekly and seasonal basis. Most people (excluding those who take their lap-tops and mobiles on the beach), at least recognize the value of this in their holidays.

Rush-bearing and Wakes Weeks

The Wakes had their beginnings in the Middle Ages. They were originally a religious festival when villagers would hold a patronal festival for the saint of their local parish church. Like a funeral wake, the name refers to the all-night vigil on the eve of the festival. The main custom during July and August was "rush-bearing." In the days before pews, people sat on rushes on packed-earth floors in churches. The old rushes were swept out once a year. New ones were brought in with a ceremony, and the rest of the day was a holiday.

In Lancashire, the tradition of a holiday in July and rush-bearing remained, and after the Industrial Revolution, in the mill towns, the factory workers would not appear at work so the Mill owners decided to close down officially for one or two weeks, often on the third Saturday in July. It ceased to be exactly the same week when it became clear that Blackpool could not accommodate the whole of Lancashire. Blackpool had become the most popular Wakes Fair of all due to the arrival of The Big Wheel and the Pleasure Beach. Even though Wakes Weeks are no longer official across Lancashire, shops, offices and factories often do take that same week off and schools are expected to finish term by then.

Pilgrimage

In many places, and especially in Ireland, the last days of July were a holiday time and many wandering monks and ordinary pilgrims set out on pilgrimages. The weather made it good for travelling and sleeping out under the stars was possible. Ireland's famous voyaging saint was Saint Brendan who set out, with a crew of monks, in search of a mysterious island called "the Land of Promise." Pilgrimages are not the same as holidays, though holidays can turn out to reveal things we need to hear once we stop being so busy. Pilgrimages are journeys to special places. These could be Christian shrines and holy places, or sacred places like burial mounds or standing stones. Avebury in England, Newgrange in Ireland, Callanish in the Hebrides, the various sacred springs and wells like Kildare, Madron's well in Cornwall, Chalice Well in Glastonbury, attract all kinds of different people. British Celtic sacred sites are far too many to mention, such is the richness of our heritage. Many have both pre-Christian and Christian overtones, like Kildare due to Brigid's wonderful dual spiritual nationality.

The Celts were said to have two homes: the house inside and the universe outside. In winter-time the hearth was their centre, and from May to November, the sun. In Ireland they imagined the world supported by invisible columns of the sky, holding up the roof of the heavens, the rafters of the firmanent and God, as the divine thatcher, building the house of the world. Rituals took place outside using the elements, and so the Celtic sacred sites are mostly outside. The church generally worships inside and so has built stunning buildings as places of worship. Some of the Christian sites remain intact like Durham Cathedral, and some are ruins, like Lindisfarne on Holy Island or the Abbey at Glastonbury. This maybe reflects the different nature of worship. Old monastic settlements like Bardsey Island in Wales and the Skelligs in Ireland are places of pilgrimage, where the harshness of the landscape is part of its attraction for the pilgrim. Another place that causes spiritual joy to almost any visitor is Iona. God is in the rocks, and her white sands, blue sea, and stones of green and red seem to breathe sacred like no other place. It is not for nothing that it is known as the "thin place."

Another place of pilgrimage that never seems to wane in popularity is Santiago de Compostela in Spain. The way, or Camino of St James, starts in France, and though it is a Christian pilgrimage to St James' shrine at Compostela, it attracts all different kinds of people. James was one of the disciples and a Galilean fisherman. The scallop shell is particularly associated with him and with the pilgrimage, and has become a symbol of pilgrims in general. They wear one on their bags, or clothes or round their neck. There is a legend that St James once rescued a knight who was covered in scallops. However, they are common features of Spanish beaches and may have had a practical function scooping water from streams to drink along the way. In churches the priest baptizes using a silver scallop shell to scoop the water from the font. This symbolizes the journey of the person's life.

Important as the destination is, it is not always the main story of pilgrimage. For pilgrims it is the journey. It is an inner and outer walk. The landscape outside, and the journey of the soul inside, become almost inseperable and both, deeply sacred. It is like a long and sometimes hard, sometimes joyful, prayer. We are meant to return changed. The word "pilgrim" comes from the

Latin word "peregrinus", which means one who travels through the land. In the Middle Ages, peregrini would set out from the known and familiar and throw themselves on the mercy of the new and different landscape. This is part of what changes us still, on our modern pilgrimage. We discover things about ourselves, resources we did not know we had, and struggles that seem hard to overcome which we learn, or fail to learn, to embrace. Pilgrimages can be undertaken alone or as part of a group.

For all of this, Brigid herself told some pilgrims, that we will not find ourselves or God if we cannot find them at home. This is congruent with the Christian monastic tradition. Russian Christians had little huts in their gardens or in the woods called "poustinias." They would consist of a bed, a chair, a table and a Bible. Set aside places in our home, if we have the space, can help our daily pilgrimage. It is often the plain little huts or stone buildings and hermitages that can be the most moving places to encounter, for example, St Peters Chapel in Bradwell, Essex or St Oran's Chapel in Iona. Their simplicity can almost strip us of pretence just by walking inside. Our soul is stripped naked before God and ourselves. Uncluttered, our true desire can be awakened and stuff shakes down revealing what is important.

Labyrinths

Labyrinths are another kind of pilgrimage that are being re-discovered across the spiritual traditions in the West. The most famous are the Cretan one and the Chartres one. The Cretan one can be seen on a wall by a water mill in Tintagel. Its shape is the most simple to re-create and so it is the one that people make on beaches, with stones and twigs outside, or draw on canvas inside. The Chartres one, which is often covered with chairs in its location in Chartres Cathedral, is beautiful to walk. It is easier to get lost in its rhythm because it is more complex, like weaving through the patterns of a petal before arriving at the central floret. It cannot be hurried. Unlike mazes, there is only one route through. You cannot find yourself in a dead-end. Labyrinths are like the spiritual path because in walking them you are aware of walking towards the middle but sometimes the path takes you close and then you seem to be on the outside again until, eventually, you arrive in the still place at the centre.

Music

For some people today there are other kinds of pilgrimage, like travelling long distances to see a singer, who has long lit our soul, sing those same songs for real in front of us. We grieve when those people die, and hearing just two bars of a song can replay a particular episode of our lives in our minds with such vivacity. Classical music similarly stirs our soul but without words. It touches us deeply. In July and August, across Britain, there are music festivals a-plenty. They grow in number as the most popular become so big that the smaller ones seem to provide quieter, friendlier environments for camping and listening to live music. Sometimes they are a great place to meet up with friends that do not live nearly. July seems a good month to celebrate the precious gift of music.

So July is about slowing down and becoming aware of ourselves as whole people, away from the focussed targets of work. It is discovering God, or our souls, in relation to the natural world, to each other and through the gift of music. Holidays are in view for many, and rest welcomed.

MONDAY House of God

On Rising/Resting

Blessed are you Sacred House-Builder
for making this beautiful dwelling for us all to live.
You thatched with sky of cloud and blue.
You laid the flagstones of earth for our feet to tread.
☼ Furnish me this day with all I need as I walk under your roof of care.
☾ Cover me this night as I lie down under your roof of care.

Praising

Praise to you Loving Home-Maker, for the peace when I feel at home
as I stand on the firm rock or yielding sand,
where the waters meet the land
and the waves crash and creep in womb-like rhythm.
Praise to you even, for the restlessness when my heart is troubled,
for the desire for peace within your house
leads me deeper into your desire, O Loving Home-Maker.

In Stillness

Be still in the silence and aware of the Love with and within............

☼ Morning Invocation

Householder of all, you made this house by hand
from sea-bed foundation to canopy of heaven.
You designed every touch and finished off every detail
and still you keep creating.
Create in me a sense of wonder at my body's doing this day.
Forgive me when I am dissatisfied with my appearance or ability.
Create in me a desire to care for the blest inheritance that is your house.
Forgive me when I put my comfort first.
Create in me a love for all who inhabit your house this day.
Forgive me when I find love difficult.
Create in me an awareness of your sacred ground
as I set foot on paving stone and work-place floor this day.
Forgive me when I am dull to all around me.
Heavenly Householder, bless the work of all our hands
so we may co-create this house with you and make it a fit habitation for all

May I cherish this house as my home this day.

✿ Opening Out

O Living One, who thirsts for peace,
how good and lovely it is when we live together in unity.
Come with Wisdom Sophia and arbitrate in the family disputes
over land and race, fuel and food for all,
those rooms in your house where we need to be reconciled this day

Bring justice to this house that we might work together
to live peaceably, each sheltered with running water,
without hunger or hatred but sharing the treasures of home.

☾ Thanksgiving

As I end this day in your safe-keeping
I count three blessings before my sleeping

☾ Night Shielding

Great Architect of this rambling mansion,
as I lie under firmament of the blue-black rafters,
hung with little white lanterns that twinkle down on me,
I feel the wildness of this great space where I lodge;
its rooms down corridors of hill and vale and ocean,
too endless for me to discover.
But here, in this small patch that is my resting place for now,
I give especial thanks for its particular beauty
and the people I have shared it with this day

Protect us this night, and give us rest,
until the sun rises on another new day in your house of wonder.

Blessing

May the earth beneath my feet be the path that you will bless.
May the air around me that I breathe be as the sustaining of your Spirit.
May the wave on the shore be as your returning mercy new every day.
May your protection keep me safe under the dome of the summertime sky
until I dwell in peace under the heavenly arch of my eternal home.

TUESDAY Rivers

On Rising/Resting
Blessed be you River of Life,
for you nourish and refresh with clear cold waters,
bringing healing and rest to all who come to you.
☼ I come down to your banks to pray this morning.
☾ I come down to your banks to pray this night.

Praising
Praise to you Sacred Spring, source of living waters,
for beside you the trees grow strong
thirst is quenched, bodies cleansed.
Even the sound of laughing brook and beck
in dappled light brings joy to troubled souls.
Take my meditation and carry it down to the sea,
where the depth, height and width of your love cannot be measured.

In Stillness
Be still in the silence and aware of the Love with and within............

☼ Morning Invocation
O River of the Spirit,
as the heat of my desire wakes this day,
flow with compassion through my eyes that I may understand before I judge.
Flow through my mouth that I may speak with words of peace.
Flow through my feet that I may find those I am meant to meet today.
Flow through my hands so I may work with gentleness.
Flow through my heart so I am unafraid to share.
Flow through my attitude so I may be easy with others.
River of Spirit flow through my life.
Flow from the rock when I pass through dry land.
Flow under me with your grace as you would carry a leaf
on silver sud of eddy and whirl.
Flow over my roots that I might grow deep down
in the river of your plentiful love that babbles through our world
offering succour, solace and a place to go,
when all has been said and done this day.

✪ Opening Out

O God of the rivers and streams and tributaries,
I thank you for Rhonnda and Avon, for Thames and for Tyne
for Liffey and Shannon, Wye, Tay, Dee and Clyde;
for the rivers nearby me that I walk beside;
for the fishes within them, stickleback trout and perch;
the gemstone viridescence of dragonfly and Kingfisher blue,
of mallard and the scarlet stripe of moorhen and her little crew;
for sewage worker, fishermen, for all workers of pipe, drain and water.
And I lament the damage caused by chemical waste, by human waste,
by neglect and rubbish, blackening the waters, darkening our care

Have mercy on us and on the waters that run through our land.
Give us awareness and impetus to change the habit of our living.

☾ Thanksgiving

As I end this day in your safe-keeping
I count three blessings before my sleeping

☾ Night Shielding

O Spirit surround and sustain me
as I go down to the riverside to lay my burden down,
to hang my harp on the trees and weep
for all the wars and fighting happening in the world this night

Pour out your streams of forgiveness on all of us
when we cause division, from the personal hatreds within each heart,
to the escalation of violence between nations.
Help me to turn to the ways of peace as I lie down this night.

Blessing

May the hand of God hold mine as I step from stone to stone across current.
May the arm of God uphold me when rushing waters overwhelm me.
May the feet of God lead me by the quiet stream of contentment.
✪ May the love of God keep me as I follow my life's course this day.
☾ May the love of God keep me as I follow my life's course, this night
and when I come to the final crossing over, the carrying of God.

WEDNESDAY Colour

On Rising/Resting
Blessed be you Great Artist of the Beginning for your wild original spark,
for thinking up the paint-box and the shapes and patterns that I see.
☼ Let me notice the miracle of your invention as I go about my day.
☾ I marvel at the glory of your artistry as I close my eyes on this beautiful day.

Praising
Praise to you Holder of the Spectrum of All.
The white light of your love refracts into dazzling difference of every shade
when it shines through every living thing.
Praise for your endless palette that causes my spirits to break out in joy.
Praise for your pencil-chewing enjoyment of variety
as you design across this whole wondrous planet
letting us know that we can never be the whole story,
and that your mystery is beyond our fathoming.

In Stillness
Be still in the silence and aware of the Love with and within..........

☼ Morning Invocation
Artist of Life, how deep your colours touch the soul.
My eyes awake to colour in my home, and clothes in which I dress this day,
natural hue of flake and nut in bowl, white of milk,
the shade of door as it slams shut.
Outside midst the common green, the pink and purple florescence of July,
and over terracotta pot with geranium red, a moth or butterfly flutters by:
nut-tree tussock, peach blossom, burnished brass and speckled wood
red admiral, purple emperor, clouded yellow and chalkhill blue.
And on the browny bark the woodpecker with his red cap,
his green brother on ground, and yellow bellied blue-tit on feeder found.
And in bright-coloured lunchbox, taut-skinned red tomato, yellow cheese,
deep magenta of beetroot and bread with brown grain,
like the soil from whence it came.
For all my eyes take in until sleep comes to close them,
inspire my life with your beauty and fill me with gratitude this day.

☼ Opening Out

Rainbow God, who brings sunshine after the rain,
how lovely is the variety that you cherish.
Paint in my hands and heart the gift of your creative life this day
that I might express the wonder of your multi-coloured love.
Bless the risk of all creative endeavour between strangers
especially where there is conflict and difficulty

May barriers break down into a place of hope,
so every colour can be honoured in a new covenant,
and the white dove fly under arc of rainbow,
leading us into the promise of your peace.

☾ Thanksgiving

As I end this day in your safe-keeping
I count three blessings before my sleeping

☾ Night Shielding

O Holy Light that contains the darkness,
there is no black, no no-colour that is hidden from your light.
As I lie down in this dense night,
protect me from all the fears that find me in the dark,
that rob me of the colour of my daytime doing
and threaten to pare me back to nothing.
Be with all who feel colourless in the dark

Let us know that with you the darkness is no darkness,
and in the clear night all that you see is coloured by the light of love.
Let me rest in that love as I close my eyes this night.

Blessing

Blessing of red earth and orange flame,
Blessing of yellow sunshine on green hills,
Blessing of deep blue sea under the night-time indigo sky,
Blessing of the violet passion of the love of God
☼ be the Rainbow blessings of God on me this day however grey.
☾ be the Rainbow blessings of God on me this night as I lie down in peace.

THURSDAY Endings

On Rising/Resting
Blessed be you O Constant One, more faithful than the eye can see.
You are the unique mystery of being alive, yet unchanging.
☼ Remain deep within me as I change and grow this day.
☾ Keep your watch over me as I lie down this night.

Praising
Praise to you Safe place of my trust,
for the shape of your love does not shift
when episodes in my life come to an end and others start.
Praise for seeing you anew as I go through change and time
and the strengthening of the roots that happens
even when I have cursed or doubted your presence
because we have travelled some.

In Stillness
Be still in the silence and aware of the Love with and within……….

☼ Morning Invocation
Steadfast Lover of my soul,
stay close to me today, in this season of endings,
before the resting of holiday or before new chapter opens.
Stay in my hands as I tidy up or pack away.
May I treasure the memories and trust my achievements.
Stay in my feet as I close the door and walk away for a little or forever.
Stay in my arms as I embrace those who have shared this chapter with me.
Stay in the salty cleansing of my tears when I say good-bye.
May I let the grieving come because I have loved here.
May I lay down any tensions now, not forget the kindness
and celebrate the time we had together.
Stay in my heart when I feel sorrow for any failure.
May I learn from my mistakes, accept your forgiveness and let go.
May I offer my sense of incompleteness and imperfection.
Steadfast One be in my eyes this day as I look ahead to new possibilities
and with thankfulness for this moment that you have given.

✿ Opening Out

O God my stay and support,
as I delight in the butterfly alighting on leaf,
remind me of the wonder that once this delicate beauty
was a long lolloping caterpillar, lovely but unable to fly.
Remind me how in chrysalis bound like a dark mummy
it died a kind of death and turned to liquid,
not knowing anymore what it was
before it emerged into this exquisite winged creature
I see before me and take pleasure in.
Be with all whose becoming feels raw at this time

May we trust that your chrysalid holding
is a cradle of hope and new beginnings.

☾ Thanksgiving

As I end this day in your safe-keeping
I count three blessings before my sleeping

☾ Night Shielding

O Spirit of love, reassure me as I lie down this night.
For as I walk the labyrinth of my inner journey,
sometimes I see only walls either side
and know I must go on without understanding.
Protect me and those this night whom I remember now

Give us the eyes of faith to walk blind when we feel far from centre
and trust that the path maps the way for with you there are no dead-ends.
O Spirit reassure me as I turn out the light and take my rest.

Blessing

Holy God, steadfast and true
Indwell your spirit of peace as I mourn the passing of the old.
Indwell your spirit of peace as I welcome the adventure of the new.
Indwell your spirit of peace as I die the little deaths
until the final changing place when I may let go of this life with peace.
✿ Bless me with thankful expectancy as I start this new day.
☾ Bless me with gratitude for the passing of this day.

FRIDAY Music

On Rising/Resting
Blessed be you, Wordless Rhapsody
composed for all the living instruments in the orchestra of this world,
to play together the most majestic symphony ever heard.
✿ I wake to sing your praises this day.
☾ I lie down singing your praises this night.

Praising
O Melody of Life, praise to you.
From cradle-song to dirge you know the soundtrack of my days.
You hear the underlying tune when we improvise together,
and the sounds I make seem just a noise.
You hear the song I long to write with my life
and leave on the air when my busking days are done.
For accompanying me through the rise and fall of every cadence,
praise to you

In Stillness
Be still in the silence and aware of the Love with and within..........

✿ Morning Invocation
O Sacred Rhythm Maker,
I was made by two folks' sultry rhythm,
until my heartbeat was formed in my mother's womb.
It pulses now and will pulse through until it stops with my last breath.
Song of life beat through my veins that I may live this day with gladness.
Beat through my feet that I may dance the dance that only I can dance.
Beat through my being that I might be in time to your movement.
Beat through my heart that I might bring harmony when I am with another.
Beat through my hands that I might hold another with a sure touch.
Yet beat through the laughter when I stand on their feet.
Beat with compassion when I am out of step with all around me.
Maker of mambo and rumba, of samba and salsa, of bebop and blues,
of ragtime and reggae, swing, jive, jigs and reels,
beat through every upbeat and downbeat phrase of my life,
in each tick and tock of this day.

✿ Opening Out

Giver of the musical gift,
I thank you for every musician that has struck a chord in my life,
who has so precisely met my yearning and makes me swoon or weep.
For the festival spirit where boundary is melted.
For the sacred connection of music as it is played,
setting my spirit free, sparking memory and desire.
Be with all who give of their musical talent

Let me live from the unreachable part music touches this day.

☾ Thanksgiving

As I end this day in your safe-keeping
I count three blessings before my sleeping

☾ Night Shielding

Spirit, you are the harmony between all things.
From the belly of my chant, I sing out my day to you.
Be my song plain and slow, soulful and sweet,
wild and free, deep and strong,
hear me and any I know who offer mournful sad tunes this night

Incorporate every discordant crotchet or quaver
into the haunting ballad of your love
and sing us to sleep with your lullaby of peace
as we close our eyes and drift away until morning chorus wakes

Blessing

Praise God with lute and lyre, with harp and mandolin,
with harmonica and saxophone, organ and drum,
with guitar and flute, with fiddle and bodhran,
with horn section, pipe-players and a whole brass band.
And with the sole instrument of the human voice stirring the angels,
my plaintive desire, the divine echo, the call and response
✿ invoking your blessing with my cry this day.
☾ invoking your blessing with my cry this night.

SATURDAY Pilgrimage

On Rising/Resting
Blessed be you Out-there In-front God,
drawing us on through our struggle and yearning
to meet you and ourselves on the journey.
☼ travel with me as I leave my home this day.
☾ thank you for travelling this day with me.

Praising
Praise to you Inspiring Spirit.
You promise to meet every pilgrim soul
who packs a bag of troubles and hopes
and sets out as a seeker with an open heart.
Praise to you for surprising me by showing me my true desire,
widening my horizons,
and honouring my sacred intent.

In Stillness
Be still in the silence and aware of the Love with and within............

☼ Morning Invocation
Wayfaring One,
up hill and mount, by well and spring, by standing stone and shrine,
how you satiate when the outer landscape teaches my inner one.
How natural to trust what I find within.
Lead naturally my booted feet when I go away for awhile.
Lead naturally my receiving hands free of daily care.
Lead naturally my body and sustain when I become weary.
Lead naturally my solitude to find my company in you.
Lead naturally my searching heart to find what I need to find on this part of
the road.
Lead naturally my meditation this day that I might see my true size in this
wide world.
Stretch my resources by your grace when I encounter challenge
and enlarge my love as I cross unknown land to find the holy place.
May I return to my home, as to my heavenly home,
changed by my walk with you this day.

☼ Opening Out

Living One,
as I set out on this broad open road,
treading the path that is mine to tread,
open my eyes to the others who share this road with me,
those joined by quest or only by being fellow-traveller.
For we all carry a scallop-shell inside, journeying and seeking,
not one of us knowing the exact way.
I particularly remember those given alongside me this day

Bless each of us to our journey,
to all that we find,
and to all that is only yours to know this day.

☾ Thanksgiving

As I end this day in your safe-keeping
I count three blessings before my sleeping

☾ Night Shielding

Dear God as I lie me down to sleep,
on little bunk with pack beside,
on my lifetime pilgrimage or shorter voyage of discovery,
I give thanks for the sacred places in my life,
those I know well and those I long to see.
Hallow each day of my pilgrim way
and those whom I hold before you now

Place your hand on our brows and smile on our effort
as we take our rest this night.

Blessing

Bless my feet in the footsteps on the well-trodden paths.
Bless my eyes as they gaze with awe where many have gazed before.
May the blessing that so many have found here
bless me as only your love can find me.
☼ As the sun shines on my journey show me your face this day.
☾ As the moon shines on my resting show me your face this night.

SUNDAY Dog Days

On Rising/Resting
Blessed be you Heart of the Silent Nothingness,
who does not call us into ceaseless activity,
but bids us come rest awhile.
☼ Be the ground of my being this day.
☾ Be the ground of my being as I close my eyes this night.

Praising
Praise to you for making rest part of the rhythm,
for knowing the sacredness of stand-still,
and knowing my need to do nothing.
For at the heart of all the activity in the world lies the still point.
Contain any fears, as I shed my doing this day
and help me to find the peace at centre.

In Stillness
Be still in the silence and aware of the Love with and within..............

☼ Morning Invocation
Living One present in the lazy hazy Sundays,
who makes the dog day sun to shine,
in the halcyon cloud-whipped Sabbath skies,
give me grace to let go as I play this day.
As my back uncurls on old rug;
as my thirst is slaked by cool drink;
as my mouth enjoys food eaten outside;
as my bare feet fondle the soft meadow grass;
as my mind absorbs only book or Sunday paper or gentle chatter;
dimly aware of the sound of children playing;
as I have time to notice butterfly or buzzard or the buzzing of bee;
let the sweet honey of enjoying the moment drip down my soul,
unaware until tomorrow how restorative is this day.

☼ Opening Out
Perspective-Giver, Holder of True,
be with all who are ruled by target and deadline.

Help us to let go of our need to be efficient this day
and the illusion of our indispensability.
Keep our feet on the solid ground of your love that made us as whole people
and not the shifting sands of a virtual world,
the number-crunching and word-spinning that misses the story.
Be with all whose stories have been missed this day
and those who have dismissed their own.

May we find head-up time to stop the treadmill,
discover life anew in all its richness and balance
and re-discover our wholeness, made holy by you.

☾ Thanksgiving
As I end this day in your safe-keeping
I count three blessings before my sleeping

☾ Night Shielding
As the quiet dog-star rises on all I have not achieved this day,
I lie down in thankfulness for the pleasure of doing nothing.
Like the soothing beat of willow on leather, in village green,
the lap lap clap of those half watching for a score,
time has moved slowly
and for the basking in it, gratitude.
At the ending of this day I remember those who need your peace

May we know the comfort of your presence this night.
I let go into the balm of your protection as I lay my body down to sleep.

Blessing
May the blessing of God shine overhead.
May the voluptuousness of God suffuse my carefree days.
May the fullness of God be in my stopping awhile.
☼ May the dreaming of God be in my slow doing this day.
☾ May the dreaming of God be in my sleeping this night.

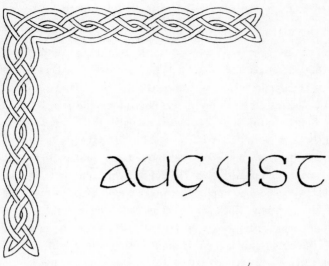

AUGUST

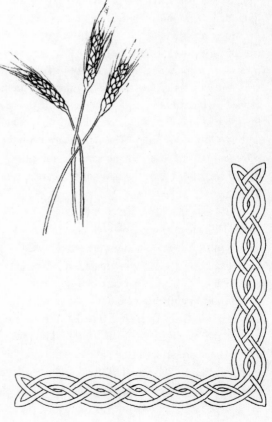

INTRODUCTION TO AUGUST

August is summer's last splurge of activity. It is thought of as the month of settled fine weather though this is not always the reality. Other factors contribute to this perception, such as memories of the long summer holiday free from school. The insects and flowers that abound remain from July and earlier months, some in full flourish. The birds, animals and flowers continue to do all that must be done to ensure the survival of their species before the cooler weather of autumn. August is the start of the birds' autumn migration, especially for waders, who pass through Britain from breeding in the Arctic en route to Africa. August is also moulting season for both the adult birds and the ones born in the spring. They get what is called their "first winter" plumage which can make them look a bit raggedy. While they are moulting they are less visible because their flight is limited. Their flight feathers drop first, one by one and are replaced quickly so they are not out of action for too long, and then their body feathers follow.

Many people make for the coast in August. Filled with childhood memories of times spent on the beach, the rhythm of the tides seems a universally restorative experience. Tides are not just the rise and fall of the water in our seas and oceans. They are the regular and predictable movement of water caused by the way the earth, moon and sun move in relation to each other and the force of gravity. This is what is read in tide tables. There are two high tides and two low tides a day. The tides caused by the moon are called the lunar tides and those caused by the sun, the solar tides. The largest tides happen a day or two after the full or new moon nearest to the equinoxes (March 21 and September 21).

Our coasts are teeming with wildlife. The wading birds like the ruffs and spotted redshanks, curlews and sandpipers feature on our coastline. In the rock-pools, the rocks, and on the shore, children and adults alike enjoy barnacles and limpets and sometimes find crabs, anemones and jellyfish. Finding a starfish or sea urchin is a rare delight. On the beach there are many hours of pleasure from collecting even the common shells of razor-shells, periwinkles, cockles, mussels, oysters and whelks. The rock-pool fish have such names as gobies and blennies. Whilst it would be unlikely to see the fish from the sea except in an aquarium or on a plate, watching the fishing boats reminds us of their existence. The wonderful experience of seeing whales, sharks or dolphins, probably involves getting on a boat. The plants around water are flowering in the summer months, like sea holly, sea spurge, sea purslane, sea sandwort and in still water, water lilies. In moorland and meadow, familiar summer wildlife in Britain includes grasshoppers and crickets. Clover, heather, fern and blackberries are there for the picking.

Lammas or Lughnasadh (pronounced "Loo-nassah")

August may represent holiday time for non-agrarian workers, but it is one of the busiest months on the land. Lammas or Lughnasadh is celebrated on August 1 or 2 and marks the beginning of the grain harvest. The cereal harvest is the first harvest. We think of September as the festival of Harvest, which is the second one of berries, apples and wine and the third is at Samhain (or Hallowe'en) October 31. This is the harvest of the earth's fruits, pumpkin, squash and nuts as well. In Ireland, the cattle and sheep were brought back from the sheilings or highland pasture by Samhain.

Lammas which derives from the Anglo-Saxon, "Loaf-Mass" has more certain origins than Lughnasadh. It is sometimes thought of as first fruits. Feasting followed the first grain being cut, threshed and stored. The grain was of corn, wheat, barley rye, oats and in Ireland, potatoes too. The word "cereal" is derived from Ceres, the Roman name for the Grain Goddess or Corn Mother who provides the fruits of the earth. The cross-quarter festivals (Imbolc, Beltane, Lughnasadh and Samhain), all at the turn of a month also mark a shift in season. The energy outside changes and this may reflect the beginnings of an inner change too. We can be unaware of this in August because of the fine weather and the holidays. However, the death part of the life-death-rebirth cycle begins here slowly. It becomes noticeable in September and by Samhain/All Hallows, death is honoured in both the Celtic and Christian calendar. So the Introductions to August, September, October and November flow together in this theme. Here, the story of the Harvest/Cereal Goddess is told which would have informed the spirituality of the pre-Christian rites, of which we know only a little. It is likely that the residual beliefs around some of the Harvest rituals described in Introduction to September, which we know a bit more about, stemmed from this story.

The grain is associated with the gods and goddesses of resurrection. At harvest, the Corn Mother Ceres, or Demeter in Greek, gives birth to Proserpine/Persephone, the seed or grain for next year's harvest. Persephone is abducted by Hades and taken into the Underworld. Demeter grieves for her and searches for her lost daughter, who is also like her younger self. This made the earth die so Zeus forced Hades to return Persephone to the earth. Persephone ate six pomegranate seeds which meant she could return for only six months each year. When Demeter and her daughter were together the earth grew abundantly but when Persephone returned to the underworld, the vegetation died again. This story was believed to explain the seasons. It is symbolic of the seed going underground for the winter in order to re-appear in the spring. Persephone is known as the goddess of the underworld.

In folklore, the popular figure of John Barleycorn, told in the folk-song which has more versions than any other in the English language, is a person-ification of barley. In 1782, a famous version by Robert Burns tells that he must die in order for new life to come from him, in the shape of beer and whisky. This is after his violent death by reaping and threshing.

So at Lammas, the doorway to the darker months is beginning to open. August is the last outside month, manifesting summer energy, before the more inward autumnal months beckon the winter on. In mystical Christianity and in the pagan tradition, darkness and death is seen as regenerative and neces-sary for incubating the seeds of new life.

Whilst there is evidence that Lughnasadh was at least kept in Ireland, it is unclear why the god Lugh was celebrated in relation to the harvest. Lugh was one of the most important gods in the deity. He was the god of all human skills – arts, magic, warfare, the guardian of roads and travellers and the patron of money-making and commerce. He was closely associated with kings and heroes. If masculine and feminine are defined archetypically, Lughnasadh is sometimes seen as a man's festival. It is opposite Imbolc in the wheel of the year when Brigid was honoured and was more a womanly festi-val. Lughnasadh falls in the outer half of the year and all festivities were held outside. In Ireland, great assemblies are recorded[6] that may have lasted three weeks. They were the gathering of the tribes where not only the first fruits of the land were celebrated but the "ripened" talents of human society. There were races, games, athletics, arts festivals, and people gathered for political and legal debate.There was horse-racing and commerce where tribes traded animals and other goods. Most Lughnasadh gatherings took place on hill-tops or by water including holy pools that would have been places of pilgrimage. There were some ritual elements like a solemn cutting of the first corn. This would be presented to Lugh. A feast with all the "new" food would be made including bilberries, often gathered on the walk up to the hill. In Ireland these festivals ended in the twelfth century after the Norman Conquest, but Lammas Fairs were popular and more widespread both in Ireland and across the British Isles, and shared similar elements.

Lammas Fairs were held on the Sunday nearest to August 1 and could last for weeks. Folks came from miles around for sports, stalls, side-shows, to sell horses, farm animals and other produce. Travelling fairs arrived. There were fortune-tellers, entertainers, dancing and feasting. Beer, wine, cider and whisky from the previous year's harvest were ritually, and non-ritually, drunk. They were also the time when rents were paid, local officials elected and common lands opened. These occasions were rowdy to the extent that they became increasingly banned, until the nineteenth century when the Victorians made them all but extinct. These non-ritual summer fairs, wakes and revels (also called "ales" and "hoppings") that took place in every village and town across the British Isles, including the Irish county fairs, remain in some form today. Often a travelling fun-fair arrives and there are stalls and games. On a larger scale, many places still have county shows in August or September. On the continent, the village festivals do not pass without feasting and dancing into the early hours, more in the spirit of the older Lammas Fair.

The wakes, fairs, revels and Lammas did have ritual elements though and this has been largely lost. Originally they were held, as with the rush-bearing described in the Introduction to June, around parish feasts. Often this would have been the actual patronal festival of the church, the day of the saint that the church was named after. People gathered together for a service in the morning and the revels began afterwards and lasted several days. They were always threatened through the centuries, by restraints of religious objection and civil order, due to the rowdy nature of the feasts. Even so, communities continued to celebrate the summer and the first-fruits of the harvest.

The most striking ritual of Lammas is the cutting of the first corn and making it into a loaf for the Mass in church on August 1st or 2nd. Alexander Carmichael[7] records that in the Hebrides, they celebrated Lammas on August 15th, the feast of the Assumption of the Virgin Mary, in a ritual that combined Catholic and pre-Christian elements. They cut the corn and made it into a loaf called a "Moilean Maire" or fatling-of-Mary bannock. Each member of the family would take a piece and walk sun-wise round the fire singing the Paean of Mother Mary:

"On the feast day of Mary the fragrant,
Mother of the Shepherd of the flocks,
I cut me a handful of the new corn,
I dried it gently in the sun,
I rubbed it sharply from the husk,
With mine own palms.

I ground it in a quern on Friday,
I baked it in a fan of sheep-skin,
I toasted it to a fire of rowan,
And I shared it with my people.
I went sunways round my dwelling
In the name of Mary Mother,
Who promised to preserve me,
Who did preserve me
And who will preserve me,
In peace, in flocks,
In righteousness of heart,
In labour, in love,
In wisdom, in mercy,
For the sake of Thy Passion.
Thou Christ of Grace
Who till the day of my death
Will never forsake me!"[8]

The idea of presenting a loaf with the new corn at the Sunday communion, was revived by Young Farmers across southern England in the 1940s and some churches in rural areas are attempting to revive Lammas today.

August then, in times gone by, was dominated by the start of the cereal harvest and the Lughnasadh and Lammas celebrations that accompanied it. The themes of gathering in what has been planted earlier in the year are community based and spiritual too. It is a pause for assessment of our own lives and of the lives of our communities. Most British people have been raised in the school system which counts the summer as the break between one school year and the next and so we carry this with us long after we have left school. The warm weather means that August is the main holiday for most. However, within this month is the portent for the darker months and the dying that must take place before the seed within the harvest starts to bear fruit again in the spring. Whilst there maybe gatherings of families and friends in August and it is a popular month for weddings, it is also a month marked by absence, the loosening of routines, and suspension of regular timetables. Despite finer weather and holiday time, it can be a difficult month for many with the "new term" of September bringing relief.

As it is the last "outward" month, the prayers continue to focus on outside themes – the sea, as many people go to be near it, mountains and hills for a similar reason and a day focussed on the world. August is the month when folks sometimes visit other parts of the world. The prayers celebrate the richness of other cultures beyond Britain's shores.

MONDAY Lammas

On Rising/Resting

Blessed are you Fruitful one,
giver of abundance and plenty,
giver of resources when stocks are low.
☼ Strengthen me with all I need as I set out this day.
☾ Grow my faith in your providence as I lie down this night.

Praising

Praise to you Unseen Love,
for you buried deep within me the seed of life
and watch me grow from newly green to golden
like the fields that turn at this time.
Praise for the tenderness of your eye
when I survey the first fruits of all that I have harvested this year.
Praise for the new seed from the old
that will flourish with the coming year
in ways that I cannot imagine.
Praise to you.

In Stillness

Be still in the silence and aware of the Love with and within..............

☼ Morning Invocation

O Bread of Life, my staple and my comfort,
who meets me in my hunger,
give me my daily bread this day, simple and sufficient,
fuel for my body, sustenance for my soul.
Feed my feet that they may walk down fertile paths this day.
Feed my heart that my love may be plentiful for those around me.
Feed my work that I may be productive.
Feed my words that I may be generous and not mean.
Feed my management of time that I may be generative and not pinched.
Feed me in my spirit so I may not go hungry
but return again to you each morning with open hand
to receive all I need for today, freeing my care for tomorrow.
Give me my daily bread as I set forth this day.

☼ Opening Out

Generous One of the Harvest,
walk alongside those who have sown in tears,
who have scattered their seed without hope,
on a land not of their choosing.
Come close to those who weep this day

Shine your abundant love on them
that they might come back singing,
carrying their sheaves of joy.

☾ Thanksgiving

As I end this day in your safe-keeping
I count three blessings before my sleeping

☾ Night Shielding

Giver of all human skills,
I give you thanks for the ripened talent of all those I know.
Protect and sustain me as I lie down this night,
and all who feel they have harvested little,
their efforts fruitless, their spirits dry, their struggles in vain.

Hold us all in the doubting of our gifts
until we can treasure in the hidden place
the unique harvest that is ours to bring forth
through good seasons and bad.
May I trust your holding as I go to sleep this night.

Blessing

Golden blessings on the oats and rye, the wheat, barley and the corn
Golden blessings on the reaping and threshing, the winnowing and storing
Golden blessings on the grinding and milling, the rising and baking
Golden blessings on the Loaf, sacred and broken to be shared by all.
☼ Blessings on all your hand provides this day by your love.
☾ Blessings on all your hand provides this night by your love.

TUESDAY Emptiness

On Rising/Resting
Blessed be you O Sacred Presence,
present when I do not feel you there,
present below the surface of all things.
✪ Let me glimpse your liveliness this day.
☾ Let me glimpse your life within as I lie down this night.

Praising
Praise to you Invisible One,
whose abundant graciousness is all around despite the nothingness inside.
Even when I fail to receive your goodness
and cannot hold it to myself like a long lost loved one,
yet will I praise you today and tonight,
and trust that one of these mornings my felt faith will return,
with the doing and the routine and the peopled days of September.
Praise you for not losing your faith in me.

In Stillness
Be still in the silence and aware of the Love with and within.............

✪ Morning Invocation
Distant God,
when my mooring's cut, my desire adrift and I am without centre,
do not become absent in the deadness around me,
the empty streets, the curtains drawn in the day,
the no-one's home of August time that awakens my homeless state.
Rather, restore to me my belonging in you.
Peg down my free-floating listlessness and ground me this day.
Ground my reluctant body as I return to work.
Ground the hidden memories of long school holidays freed from timetable.
Ground my focus when lack of clamour obscures my purpose.
Ground my connectedness when friends are far away.
Ground the soles of my feet on the earth as I tread each day anyway.
Ground my eyes as they alight on your works and take me out of myself.
Ground the doing of my hands that I might remember my usefulness.
Ground my insecurity in your unwavering love as I set out this day.

☼ Opening Out

Comforting Spirit who knows our emptiness.
In the hollow days of the holiday time
when everyone is coming and going with packs and cases,
be with all who struggle through this month,
those pulled by many different calls who have little time for themselves,
those with endless care for children,
those who work and cannot go away,
those who feel alone

Be with each of us and give us glimmers of your care,
like the sun that breaks through in the late fading days of summer.

☾ Thanksgiving

As I end this day in your safe-keeping
I count three blessings before my sleeping

☾ Night Shielding

Secret God as I lie down this night,
I long for the darkness to cover the emptiness and make me forget
until a change may come with morning light.
But when my love seems inadequate and flat,
grace me with the accepting heart of a mystic
and let me trust your hiddenness within my soul.
Be with all others I think of now who need your love tonight

Thank you for the gift of dry and discontented times
when we come to understand the covering of your love in the darkness.
Secret God, hide me, as I take my rest this night.

Blessing

Bless my vacant spirit with your fullness
My hollowness with your meaning
My palling with the reviving of your Spirit.
☼ Let me not miss your blessing at this day's beginning
☾ Let me not miss your blessing at this day's end.

WEDNESDAY Sea

On Rising/Resting
Blessed be you O Great One,
wild and tempestuous as the waves crash on the rocks,
peaceful and rhythmic as the tides move across the sands.
☼ Grace me with your wildness and your peace as I go about my day.
☾ Grace me with your wildness and your peace as I let go this night.

Praising
Praise to you O Holy One of the Sea,
for the gift of eternity when I stand on the shore
and know your vast wonder as the waves lap over my feet.
When I am here like a child,
with pocketfuls of shells and stones and sea-glass,
I seem small and so do the troubles I bring,
before the epic arrival of each wave
causing tears of healing and awe.
Praise to you.

In Stillness
Be still in the silence and aware of the Love with and within.........

☼ Morning Invocation
Holy Anchorage,
you are my security when stormy weather tosses me about
and in fairer times, under mackerel skies, on breeze-ruffled waters.
Guide my spirit this day with still contentment like the seal.
Guide my spirit with playfulness like the otter,
with quirkiness like puffin, purpose like sandpiper and curlew.
Guide my spirit with child-like joy at rock-pool's edge,
with the delight of your creation seen in starfish, sea-urchin and crab.
Guide my spirit by the holy spiral as on periwinkle and ammonite.
Guide my spirit with steadfastness like barnacle and limpet on rock,
friendliness like dolphin, large gentleness like whale.
May your Spirit blow my boat on the waves of this day before me.
And may the sun go down on steady waters as I return
to the safety of your evening harbour, the window-lights of home.

☼ Opening Out

O Man of Galilee who walked the shore in the first light of day
when all seemed lost and gone,
appear on the edge of the horizon for all who feel washed up,
their brokenness like flotsam and jetsam after the wreckage,
those floating like driftwood brought on the surf,
those who cannot get back on course,
or who fish and fish without bite or catch

Rescue our lostness from the fathoms green darkness.
Reveal the pearl made there from the grit, risen up, shiny white and new.

☾ Thanksgiving

As I end this day in your safe-keeping
I count three blessings before my sleeping

☾ Night Shielding

I lie down in wonder at the power of your Spirit this night
You swathed the sea in blue and green with silver sequins,
covering hidden depths as your love enfolds mine.
I ebb and flow in glimpsing your mystery
that hovers with mists of unknowing as at the beginning
when you first appeared on the water making all from love.
Keep me open to your Spirit and surround all who need your peace.

Like the full moon on dark waters, watch over us as we sleep this night.
In my waking, may I reflect the love that shines upon me always.

Blessing

May the might of the waves strengthen me, the ancient rocks ground;
the wind in my hair and spray on my face connect me;
the sun and moon that move the waters, move me to see your blessing
☼ as surely as the tide goes in and out this day
☾ as surely as the tide goes in and out this night
and at journey's end be waiting on the strand in morning light

THURSDAY Celebration of the World

On Rising/Resting
Blessed be you Maker of all,
you hold the whole world in your hands,
the mountains and plains, the rivers and oceans.
✿ Hold me as I walk in the world this day.
☾ Hold me as I lie down in the world this night.

Praising
Praise to you Bearer of our Home Planet,
who made and loves the intense variety of our kind,
the colours and shapes of our features,
the desires and ways of each tribe.
Praise to you who weeps with us
when we fear those that are different,
and wound and spill blood in the name of our own,
and worse, in the name of you, Keeper of all.

In Stillness
Be still in the silence and aware of the Love with and within...............

✿ Morning Invocation
Blessed Inspiration,
the spark of your infinite joy is in every living thing.
Come to me this day and delight with the gifts of the nations.
May those rich in coloured textiles and painted houses inspire my creativity.
May those good at invention inspire my thinking.
May the varieties of humour inspire my conversation.
May the peaceful and gracious peoples inspire my way with others.
May the pioneers of every land inspire my risk-taking.
May the embrace of the good and simple things inspire me to let go.
May the easy living and slower pace mellow me.
May the seamless join of earthed and spiritual inspire my faith.
May those waiting to be free inspire my courage.
May the joyful who know suffering inspire my belief in the human spirit,
as I walk the wonderful world with thanksgiving this day.

☼ Opening Out

O Sorrowful One,
lament with us the shadow cast by our special gifts.
The strength of identity that becomes unlistening;
the passion of faith that becomes certain;
the tolerance that becomes intolerant;
the power that becomes corrupt;
the history that becomes a battlefield.
I think of places of conflict this day

Grant us a peace that is wise and sustaining
and values our different stories.

☾ Thanksgiving

As I end this day in your safe-keeping
I count three blessings before my sleeping

☾ Night Shielding

Patchwork Spirit spread over each one of us this night.
Cover those in hemisphere dark and those not long arisen,
those whose season brings the sun and those in wintry climes.
Let your love stitch and strengthen our fragile co-existence together
that our children may honour the multi-coloured patches of land
and the peoples that live there, remembering especially

Tuck all of us in under the quilt of peacemaking,
for blest are those children of God who follow the way of peace.
May I sleep with safety and wake with praise in this world.

Blessing

Blessing of the sun that shines upon us all, blessing of the moon.
Blessing of the waves that crash upon our shores, blessing of the skies.
And in each land, the different tongued blessing of God upon one and all.
☼ Bless the understanding in the world this day.
☾ Bless the understanding in the world this night.

FRIDAY Cherishing

On Rising/On Resting

Blessed be you Bringer of Gifts in due season,
for the flourish and zenith of summer,
bearing first fruits and full growth.
✿ Brim me over with gratitude as I walk out this summer's day.
☾ Settle me deep with gratitude as I lie down this summer's night.

Praising

Praise to you for walking in the garden of this lovely day.
The flowers have not yet faded though soon they might.
Some of the blackberries are fat, some tart and some just right.
The nights are falling slowly, and the mellow evening light is warm.
Praise to you in this sacrament of now.
Give me grace to hold this moment that you have given to me,
to cherish it before it passes with the autumn glow,
to gather the plums and pears that have fallen to the ground,
and to taste the sweetness of today.

In Stillness

Be still in the silence and aware of the Love with and within...........

✿ Morning Invocation

Loving Spirit, pour down on all I do this day.
Make me as a bowl ready to receive, hands cupped in supplication
noticing your love as it happens, not afterwards.
Pour down on my empty hands that I might know your Spirit this day.
Pour down on my eyes that I might truly see.
Pour down on my ears that I might leave a space to listen.
Pour down on my tongue that I might relish each taste of good nourishing.
Pour down on my feet that I might be ready to be guided.
Pour down on my body that I might be open to the other's touch.
Pour down on my heart that I might hear another's need.
Pour down on my hunger, absorb the wanting that delays today.
Make me as a bowl, ready to receive your love,
and know how beautiful is this summer's day before it passes.

☼ Opening Out

Source of life,
as the season fades and the grasshoppers quieten,
help me to see the freshness of the first-fruits around,
the ripening fruit falling from the tree,
the rolls of straw in the fields,
and in my own life, the new growth to be celebrated this year.
I offer any struggles to see my gifts.
Be with all who cannot feel your favour

Shower our poverty with the riches of your grace
and our wealth with your simplicity as we rise up this day.

☾ Thanksgiving

As I end this day in your safe-keeping
I count three blessings before my sleeping

☾ Night Shielding

Protectress of the night,
still me when I become afraid
for all the living know that the dying days must come.
Be with all those who live with diminishment at this time

Thank you that you are not a fair weather One but with us always.
May we cherish the sunny days of our lives
so we may embrace the darkness without fear,
and know that without the winter, no spring can come.
Restore me in sleep this night so I might greet the day.

Blessing

God of the golden dawn keep me with blessings from above.
God of the mid-day sun, shine your rays of warmth and life.
God of the silver dusk keep me in the twilight of my days.
God of the night-time deepen me to walk in the morning light.
☼ Bless me in awareness of the gift of this new day.
☾ Bless me in awareness of the gift of this new night.

SATURDAY Mountains and Hills

On Rising/Resting
Blessed be you Presence of the Mountain,
shrouded by cloud, the misty numinous meeting
amidst the sky, the floor of heaven.
✿ Meet me on the ground this day and in every step I take.
☾ Cover me with your presence as I lie me down to sleep this night.

Praising
Praise to you Maker of mountain and hill
of crag, fell and pike, of moor, tor and down;
for the walking through heather and fern, leaving my ground-level routine
and up to the magnificent isolation and silence of the high places,
to the holy mountain top, where I can see more clearly,
and gasp at the marvel of your handiwork,
across rocks and mountainsides and down into the valleys,
and know that I am part of all that is made.
Praise to you

In Stillness
Be still in the silence and aware of the Love with and within...........

✿ Morning Invocation
Long-time Companion of my soul,
I lift my eyes to the hills of my life this day.
My weariness can assail me from so near the bottom.
The top can seem too far away and is not within my view.
I can only put one foot in front of another.
I cannot go back and doubt my strength to go forward.
My foot stumbles on loose stones, my short-breathed body aches.
I fear the darkening day with no signs to point the way.
Come to my aid, my Journey Friend, do not leave me on my own.
I pass cairns and know others have trod this way before.
I stop to take my shelter in a rock and look back.
A bird soars, a flower at my feet stares at me, happy here.
I see where I have travelled and slowly glimpse your hand.
Place it in mine and let me trust your walk beside me

as I set out again this day.

☼ Opening Out
Keeper of the way,
walk close beside all those who feel alone,
whose path is all uphill at this time.

May our help come from you.
Do not let our feet slip and be our shade by day.
Keep us on our setting out and on our returning,
this day and always.

☾ Thanksgiving
As I end this day in your safe-keeping
I count three blessings before my sleeping

☾ Night Shielding
Guarding Spirit,
as I lie down this night tucked up, and sheltered,
I think of Cairn gorm and Sca Fell and great Ben Nevis,
of Croagh Patrick, Cadair Idris and Helvellyn,
of Sugar Loaf Mountain, Bessy Bell and Dollywaggon Pike,
and the mountains and hills nearest to me.
How marvellous the same dark
covering their grandeur covers me.
Protect all who need your safety this night

Keep fear without and love within
as the lamp burns low on this night, in this land.

Blessing
O Hand-Holder, who walks with me,
bless my heart with courage when fears creep.
Bless my feet upon the path when it turns steep.
Bless my eyes with gratitude for the wonders you have shown me.
Bless my hands with trust in your hands that will never disown me.
 ☼ Walk beside me this day, for long is the trail and sacred is the journey.
 ☾ Keep me this night for long is the trail and sacred is the journey.

SUNDAY Holidays

On Rising/Resting

Blessed be you Sabbath Giver, who rested from your labour,
and sanctifies change and rest as holy days.

☼ Renew and refresh me in different climes as at home this day.

☾ Renew and refresh me when I lie down in different bed or at home this night.

Praising

Praise to you Bringer of Sunshine,
for this last bright month of summer days,
for time spent away from home with friends and family,
for the rounding off of the year,
for precious time to be and play in the adventure of your world,
see different lives and return,
with summer-golden skin and softened body and soul.
Praise to you

In Stillness

Be still in the silence and aware of the Love with and within..........

☼ Morning Invocation

O Maker of all the world where I can roam,
you give me the life that I have made and know my need to rest.
Come to me with your peace, at home or away, as I set out this day.
Come to my mind, take the stress and strain of my daily habit.
Come to my sleep and restore me from my weariness.
Come to my eyes as you show me new sights and points of view,
or those I have loved and return to again.
Come to my tongue as I savour tastes strange to me.
Come to my hands as I try things I have not tried before.
Come to my feet as I walk where many have travelled.
Come to my homesickness and assure me of my true home within.
Come to the freedom I feel when I am away,
that has tried to break through my working days,
and might be longing to whisper something important.
Come to my vision and show me what I need to see this August day.

☼ Opening Out

Divine Keeper,
Be with all this day who find it hard to holiday,
those who are afraid to leave routines of safety,
those who have no-one to travel with,
those who have no money to go away,
those who struggle to let go of screen or phone,
those who feel the tensions of free time with family,
those who have memories of family times now gone.

Give us grace to survive what we cannot change
and hope where change may come, as we spend this day in your love.

☾ Thanksgiving

As I end this day in your safe-keeping
I count three blessings before my sleeping

☾ Night Shielding

Creator God you gave us one life and dreams to fly,
surround and sustain me where I lie down this night.
As the birds around me moult and cannot fly until new feathers come,
be with me as I stop for awhile and shed my skin of the year.
And when I prepare to take off again,
give me wisdom to know what to let fall and what to take with me.
Be with all I think of now who need your care

Bring us your comfort as we lie down to sleep.
Replenish me as I rest this night and make me ready to greet the day.

Blessing

The blessing of God when I am far from home.
The blessing of God when I am near.
The blessing of God on my venturing and exploring.
The blessing of God on my homecoming and belonging.
The blessing of God on my going out and coming in this day/night and always.

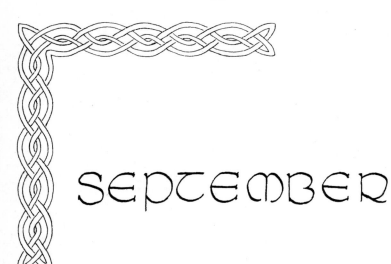

SEPTEMBER

INTRODUCTION TO SEPTEMBER

"Harvest home! Harvest hum! Harvest home!
We've ploughed, we've sown
We've reaped, we've mown
Harvest home! Harvest home!"[9]

Autumn, or Fall, whichever evocative word our culture uses, is a much beloved season. Keats' "season of mists and mellow fruitfulness" is oft-quoted because, like all great poets, he says it in six words. Autumn has been the inspiration for poets, artists and musicians down the centuries. The gathering in of the fruits of the earth as the colours turn to golds, russets, fiery oranges and rich browns like the soil and the sun themselves, warms our spirits. In fact just describing the fruits and the colours with no poetic artifice feels delicious. September is a time for ripening berries and nuts, hips and haws, blackberries, scarlet rowan berries, elderberries, blueberries, loganberries, sloes, rosehips, hazelnuts, and sweet chestnuts. Childhood memories are evoked by the first sight of acorns and conkers. Seedheads on plants like thistles and teasels feed the birds during September. Fruits are gathered in abundance: apples, damsons, greengages, pears, plums, and squashes and marrows. Corn on the cobs dripping with butter are a seasonal treat. Although we no longer have that visceral sense of needing to lay up stores for the winter, and fears for our survival if the harvest has been poor, we seem to have retained the residual feeling that being more home-based again after the summer, is comforting. It is a time for gathering in and preparing for the winter months: storing all that fruit in jams, preserves and chutneys. It is the time for finishing the outdoor jobs, cutting back branches and planting bulbs for the spring.

There is a safety in the weather too. September rarely has the harshness of winter though can be rainy, windy and cold. It is more often mild and Indian Summers are not uncommon. The summer, though dying, is still in evidence and the light is soft. Many of the wild flowers and garden flowers, like marigolds, remain, as do insects. In fact daddy long-legs have their own kind of abundance! The leaves are, for the most part, still on the trees and still green. However, the days are getting shorter and colder and the sun's power is waning. The earth's energy is changing and moving quite fast. Starvation is not a reality for people, but it is for the creatures that live in our land. They know that winter and lack of food is coming and they need to prepare. Most visibly, the squirrel is out and about, with nuts in mouth, laying up her store for the winter months. Lucky folks in the north of England and Scotland and very select spots, south, may catch the classic sight of a red squirrel, with her tail curled up her back, tufted ears, nut in claws.

In September a miracle happens above our heads - that of the migrant birds. A recognizable sight is the martins and swallows all lined up on telegraph wires ready to make their long journey back to southern Africa. It is amazing that they get there and amazing that they return, often to the same nest. Surprisingly, the newly fledged birds do not make that first journey with their parents but with their peers. They navigate by the sun at day and if they travel at night, by the stars. They are tuned into the earth's magnetism, echo sounding and "landmarks" like the Eiffel Tower!

Autumn Equinox (sometimes called Mabon)

Whilst Lughnasadh, at the beginning of August, is thought to be the beginning of the changing energy, most of us are much more aware of it in September. In August the evenings are still predominantly light but in September we noticeably approach another equinox when day and night are of equal length all over the world. It happens around September 21st and is opposite the spring equinox around March 21st. Both are months of transformation when one season clearly moves into another. There is thanksgiving for all the earth's abundance but there is also a letting go of the summer. There is a movement of going underground and more inward as we step through the doorway into winter. The double spiral is the symbol of the autumn equinox as we are poised between the outward harvest of the past year and prepare to journey in towards the darker months. The balance of the equinox celebrates the wholeness of light and shadow, the seen and unseen, the known and unknown, death and re-birth, creation and destruction. Spiritually, if we are to make space for the new, we need to embrace rest and renewal, almost like brushing the fallen leaves of the soul to clear a path for what will come. We plant bulbs now and keep them in the dark until they are nourished and ready to come up into the light later, changed and transformed by their time beneath the surface.

September is also a time of change because children, who remind us of our earlier lives, go back to school. Even beyond school, new "terms" start up. In the collective psyche, September can mean new, regardless of the rhythm of our job.

Harvest

> "Come ye thankful people come
> Raise the song of Harvest-home:
> All is safely gathered in,
> Ere the winter storms begin;
> God our Maker, doth provide
> For our wants to be supplied"[10]

Another memory from school days is the Harvest Festival. Many people decorated their shoe-boxes (fresh from containing their shiny new shoes), and packed them full of tins for old or homeless people and carried them to school or church for the Harvest Thanksgiving. School halls and churches were decorated with sheaves, marrows, apples, grapes and loaves. Even today, schools and churches, especially in rural areas, keep Harvest Festival. Villagers who are not regular church-goers often go, as they do at Christmas, Remembrance and Easter. It is interesting to note that all these festivals echo the natural world at the time in which they fall.

Harvest Thanksgiving may appear to be a Christian festival but its ritualistic roots are pre-Christian and the Harvest Festival is a relatively recent invention. Rev. R.S. Hawker, a vicar in Cornwall, is credited with starting it in 1843. He invited parishioners to receive the sacrament (eucharist or communion) in the bread of the new corn. It became incredibly popular and remains so, even with greatly reduced congregations. Like it's mediaeval predecessor, it combined parochial organization and all-age entertainment. Parishoners were allowed to decorate the churches with their own ornaments for the first time since the Reformation.

If Lammas celebrated the first corn being cut, Harvest-home is the celebration of the last sheaf being reaped. It is the Harvest supper, the communal meal, given by the farmer and his wife to all the labourers on their estate as a reward for their hard work, after the last load had been carried in from the fields. It took place in the farmhouse or in the barn and was an occasion of great feasting and much drinking. In England they ate beef and plum pudding, and drank beer. The Scots fared less well and feasted on beer, bread and cheese or oatmeal. However, across the land there were local specialities and there was singing and dancing as well as feasting. Harvest-homes were widespread from mediaeval times until the nineteenth century when agricultural machines were introduced. The Harvest Festival was well timed to gradually replace the much-loved Harvest-home.

There were many regional variations around the beliefs and practises of cutting the last sheaf. The Devon and Cornish practise of "Crying the Neck" is the most famous. All the workers would stand in a circle around the last sheaf, or "the neck" or "the mare". They would throw their sickles at it. Although this was light-hearted, it arose from a belief that the spirit of the corn was in the sheaf and so nobody wanted to be the last one to cut it for fear of killing the spirit. The man who threw the last sickle, cut the sheaf. The men in the circle took their hats off and bowed to it in homage to the earth that had provided. The sheaf was raised and they threw their hats in the air with laughter, crying "a neck, a neck, we have one." Some sang and chanted in rising harmony. The actions of the men in the circle might have originated from the belief in the dying of the corn spirit, as they bowed down and then their joy as they rose and sang or cheered, at her bringing forth new life as the seed of the next year's harvest. Then one of the men would seize the neck and run to the farmhouse, followed by the others. One of the maids would be waiting by the door with a bucket of water or a kiss.

Some areas had a cart like Robert Herrick describes in his poem "The Hock-cart."[11] It carried the last load from the fields and was decorated with country arts. A Harvest Lord or Queen sitting on top, was crowned with ears of corn or a wheaten hat. It too, was greeted with buckets of water as it arrived at the Harvest-home. There was some element of a race to the Harvest celebrations and nobody wanted to be the last to bring the harvest home. Pranks were played on the last farm to be harvested.

The last sheaf of corn was the focus of any spiritual beliefs. As at Lammas, the goddess of the harvest was Ceres. The last sheaf was made into a woman, adorned in ribbons and often a dress. It is the origin of the corn dolly. All the different names for her like "the Cailleach", "the Old Witch", "the Maiden", "the Queen", "the Mare" "the Gander" (hence the "neck") "the Bitch" might have originated from a veneration of the goddess. She was feared and honoured in different ways shown by the particular ways she was treated. The Cailleach was hung in the home until Candlemas/Imbolc when she became Bride's bed (see Introduction to February). Sometimes the harvest goddess was seen as another aspect of Brigid. In Shetland though, the last sheaf called "the bikko bitch" or straw dog was tossed into the field of the farmer who was late harvesting and then he was "barked" at.

It is easy to see why any spirit or goddess of the harvest was either feared or honoured when people's survival depended on her. The names given to the last sheaf testify to the worship and fear that women have always attracted in our culture. The story of Ceres/Demeter (see Introduction to August), contains archetypal aspects of woman that evoke awe and hatred. She is the earth mother/provider in Demeter and the concomitant suffering in her grief-stricken wandering around the world searching for her child. In Persephone, goddess of the Underworld, the dark mystery of womanhood is embodied. The twist that she is Demeter's younger self also speaks of the paradox that women can seem both unreachable and all-giving. In relation to harvest, the goddess, like John Barleycorn, like Jesus Christ, must die in order for new life to come. It is a spiritual reality that is concealed in our particular culture because death itself is so hidden. It accompanies every change we make including the changes of September, harvest and birth. It is not for nothing that Earth is conceived of as Mother. All things proceed from her and to her all things return.

Trees and Fungi

This life–death–rebirth cycle can also be found in our woods and forests at this time of year. Folks swoon at the marvels of new life in the spring but the less perceptible workings of the circle of life above and below us in the autumn are awe-inspiring. At the foot of the trees are little recycling centres. Mushrooms and toadstools suddenly appear. They have actually been there all along as tiny threads in moist places drawing nutrients from decaying organic material. With the damper weather of September, the threads grow into mushrooms and toadstools. Later in the autumn, they die releasing their nutrients back into the soil and feeding the plants and roots of the trees. We have given our fungi such endearing names that they are worth telling. The classic red toadstool with white spots that pixies sit on is called "fly agaric" because its scent kept insects out of people's kitchens. There is also the fairy-ring champignon, the destroying angel, the coconut-scented milk-cap, the horn of plenty, the wood hedgehog, the arched woodwax, the yellow knight, the slippery jack and velvet shank, the aptly named ox-tongue, oyster, giant funnel and parasol, all of which look like their namesakes; as well as the puff-balls and ink-caps that may already be familiar!

Trees have a special place in Celtic spirituality and symbolize it well. They are rooted in the ground and reach up to heaven. There are many beliefs and lores in the properties of each tree. The Celts had a tree ogham. This was a system used to encode the symbolic and divinational meaning in each tree. The meanings vary with the sources but some of those special to the Celts were Oak (doorway to the mysteries, strength of change), Holly (good fortune, evergreen), Yew (transformation, long-living), Birch (beginnings), Ash (link of inner and outer world), Beech (stability, evenness), Hazel (wisdom) and Willow (feminine, watery, healing due to salicin being the active ingredient in aspirin).

Trees partake in the extraordinary circle of life and stand for us, as important pictures of the spiritual journey. They draw up water and minerals through their roots from the humus, the organic matter in the soil, and carry them to the leaves. The leaves draw in the sunlight turning the carbon dioxide into oxygen and helping us human beings to breathe. So living things are scientifically and spiritually connected to each other. By the end of September through to November, the diminishing light and warmth from the sun starts to turn their leaves the magical fire colours we associate with autumn. This process which is a feast for our eyes, is actually a dying process. Within, the tree, the sap descends but this gives the roots energy. The sleep, and rest above ground, hides the deepening roots underground, renewing the young trees and plants and making them stronger.

In Britain we have cleared much of our land but we still have wonderful forests and woods. Up to about 4000 BC, our country used to be covered in forest, called the "Wild wood". It is said that squirrels could jump from one branch to another and cross from the southern coast of England to the northern tip of Scotland without touching land. Dramatic declines started and then Neolithic peoples began the process of clearing the wild wood. In the prayers, September is a good month to celebrate our trees.

The apple tree is especially thought of in September because of the apple harvest. In every country it is sacred and symbolizes fruitfulness, abundance, love and immortality. In Genesis 3 in the Bible, the story is told of when Eve took the fruit from the Tree of Knowledge in the Garden of Eden. This is often thought of as an apple. This has been held against women for over two thousand years of Christian history, apparently redeemed by the perceived passivity of Mary, the mother of Jesus, in the Gospels. It is plainly ridiculous to suggest that one gender has a monopoly on temptation. Eve's spunky act of finding out for herself must surely symbolize the route any of us go, to discover who God is and how we learn about ourselves. She powerfully represents the human dilemma of wanting to know and reaching out and tasting, knowing it can lead into dangerous waters where there is no going back. Ignorance, as they say, may be bliss, but reaching for the stars is part of the richness of being human.

Genesis was written to be a creation myth by the Hebrew men of that time. A myth is a story that expresses the ideology of a culture and as such, it works well. Its potency persists way beyond Judeo-Christian doctrine because it still has resonance in our culture. Many people in the street today could tell the story of Adam and Eve, but would be unable to recall most other Biblical stories. Sadly, it works because it continues to contain a truth about how men and women relate to each other and how men and women together, relate to the earth. Feminists have re-appropriated the apple tree as a symbol of women's knowledge and wisdom in defiance of the way the story has been used against women.

Harvest Moon

The harvest moon is the full moon nearest the equinox. It is often afterwards and can be in October. At this time, the moon rises at a point which is opposite to the sun, close to the eastern point of the horizon. It looks larger because it hangs lower. This is similar to the moon on the other side of the wheel, at the spring equinox. The harvest moon is so called because workers in the fields could work by her light as the days grew shorter, in order to get the harvest in. Each moon in every month has a particular name. The name for the September moon is the Vine Moon. This is because the grape harvest is picked at this time.

"Like the vine I bud forth delights,
and my blossoms become glorious
and abundant fruit.
Come to me you who desire me,
and eat your fill of my fruits."

- Sirach 24.17-19

Thus speaks Wisdom in the book of Sirach. In some Bibles there are a series of books called "the Apocrypha". They can be found between the Old and New Testaments. They were excluded when the church decided which books would make up the Bible. Several of these books (Sirach and the Wisdom of Solomon) and some of the Old Testament (Job, Proverbs and Ecclesiastes) are called "Wisdom literature". Wisdom is an ancient Israelite way of looking at the world that flourished during Bible times. Some of the Psalms and the sayings of Jesus reflect Wisdom perspectives. Wisdom starts with experience rather than what God says about the world. So it is earthed in ordinary life.

Wisdom believes in God as Creator and that as creator, truth is embedded in all of creation so our finding out about God can start with life around us. Wisdom is always personified as female. She was there from the beginning and playing while the world was created (see Proverbs 8 for the hymn to Wisdom). Christian feminists are re-discovering her, feeling she has been too hidden. She is consonant with Celtic spirituality because of her earthedness. She is also abroad in the intentional spiritual paths that people are increasingly embarking on in our time. So there are prayers celebrating the divine feminine in September.

St Michael and all Angels

Michaelmas is celebrated on September 29. Its proximity to the equinox means it is associated with autumn's official start and the shortening of the days. Some universities and other old institutions call the autumn term Michaelmas term. The feast's proper name is Feast of Ss. Michael, Gabriel and Raphael. St Michael is leader of the angelic warriors and is pictured in armour on a white horse, often slaying a dragon. He is seen as a protector against the darkness in his role of conveying souls to heaven. This is maybe why he is associated with high places like Mont St Michel in Brittany, St Michael's mount in Cornwall and the Skelligs in Ireland.

St Michael and all Angels was a day in the British Isles when accounts had to be settled. There was a traditional meal of goose. In Skye, they had a procession and ate a cake called the St Michael's bannock. In the Western coast and isles of Scotland they made a "struan" from the new cereal, baked on a lambskin and moistened with ewe's milk. It was taken to the church to be blessed and afterwards, they ate it with lamb. The priest led a procession around the graveyard on a white horse singing a song to St Michael.

Angels are messengers of God and are surprisingly popular in our culture. There are many different beliefs about them but a lot of people feel they have a guardian angel. Less specifically, they feel there is angelic presence in their lives at certain important times. This could refer to either visionary phenomena or ordinary human beings placed in the right place at the right time that demonstrate God/Someone caring. The reality of actually feeling or seeing angels is true of religious and non-religious people alike.

So September is a time of change and transformation. There is thanksgiving for all the fruits of the earth and of our labours. It is a time of letting go and letting die in order for our inner journeys to be strengthened in darkness and quiet, that the newness of our next harvests might grow. This is mirrored all around us in the natural world. It is a time to celebrate the wonder of our bodies and souls being connected to the earth. Historically, this has been seen to be more womanly and relegated as less important than other kinds of knowing. So there is a restoring of the balance that has been lost, in this equinox month, when balance is celebrated.

MONDAY Autumn

On Rising/Resting

Blessed be you Balance-Holder,
unafraid of the dark from which all newness must begin,
giver of light that draws us on and out into fullness.
☼ Help me to balance my need for outgoing and restoring this day.
☾ With thankfulness for my going out, restore to me my rest this night

Praising

Praise to you Sacred Spirit who ripens and brings to fruition,
who knows the right time for things.
You know the quivering poise between readiness and fall,
the delicate tension between gathering and letting go.
Give me grace to know what is my season
in the rhythms of my flourishing and fading
as your love ever ripens in me.

In Stillness

Be still in the silence and aware of the Love with and within.............

☼ Morning Invocation

Embracer of all, who held out your arms and joined up the circle of life,
embolden me to believe that my lessening will bring new growth this day.
Embolden me as I cut back the branches and trust the bud will come.
Embolden me as I sweep the leaves and make a pathway through.
Embolden me as I clear a space and allow my autumn work to unfold.
Embolden me as I sit in the silence and let you be the all in all.
For in the pounding of the grain is the sharing of the bread.
In the crushing of the grape is the pouring of the wine.
In the falling of the leaves is the feeding of the roots.
In the disappearing of the creatures is the survival of their kind.
In the cutting of the corn is the new seed that will rise again.
In the dying time and darkness is your promise of hope renewed.
For you have lain in the deathly grip and felt the power of love's release.
Release in me the power of love as I set out this day.
Release in me your love.

☼ Opening Out
Brooding Spirit,
you warm and overshadow me so I can grow.
As the squirrels bury their nuts for future days when the frost will bite,
give me prudence to know what to store and to treasure,
what needs slow tending and incubating in your mercy.
Give me the humility to know when things are not yet ready,
though my passion would overtake my patience.
Be with all those this day who are yearning and longing for change

May we trust that the waiting is part of our ripening.

☾ Thanksgiving
As I end this day in your safe-keeping
I count three blessings before my sleeping

☾ Night Shielding
Nurturing One,
keep me close in the darkness as I let go into my rest this night.
For without the gift of sleep, I cannot be restored to the day.
Deepen the roots of my being and hide the fragility of my spirit
when I feel as a seed or pip or grain
with no sense that I will grow here.
Be with all who feel insignificant this night

Give us grace to trust our smallness and hope when we cannot see.
May your love transform me even as I sleep this night.

Blessing
May the autumn blessings of God be upon me
in the preserving of the fruitfulness you gave to me this year,
in my letting go of the old as the leaves fall to the earth,
in my holding a space so your peace can replenish, as the darker days come.
☼ As my time creeps on, may your love mature in me this day.
☾ As my time creeps on, may your love mature in me this night
until my final fulsomeness, when I will be plucked and my body return to the
soil on which I stand, and my soul complete in heaven.

TUESDAY New

On Rising/Resting

Blessed be you Living Presence,
for you come to me new with the dawn each morning
though you never deserted me through the night.
✿ Come with fresh grace as I rise this new day.
☾ Enfold me with your care at the ending of this day.

Praising

Praise to you O Faithful One,
for bringing me safely to this threshold.
You have been within me and watched over me
through change and chance, through troubles and joys.
And you are with me now as I stand at the doorway of this new place.
Bear my hopes and fears and walk with me into the unknown.
for you will keep me now, as you have then,
and for that, O Faithful One, praise you.

In Stillness

Be still in the silence and aware of the Love with and within...........

✿ Morning Invocation

Companion of the Way,
you know the place where I have come from, those I have loved and left.
You know those things I have longed to bid farewell to.
Accompany my trembling feet as I step onto a new road now.
Accompany my quivering hands as they grapple with unfamiliar things.
Accompany my memory as I absorb new information.
Accompany my wandering legs when I get lost and disorientated.
Accompany my heart that I might be open to new possibilities of friendship.
Accompany me when I tarnish the new place with my old mistakes.
Take my brave face in your hands and my fears in your love.
Take the strain of being a beginner and not yet competent.
Take the exhausting alertness of being unknown and not yet loved
until I can return to those who love me and tell them my story this day.
Accompany me as I enter this chapter on my own, dear Companion of my
way.

☼ Opening Out

God of new things
encircle us in the constant movement of our lives.
Flow in us when the honeymoon is over in our new stage
and we accept the everyday and disappointing features of our days.
Encircle those loved ones going through change,
those in new schools, new homes, new places or strange lands,
those who have not chosen this, those for whom it is too much

Beloved, be the asylum we seek in the new surroundings
and in the memories that rise up and pierce the daily round.

☾ Thanksgiving

As I end this day in your safe-keeping
I count three blessings before my sleeping

☾ Night Shielding

Ground of my being in whom my roots grow,
let me know that your love never changes as I lie down this night.
Hold me strong and close, for you alone know.
Give me courage when outside things are strange
until they are part of my familiar.
I offer everything in my day to you in the silence of now

Graft the surprises and struggles of this time into my becoming,
which I entrust to you, as I close my eyes and take my rest.

Blessing

Ancient One who makes all things new, bless me with your eternal love.
Bless me with your faithfulness when time has not yet forged loyalty and care,
and when I get worn and stuck, bless me with the hope of newness.
☼ Settle me with your ageless love as I set out on this first day of all my tomorrows.
☾ Settle me with your ageless love as I lie down to sleep this night.

WEDNESDAY Trees

On Rising/Resting
Blessed be you Tree of Life,
with your roots reaching down to the dark centre of the universe,
your leaves yearning towards the light beyond heaven.
✿ Shelter me with all your creation as I rise up this day.
☾ Shelter me with all your creation as I take my rest this night.

Praising
Praise to you Ancient and Strong,
for the wild sanctuary of the wood
where I can praise you midst the barky columns
and the branch-beamed roof.
Praise even for the fearsome darkness of the forest
where I can lose my way for there are no roads.
Show me your awesome presence in the temples of trees
and reveal your beauty when I am overwhelmed by unknowing,
so I may praise you on the pathless way.

In Stillness
Be still in the silence and aware of the Love with and within..............

✿ Morning Invocation
Source of all Being,
you know my little dyings; you know my greening and renewal.
You know every inch of every ring within the trunk of my life.
You know the spiral of my inner ways.
May your Spirit blow through my leaves this day
that my prayer might inhale heaven as I exhale on earth.
May your Spirit be the sap that feeds my roots when my energy descends.
May your Spirit be the love that turns my leaves to flames,
as a quieter passion flares with aging loveliness before it falls.
May your Spirit make me receptive to all I must let go,
like the soil that is nourished by the dropping leaf.
May your Spirit bless me in my diminishing like the toadstool at my feet
releasing goodness as it withers, beyond where the eye can see.
Source of all, you turn the circle of the earth, of my life, of this day.

Come with your windfall grace as I offer you my day.

☼ Opening Out

Sheltering God, you grow a love in us greater than acorn to oak,
more surprising than the smooth mahogany of conker after spiky case,
more healing than the willow's graceful bend by stream,
more transforming than the long life of yew, more evergreen than holly,
wiser than hazel, more joyful than vine, more stable than beech;
began even before birch, more eternal and wondrous than apple,
more trusty than oak, are you, O Sheltering One.
Make your love more real than a great mighty tree for

May we feel your strength as we lean against you
and know your sheltering at the beginning of this day.

☾ Thanksgiving

As I end this day in your safe-keeping
I count three blessings before my sleeping

☾ Night Shielding

Maker of forest, woodland, and orchard, of trees in fields and on hills,
as the light shortens and hides the land this night,
give us wisdom to know how to co-operate with caring for the trees.
Thank you for soil and humus and water and sap
for leaves and sunlight and the air that we breathe
for the darkness and leaf drop, the rain and the resting.
Forgive us when we break the cycle of our sacred connection

Maker of all, guard us and teach us to protect each other,
as we close our eyes and sleep in your care this night.

Blessing

Creator of the Blessing-Tree
Bless each fruit and each flower, each insect and bird
Bless each creature on the ground or moving in the sea
Bless every man, woman and child in the shade of your holy care.
☼ Bless me as I spend my day with all under the shelter of your Tree.
☾ Bless me as I lie down with all under the shelter of your Tree.

THURSDAY Sophia

On Rising/Resting
Blessed be you Sophia Wisdom,
you call on the hilltops, the city streets and at the cross-roads.
You call out with honesty and know no guile.
✿ Help me to be straight forward and clear this day.
☾ Help me to be straight forward and clear this night.

Praising
Praise to you O Knowing One,
not discernible without listening to the heart
and whose discerning is worth more than security.
You were there before the earth came into being,
before a ring was drawn on the surface of the deep.
You were at play at creation,
delighting to be with the sons and daughters of the earth.
You were there in the garden when we were finding out for ourselves,
and the layers began.

In Stillness
Be still in the silence and aware of the Love with and within

✿ Morning Invocation
O Holy Wisdom, come to me in the morning light,
as gentle as the dew on the grass in the still darkness before dawn.
Playful Spirit I cannot find you by rote or by thought, by book-reading or by
hard work,
but you will choose to come when I am open to the search.
Come to my hands as I seek to work for you.
Come to my feet as I seek to walk in your ways.
Come to my mouth as I seek to speak your words.
Come to my ears as I seek to listen more than I speak.
Come to my heart-mind connection as I seek you beneath my thinking.
Come to my eyes as I seek to see beyond what I am shown.
Dance playfully through the world that I walk in this day
that my life might not conform to its straight lines
but delight in the curves you throw and the arabesques of your justice.

✿ Opening Out
Creator of all, your wise Spirit connects not divides.
Be in those workplaces this day that do not know your connectedness
where box-ticking defines the space and story counts for little.
Snake through the slippery tricks and traps that tempt us all
as we find our way in organizations.
Give us the wisdom of a serpent to be bilingual
but the innocence of a dove that we may never speak with forked tongue.
I offer particularly this day

Bring your healing to our workplaces so freedom and integrity may flourish
and every person's story may be honoured.

☾ Thanksgiving
As I end this day in your safe-keeping
I count three blessings before my sleeping

☾ Night Shielding
Sacred Sophia,
shining with the vine moon on the world this night,
come down to the midnight garden where the sweet grapes grow.
Bud forth your abundant fruit and open my heart like a chalice.
See my desire for you, even when I am outside the gate looking in.
For I thirst for your wine made at the beginning, poured for all.
Shine on those who need your wisdom this night

Give us patience to trust as we drink of your blessing cup.
Enfold me in your peace as I close my eyes and keep me until morning comes.

Blessing
May Wisdom's long-lasting blessings be upon me.
Keep me from short-sightedness and the ease of the crowded road.
For narrow is the way and full is the heart on the path of your blessing.
✿ Keep me on that path as I set out this day.
☾ Keep me on that path as I lie down this night.

FRIDAY September Sun

On Rising/Resting

Blessed be you Rhythm-changer,
for coming round the corner with your golden glow
as the flowers fade and routine is returned.
☼ Be the gentle haze of grace within my life this day.
☾ Be the gentle haze of grace within my life as I lie down this night.

Praising

Praise to you in the morning when
the comings and goings of schoolchildren lengthen the daily routes of all.
Praise in the evening when
the shadows slant across the house in the mild light of day's-end.
As swallow and martin line up on the wire to go,
settle me back into my biding below.

In Stillness

Be still in the silence and aware of the Love with and within............

☼ Morning Invocation

Radiant One,
more beauteous and eternal than the late summer sun,
brightening the berries cased in nature's plastic; hardening the shell of nut.
May your Spirit grow me from seed within and protect me without
that I might bear kind fruit in all weathers this day.
Be the kernel of love at the centre of my life.
Be the kernel as I go about my busyness this day.
Be the kernel as my feet go from place to place.
Be the kernel as I keep my hands open to what might be.
Be the kernel as I welcome another and listen to their story.
Be the kernel that prompts words of gentleness.
Be the kernel deep within when my troubles overwhelm.
Be the kernel softening my boundary when fear has made it impermeable.
May I know your presence at heart so I may have an earthed generosity
until the saffron rays have gone down on the world this evening,
as I make my way this day.

☼ Opening Out

Giver of night and day,
so nearly equal in length, so constant in movement.
Be with those who feel balanced in their life and work
and those unbalanced by hardship.
Be with those who find you in order and moderation
and those for whom extremity is home.
Be with those trained in security and those trained in turmoil.
Be with those who crave action and those who crave stillness.
Help each of us find the right measure for our well-being

Thank you that our wholeness looks different for each one of us,
though your healing love is the same.

☾ Thanksgiving

As I end this day in your safe-keeping
I count three blessings before my sleeping

☾ Night Shielding

Still Spirit of God, midst the waning sun and the rolling moon
sustain me in peace in the turning of my days.
As I let go of the outdoors of summer, now gone,
let me welcome the lustre of autumn.
Still Spirit of God lead me inward
to know the warming of your love as the colder season calls.
Be with all who need your warm love this night

Give us the contentment of the home within where you reside.
I shut my eyes to the world this night, and entrust it to your care.

Blessing

Gleaming God who beams on us with adoring gaze,
as the broad bright summertime sun takes its leave
and the mellow autumnal sheen creeps in,
bless me in this season and the next,
in this life and the next,
when the course of my days will end in the light of your eternal peace.

SATURDAY Angels

On Rising/Resting
Blessed be you Sender of angels,
to guide and comfort and assure us of your care.
☼ May your angels watch over me as I go about this day.
☾ May your angels watch over me as I lie down to sleep this night.

Praising
Praise to you O Shining One,
for your divine companions moving up and down the ladder,
planted in the earth, reaching to heaven,
witnessing to our spirits your visceral presence.
Unsought, unasked for, just given for the moment
to draw back the veil, to reveal the beyond within,
the shimmering holiness of everything.
Praise to you.

In Stillness
Be still in the silence and aware of the Love with and within...........

☼ Morning Invocation
Guardian of my spirit,
Shelterer of my story and my innermost being,
guard my body with your wing as I touch the earth this day.
Guard my words from being hollow that I may speak in tongues of love.
Guard my feet in my travelling that I may walk in the ways of peace.
Guard my prayer from delusion that I may open myself to heaven's ways.
Guard my eyes that I may catch a glimpse of the mystery in ordinary.
Guard my heart from grasping that I may point away from myself.
Guard my hands that you may inspire my work.
Guard my name that you knew before it was given,
for it tells my story now and will bear my sojourn here,
until you have called it on the wind, left it in the hearts of my loved ones
and sent your flight attenders to carry me home.
Attend to me this day that I may know you with me,
know you with me this day.

☼ Opening Out

Winged announcers, warners, protectors, guides,
surround our world with the company of heaven.
Give governments the courage to rule with compassion.
Give vision to leaders that they may be prophets.
Give prophets the hope to keep crying in the wilderness.
Give to the lost and the outsider deep knowing that they belong.
Give to those who mourn the comfort of your peace that keeps their loved one.
Give those who fight for justice the strength of your holy batallion.

Give me the wisdom to know that the centre reaches to the edge
and there is no edge to the heavenly realm
for your love encircles us all.

☾ Thanksgiving

As I end this day in your safe-keeping
I count three blessings before my sleeping

☾ Night Shielding

Comforting One,
who lengthens the nights as I lie down in this season of Michaelmas,
may your angels bend to hear my plea
that in the darkness I may see your presence with mine inner eye.
Show me your care in the unexpected kindness of others
and give me visions in the outer world that echo my spiritual flame within.
May your angels keep all who need message of your love this night

Comfort all your little ones, the weak and the weary ones
and protect our dreams as we sleep.

Blessing

Holy God and all your angels,
bless to me the brightness of your joy,
the hope of your peace,
the knowledge of your presence
and gratitude for your gift.
☼ Shine on me with your love as I do my earthly work this day.
☾ Shine on me with your love as I lay down my earthly work this night.

SUNDAY Harvest

On Rising/Resting
Blessed be you Mother Abundance,
with your apron full of fruits and berries, nuts, hips and haws
for by your hand, you nourish all the creatures you have made.
☼ Provide me with all that I need as I set out this day.
☾ Thank you for providing me with all that I have needed this day.

Praising
Praise to you Generous One
turning the wheel of each season with your invisible care
for you know what is needful to bring forth the fruits.
You know that a grain of wheat remains a single grain unless it dies
but when it falls into the earth and dies, it bears much fruit.
Enclose me in your sacred darkness where new things are safe,
until the tender gift is ready to emerge into the light.

In Stillness
Be still in the silence and aware of the Love with and within...............

☼ Morning Invocation
Mother of the Harvest,
gather me in when the dark underworld fears of death overwhelm.
May I deeply trust in the home of your Body and know that birth will come.
Love me home in my own body as I set out this day.
Love me home in my feet as I walk this fecund earth.
Love me home in my breast as I gather in all given to my care.
Love me home in my belly as I feast on the gifts spread on the table from field.
Love me home in my hands as I share my creative craft with you.
Love me home in my heart as I plunge myself into the mess of daily living.
Love me home in the bodily exchange of my love-making.
Love me home in my singular flesh as I try to live out my dying and growing.
Gather me in Mother God as I resist and trust your strong arms that will love me home.
Love me home on my setting out and on my returning this day.

☼ Opening Out

Life-giving One, by your hand, bramble and blackberry,
scarlet rowan and blue berries, hazelnuts, sweet-chestnuts,
shiny rose-hips, rich red haws and deep black sloes.
Squashes, gourds and marrows sitting on the soil,
apples, damsons, greengages on the soft grass all ready for picking.
Seedheads on thistle and teasel feeding the winged ones above.
And yet, amidst the riches of your providence,
in other places, the rains won't come or floods rob the yield.
Be with all men, women, children, and creatures
who do not have enough to feed themselves or their family this day

Have mercy on them and inspire us with your creative love
to partner with you and share the harvest with all the world.

☾ Thanksgiving

As I end this day in your safe-keeping
I count three blessings before my sleeping

☾ Night Shielding

Nurturing Spirit, who rests the fields, the orchards, and allotments,
guard me as I lie down below the sacred harvest moon, this night.
Nourish me as I still myself beneath her, after activities spent under the sun
that I might grow in the dark holding of your love, like a pressed down bulb
tended by the mucked-in wisdom of dirty hands.
Comfort all those who mourn or feel fallow within tonight

May your slow and hidden grace nurture us in our sorrow
even when we are unaware of your process.
Hold me as I sleep in the darkness this night.

Blessing

Tender Mother, come with your instinctive knowing, your generous bosom,
your earthed kindness and bless me with the solidity of your caress
that I might trust you for the dying time.
For all blessings come from you and to your blessing will I return
☼ Grant me the fruitfulness of faith as I go about my day.
☾ Grant me the fruitfulness of faith as I close my eyes this night.

OCTOBER

INTRODUCTION TO OCTOBER

For lovers of autumn, October is the crowning month. The leaves are in full glorious colour either overhead or underfoot. The falling and fallen leaves in the colder and sometimes windy weather, have their own kind of beauty. The summer flowers are in their last days and the insects are disappearing, but all is not dead and gone yet. The berries and fruits still brighten the trees and feed the birds. Woodland birds like woodpeckers, jays, or tits can still be seen. Migrating birds are both departing and arriving. On the coasts, ducks geese and swans are arriving from colder climates where they have been breeding. Those fortunate enough to live near the sea could see grey seal pups at this time. By rivers, in parts of Scotland, there is the wonderful vision of salmon leaping. In other parts of the British Isles, this is the month to see rutting red deer. It is a spectacular and often bloody sight to see the stags fighting it out to win the hinds. The squirrels continue to collect their nuts and foods to keep them through the winter. Less easy to see but all around us are dormice, hedgehogs, bats, and other creatures preparing to hibernate. Hibernation is a deep sleep that some animals go into because there is not enough food, and it is too cold for them to survive in the winter. In September and October, they eat enough to lay down fat reserves in their bodies so that they can get through several months of not eating. They hibernate somewhere safe so that they will not be attacked because they rarely wake up until the ground is warmer and spring is on its way.

October is the third and last harvest. It is the harvest of nuts and fruits of the earth, like pumpkins, gourds, squash, turnips, parsnips and swede. Samhain, on October 31, was a Celtic festival, certainly celebrated in Ireland, but there is evidence for it elsewhere too. It falls opposite Beltane on May 1. It is the time when the animals were brought back from the summer pastures for their winter confinement. The word "Samhain" comes from two old Irish words meaning "summer's end." By October 31, there is a definite shift of season abroad. It is colder outside. We re-fuel with jacket potatoes, stews, pies and crumbles. The clocks have changed and the afternoons darken. From here until the shortest day at Winter solstice, 21 December, it is going to become darker at both ends of the day and colder too. Autumn is over. Winter has begun.

Samhain/Hallowe'en (pronounced "Sow-en," where sow rhymes with cow).
There is the extraordinary trilogy of festivals From October 31 to November

2. Samhain/Hallowe'en (October 31) followed by All Hallows/Saints (November 1) and then All Souls (November 2). It seems wrong to separate them because they are a series of the most marvellously intertwined pagan and Christian customs and beliefs. However, the prayers will remain in the month that they fall in. It is possible, but not necessary, to follow the subject rather than the day for these three, so to pray Samhain, on the day it falls, even if it is not on a Monday. However, our festivals from both traditions are seasonally based and seasons do not change overnight. The feeling of death and darkness creeps, and is around us for several months. Our rituals must be assigned to a particular day as they are community focussed, but our prayer, which we do on our own, need not be.

Samhain is pre-Christian and so pre-dates the others. It is now thought of as Hallowe'en, meaning the eve before All Hallows or All Holy Ones (All Saints). As All Hallows is a Christian festival, Hallowe'en is a later name for Samhain and has absorbed some of the Christian meanings that have been overlaid on Samhain. Hallowe'en though, is the most important night in the neo-pagan calendar, which has turned some Christians against it. Hallowe'en today, helped hugely by the supermarkets and card shops, grows in popularity by the year. Little do children know when they go about trick or treating that they are participating in one of the most successfully revived community customs in the land. Throughout all of the history of this night, the one constant factor is that it is a night full of superstition. Deep-rooted and unfounded belief about Hallowe'en flourishes in every quarter.

At Samhain, in early mediaeval Ireland, there were huge tribal assemblies at Tara. Local kings would gather for six days for games, entertainments and feasting. This was to celebrate summer's end and the beginning of winter. Even at that time, there were stories of the faerie folk and evil spirits being out and about, "making mischief." In Ireland, it was called "Puca" (Goblin) night. There is no evidence that it was a widely held festival, although Wales also held a celebration for summer's end, and when some of the Irish moved to Scotland, they took Samhain with them. In recent times, Samhain has been thought to be the Celtic New Year, but this is unlikely. It was the most impor- tant of the three Spirit nights, the other two being Beltane and Midsummer Eve, and it was the doorway to the dark half of the year. Originally, it was not particularly associated with the dead, but once the church had initiated the feast of All Saints in the ninth century, and later, around AD 998, All Souls, the customs between October 31 and November 2 became closely related. Hallowe'en took on its connotations of being a night when dead spirits were close and ancestors remembered.

The time of year seems to lend itself to these beliefs though, as they layered on top of each other. Samhain and later Hallowe'en fires were widespread on the hilltops to invoke the sun's power as it waned, and to guard against the spirits as they entered winter darkness. People would light their new house fires from the communal fire. It is no coincidence that we continue to keep bonfire night around this time. It is a night when our fears of change and death become uncovered, when we enter the realms of myth and imagination. Both death and lack of light are two of our most primitive fears. As Jung said about the shadow, "one does not become enlightened by imaginary figures of light but by making the darkness conscious."[12] Hallowe'en has an important function in allowing our fears to be looked at before being flooded with the light of All Saints.

For this reason, tricks and guising are associated with Hallowe'en. "Mischief night" or "punky night" or "spunky night" was a night when children and adults would carve out turnips or mangel-wurzels as hideous faces and put candles in them. Later they were called "Jack o' Lanterns". This was either to look frightening like an evil spirit or to scare off the evil spirits. They would dress up as fantastical figures sometimes with blackened faces to hide from the dark spirits or witches that might be about that night. This happened in the eighteenth century but there were door-to-door gatherings on All Souls night much earlier (see Introduction to November). They would dare each other for example, to go to the graveyard and get a dead man's bone, or to gather fernseed at midnight in a wood. They would go round neighbours begging for goodies like apples and nuts. Dressed and masked like archetypal figures they symbolized what they believed to be the actions of the dead: if the good things were refused, the household was inviting revenge upon itself, which the group enacted by making mischief. The tricks that people played were tricks like emptying rubbish bins on the path, rubbing soap on the windows, smearing doorknobs with treacle, removing gates. They would return home and have a celebratory meal. In Ireland they made "the mash of nine sorts" from root vegetables and milk. In the nineteenth century, there were many Irish immigrants who went over to the United States and took this custom with them. The Americans embraced it whole-heartedly, christened it "trick or treat" and its popularity grew back in the British Isles through the twentieth century, with the increasing influence of the United States on British culture. Although trick or treating is now associated with children, the drama of our own fears that they enact for us in their play, when they put on their masks and lanterns, is deep-rooted. This seems particularly so in our culture where religion no longer plays that sacramental role for many.

Given that Hallowe'en is so laden with strong spiritual meaning, it is not suprising that the beliefs around on this night are far too numerous to mention. Suffice it to say that it was the night for divination and scrying (looking into the future) and many customs abounded. Children born on October 31 were thought to have second sight. Apples featured strongly because it was the apple harvest. Avalon "the isle of the apples" was believed to be a magical place and apples were thought to be sacred and confer immortality and so represented death and re-birth. Apple-bobbing was and is a popular Hallowe'en game, and the combination of water and apples maybe reminiscent of the journey to Avalon. There are numerous divinations for young girls eating apples on Hallowe'en. One was to look in a mirror lit only by a candle and eat an apple, and the face of her future husband would appear behind her. Another was to peel an apple with the skin in one piece, throw the peel on the floor and the shape would be her future husband's initial. These are but two!

Summer's End

Samhain and Beltane (May 1) fall at more definite changes in season than the other festivals. At Samhain, this is helped by the clocks going back and the darkness being more suddenly apparent. This awareness of the season changing is marked in the prayers by using the wonderful text from Ecclesiastes in the Old Testament.

"To every thing there is a season, and a time to every purpose under the heaven:
A time to be born, and a time to die; a time to plant, and a time to pluck up that which is planted;
A time to kill, and a time to heal; a time to break down, and a time to build up;
A time to weep, and a time to laugh; a time to mourn, and a time to dance;
A time to cast away stones, and a time to gather stones together; a time to embrace, and a time to refrain from embracing;
A time to get, and a time to lose; a time to keep, and a time to cast away;
A time to rend, and a time to sew; a time to keep silence, and a time to speak;
A time to love, and a time to hate; a time of war, and a time of peace."

- Ecclesiastes 3.1-8

The onset of winter by the end of the month and being indoors invites the more contemplative part of us and so the prayers celebrate the gift of silence.

Witches

The third aspect of the triple Goddess is the Crone. Her Maiden aspect is celebrated in the Spring, her Mother from the fruition of Lammas onwards and now is the time for the Crone. In Scotland she is known as the Cailleach. She is the Hag Queen who rules over the winter months until February, when Bride returns. The harshness of the winter weather is sometimes called "Cailleach weather." Cailleach was the Earth Shaper and Mountain Mother. Scotland is called Caledonia which means "the land given by Cailleach." The goddess associated with death and chaos appears in many cultures. In the Celtic world, she also appeared as Morgan le Fay, Rhiannon and Cerridwen. She was thought of as a dark goddess and feared in the Middle Ages as the Queen of Witches. Hag originally meant holy woman or wise or healing woman but the archetype of the wise woman is either absent or perceived negatively in our culture. This was scandalously apparent during the witch-hunt years. We do not burn wise women today but instead, we ignore them. However, with the decline of the patriarchal (traditional) religions, feminine wisdom is breaking through, albeit slowly and of course, from the margins. The word "witch" comes from the Anglo-Saxon "witan" meaning to see or to know. This kind of knowing that cannot be gained by outer acquisition but from understanding within has always been feared, and considered dark. Maybe the shameful force that sought to banish it was darker still. Many of the Hallowe'en customs were believed to be protections against witches. Witch effigies were sometimes burned on top of the Hallowe'en fire.

Saint Francis

Saint Francis has already been lauded in the Introduction to June. His feast day is October 4. He was born at Assisi in 1181 and died on October 4 1226. Although he was born the son of a rich cloth merchant he refused the privileged path laid out for him. He had fought in the Perugian war, but devoted the rest of his life to peace. He wed himself to "Sister Poverty", clad only in a rough brown robe, which can still be seen in Assisi today. He started an order of brothers and later, through Saint Clare, of sisters, the Poor Clares. He found God in animals, birds and the environment. He worked with his hands, including the restoration of a church and he also cared for lepers. His radical lifestyle attracted the attention of the Pope but Francis never compromised his vision. The clarity of his spiritual call can be seen in the wondrous prayers that he wrote. This, known as the prayer of St Francis, is his most famous, along with the Canticle of the Creatures. Impossible to live out in our strength alone, it sparkles as a pattern for how to live peaceably and remains one of the best-loved prayers ever written.

> Lord, make me an instrument of Thy peace;
> where there is hatred, let me sow love;
> where there is injury, pardon;
> where there is doubt, faith;
> where there is despair, hope;
> where there is darkness, light;
> and where there is sadness, joy.
>
> O Divine Master,
> grant that I may not so much seek to be consoled as to console;
> to be understood, as to understand;
> to be loved, as to love;
> for it is in giving that we receive,
> it is in pardoning that we are pardoned,
> and it is in dying that we are born to Eternal Life.

So October is the last month of summer or more specifically autumn. Its last day is the gateway to the darkest months of winter. The spirits within in the shadows of our minds, and those without, in the shadows of the night, were thought to be abroad. It is a time for attending to our fears, including that of death, and for remembering our loved ones. It is a time for journeying within, seeking wisdom, however hidden or feared, and seeking too the paradoxical way of peace.

MONDAY Hallowe'en

On Rising/Resting

Blessed be you O Hallowed One,
for when the flowers have fallen and the nights have drawn in
your love does not wither or fade but remains in the stillness.
☼ Remain in me as I rise up this day.
☾ Remain in me as I lie down this night.

Praising

Praise to you whose holiness sparkles
because you have visited the night,
and refused to stay pure and separate.
O Healing One, visit me now.
See all that I would banish from myself and so fail to become whole.
Let me not be beguiled by imaginary reassurances of light,
but let me trust your mercy as I face the darkness.
Praise to you

In Stillness

Be still in the silence and aware of the Love with and within............

☼ Morning Invocation

Protector of all souls, guard me on my sojourn through this day I pray.
Guard my feet as I cross into the dusk of winter.
Guard my body from feeling poorly with the coming cold.
Guard my pride from not resting when I need to.
Guard my sexual place with your cherishing
and if you have so gifted me, the sweet keeping of another's love
Guard my mind from all my demons and the traps that are peculiarly mine.
Guard my heart when you reveal to me what I am blind to.
Guard my self and my kin from all that might harm.
Guard my faith when I walk in the valley of shadows.
Guard me with your presence when I make my last journey alone.
In the hastening darkness of the evening at this day's end,
be the arms to welcome me home.

✿ Opening Out

Divine One you have graced me with knowing
and you are present in my unknowing.
Be with me in all the in-between places
where I do not know what creeps in the shadows,
the past that haunts and the future that frightens.
Let my heart's aim be true in the daily ordinary uncertainty
for it is from this place that I must live and choose and trust.
Be with all those who feel tricked by life this day

Soften our hurt with the treats of your love so surely
that we might risk again and know that no bad thing comes from your hand.

☾ Thanksgiving

As I end this day in your safe-keeping
I count three blessings before my sleeping

☾ Night Shielding

Hallowed Spirit, come with compassion this night
for though I will lay my plans out ready for the morning,
I know you might make mischief with my ordered ways.
Enlighten my nakedness gently as I unclothe in prayer
and your love reveals my shadow which I am afraid to see.
May I trust you to show me when I am ready.
Come to all who do not feel brave tonight

As the lantern glows in the darkness, shine on our faith with your love
that we might see enough for our steps tomorrow.
Come with compassion as I lie down at the ending of this day.

Blessing

Source of all, from the realms of grace, keep me on the hallowed path.
Keep me from fiend that I have met along the way.
Keep my fears of unknown foe at bay.
Keep me from evil, keep me from harm.
Keep me and lead me with outstretched arm
until I pass through heavenly veil where danger can no more prevail
and I am kept by your love eternally.

TUESDAY Francis

On Rising/Resting

Blessed be you O Radical One,
who pours the riches of your grace on our poverty,
whose wealth cannot be measured by the rules of this world.
☼ Grace me with your radical spirit as I walk the earth this day.
☾ Grace me with your radical spirit as I reflect on this day with you.

Praising

Praise to you Voice of the Prophets
for giving the uncomfortable words and inspiring the uncommon lives.
Praise to you for the gift of simplicity.
May I refuse the easy lifestyle laid before me
and embrace the difficult call of integrity.
Give me the grace to be the change I want to see
to look to you for the courage I need,
to surrender what must be given up
and to praise you, O Prophetic One.

In Stillness

Be still in the silence and aware of the Love with and within............

☼ Morning Invocation

Presence of Divine Love, open my life that your peace may flow through.
Where there is fear let me learn to trust.
Where there is apathy let me bring hope.
Where there is slander let me speak kindly.
Where there is wrong-doing, let me show mercy.
Where there is prejudice, let me show welcome.
Where there is injustice let me work for freedom.
Where there is cynicism let me bring vision.
Where there is suffering, let me bring comfort.
O Living One may I seek to be more grateful than to grasp;
to love the world more than have the world love me;
to follow the call in my heart more than follow the crowd.
For it is because I am loved that I can love,
because I have been forgiven that I can forgive,

because I need your blessing more than I can bless.
Open my life that your peace may flow through, this day and always.

☼ Opening Out

Praise to you my Maker,
you who are both balm to my soul and call to action,
take my self-gazing, however wounded,
and transform my weakness for love's purpose this day.
Show me the lepers of my time.
Create in me a humble heart that I may not be beguiled by shiny happiness
but see your Spirit in the forsaken, the broken, the unheard,
and understand my common creatureliness with all you have made.
Pour your healing grace on

Praise to you Our Maker for by your hand you heal and inspire.

☾ Thanksgiving

As I end this day in your safe-keeping
I count three blessings before my sleeping

☾ Night Shielding

O Holy One present with me now, you have made Brother Sun to go down
and set Sister Moon high in the sky.
Let me lie down under her, as if under your gentle face
that looks tenderly on all I have done this day.
Do not withhold your presence from me,
but beam on all who need your love this night

Let us know our place in the family of all that live.
Let me enjoy our kinship by your grace, as I take my rest tonight.

Blessing

The blessing of God on each creature under the sun.
Bless with peace in your war-torn world.
Bless with mercy where hearts have grown cold.
Bless with courage that my faith may grow.
☼ May I dare to cross the margins for your love this day.
☾ May I dare to cross the margins for your love this night.

WEDNESDAY Bodies

On Rising/Resting
Blessed be you Embodier of Love,
whose soles of feet walked this earth,
who made our flesh with loving hand.
☼ Embody your love in me as I set out this day.
☾ Embody your love in me as I lay me down to sleep this night.

Praising
Praise to you Creator of all,
for the beauty of your handiwork in russety crimson, ochres given,
orange flames of fire and earth, overhead and at my feet.
And for the gift of my body in the autumn breeze, praise to you.
For the divine flow from the earth which feeds bones and flesh and skin,
until in good time our bodies return.
Creator of all, praise to you.

In Stillness
Be still in the silence and aware of the Love with and within.............

☼ Morning Invocation
Divine Wonder,
source of the patterns in all my systems and workings,
let me honour all my body does this day.
Gratitude for the sleep that rests and replenishes.
Gratitude for my breathing and rising and taking it for granted.
Gratitude for the soap from plant and the washing of my skin.
Gratitude for the pleasure of eating delicious offerings of nature.
Gratitude for the excreting of my body, the earth's receiving of my waste.
Gratitude for the joy of touching another's body, in kiss or handshake,
in the affection of children, or the cling of love's exchange.
Gratitude for my well-being, mobility and health.
Mercy on my ill-health, my disablement and all that I struggle with this day
for you hold my bodily being until I let go into the divine embrace.
May I respect the miracle of my body as I set forth this day.

☼ Opening Out

Lover of my Body-story,
you know the suffering held in our bodies,
the traces and scars left by another that do not easily heal.
You see the tyranny of symmetry and monochrome beauty
that fails to see the sublime variety of all you have made.
You know the choicelessness of those who need daily help with their bodies
and those who have accepted their bodily difference
but receive cruelty from their own kind.
Have mercy on all who do not feel at home in their own skin

Let us know that you are our true home
so we come to trust the flesh you gave us to inhabit.

☾ Thanksgiving

As I end this day in your safe-keeping
I count three blessings before my sleeping

☾ Night Shielding

O loving God who came in flesh,
you know our joy and laughter, the sorrow we bear and tears we shed.
Hide my wounds in your love as I lie down to sleep.
Help me each day of my journey to nourish myself,
to take care of my body, to trust the strong earth to bear my weight,
and to rest when I am weary.
Be with all who need your healing this night

Mend our sadness when we feel divided from our bodies.
Give us touchable folks able to reflect your loving gaze.
Enfold me in peace as I close my eyes to rest this night.

Blessing

May the ground of God bless my feet, the strength of God bless my legs.
May the mystery of God bless my hidden place.
May the passion of God bless my belly, the breath of God bless my chest.
May the bearing of God bless my back, the embrace of God bless my arms.
May the love of God bless my face so I may shine with your presence
as I celebrate the life you have given me this day/night.

THURSDAY To Everything a Season

On Rising/Resting

Blessed be you, Holder of the world in your hands.
You give to everything a season as we travel on our journeys
☼ Walk with me through this season as I set out today.
☾ Hold me in this season as I take my rest this night.

Praising

Praise to you O Divine One,
for though you never ordain suffering,
you help us to make sense of love's purpose when hardship befalls.
Reveal the meaning of this time that you have gifted to me.
Help me so to trust you that in every season, I may say
Praise to you.

In Stillness

Be still in the silence and aware of the Love with and within...........

☼ Morning Invocation

Loving God, you have loved me through every season,
from the time of my birth, until my time to die.
Walk with me in my season this day, for you know there is
a time for wounding and a time to heal,
a time to mourn and a time to celebrate,
a time to be creative and a time to survive,
a time to surrender and a time to rebel,
a time to embrace and a time to be self-contained,
a time to speak and a time to keep silence,
a time to be there and a time to stay away,
a time to take charge and a time to let be,
a time to reach beyond and a time to consolidate,
a time to be moderate and a time to be outrageous,
a time to be anxious and a time to be at peace,
a time to stay and a time to move on,
a time to care and a time to be cared for,
a time to generate and a time to lose,
a time to love and a time to let go.

☼ Opening Out

Bearer of the world, though there is nothing new under the sun,
you bear me through time and change and what is strange and new.
When life is unfair, you weep with the injustice of the world.
When the season is cruel, you never withhold your love.
Be close to all this day who feel that everything is futile,
all haunted by dreams of an unlived life or feel that it is too late;
all who are in a time of grief or a time of diminishment;
all who find the memory of better times unbearable;
all who consider cutting their time short

Bear us through this time, you who bear our pain and longing.
Let us hear your voice whispering "All is sacred. It is your time."

☾ Thanksgiving

As I end this day in your safe-keeping
I count three blessings before my sleeping

☾ Night Shielding

Sustainer of the hours and minutes,
bring the resting of sleep as night falls on another day.
I lay before you this day whether seized or ungrasped,
whether special or ordinary, whether struggled through or delighted in,
for it has yielded another span to give and receive love.
Be merciful on my failure to love and on all who need your peace this night.

Sustainer of all, hold our time with compassion.
Keep my dreams with your tenderness as I go to sleep this night.

Blessing

Beloved One, my Beginning and End,
For every season I have journeyed, gratitude;
and for those that are to come, I trust.
Bless the time that I spend now in this turning world
until I reach the place where there are no seasons but only your peace.

FRIDAY Crone

On Rising/Resting

Blessed be you Wisdom of the Ages,

you know because you made the earth and understand her ways.

✪ May your spirit be grounded in me as I rise up this day.

☾ May your spirit be grounded in me as I close my eyes this night.

Praising

Praise to you Great Healer,

fecund with crone-spirit,

for you are not dry but moist with healing,

longing to meet our thirst in this brittle place.

Praise to you for carrying the world on your hips,

for never uttering "I told you so,"

rather twinkling with compassionate eyes,

and leading us into deeper loving.

In Stillness

Be still in the silence and aware of the Love with and within…………..

✪ Morning Invocation

O Heart of Sacred Intuition,

your wholeness is embodied in the Oneness of all that lives.

Come and earth your slow-grown understanding in me this day.

Come with your mercy as my folly melts before your knowing.

Come with your tears and weep with me when I fall down.

Come with your juicy ways and smile when I am ripe with hope.

Come with your deep laughter and rejoice with me when I have overcome.

Come show me the lessons of the trees and flowers, the sun and moon

for all your creation has secrets to share.

Hitch up your skirts and teach me to dance to the rhythm of the earth.

Come with your sheer silent voice on the breeze,

that does not proclaim itself but waits to be discovered,

and show me how to listen better to the heart-beat of your world this day.

✪ Opening Out

O Holy Mid-wife

who holds and guides me as I birth the story of my life,
with your sacred with-craft.
I confess before you my sorrow
at the scandalous violence of the putting to death of the wise woman,
the voiceless crone, the witches burnt,
the priest denied, the priestess hidden from sight.
I offer to you women's knowing borne in the dark and on the margins,
and the fear of it that remains this day.

Forgive us holy God, genderful and strong,
for without your gift of woman no healing can be complete.

☾ Thanksgiving

As I end this day in your safe-keeping
I count three blessings before my sleeping

☾ Night Shielding

Bright Mystery
Settle and sustain me under the shrouded light of moon,
as I unlayer myself of my day spent on the turning earth.
Let me bring to awareness all that I have seen this day
as the leaves fall and die and return to the dark soil.
Let my clothes drop to the floor, my energy to its slumber,
my waking mind down to the ground of my being,
my prayer to the source of the One who sees all.
Be with all who need your love this night

Bright Mystery, help us find a way of seeing in the dark.
For you give your gifts even as I sleep this night.

Blessing

Bless to me O God, the wisdom of the earth,
the intuition of the listening heart,
the understanding of one who dares to love,
the sensing that comes from respect for my body,
the quiet knowing of being at the edge.
☼ Bless to me your wisdom as I walk the world this day
☾ Bless to me your wisdom as I lie down to sleep this night.

SATURDAY Summer's End

On Rising/Resting
Blessed be you for Mother Earth, for her fruits that we may not go hungry.
Blessed be you Creator of all, for supplying the sun and the rain.
✿ May I co-operate with your providence and know your blessing this day.
☾ May I co-operate with your providence and know your blessing this night.

Praising
Praise to you Generative Spirit, for as the wind blows the leaves,
and all around crisps and curls with brownness and death,
you show your care with pumpkins, squashes and gourds,
golden and ochre, bulbous and buxom.
And underfoot, cream and magenta root vegetables ready to pull,
hardy turnips, parsnips beetroot and swede.
On tree and bush, clusters of berries in scarlet and October orange,
and nuts cradled in silken case within hard clasp of shell,
feeding birds and squirrels in scarce times.
Praise to you.

In Stillness
Be still in the silence and aware of the Love with and within..............

✿ Morning Invocation
Strange God who made dying beautiful,
I abandon myself to your curious beauty this day.
Let me cherish the blood and bone of all the life you have given
when the fears of no-life creep in and I am cold.
May I befriend the dark with open eye at summer's end.
May I stoke the feisty fire of my desire as vibrant as the leaves I see.
May my creative impulses leap like the speckled salmon as I embrace the
fertility of winter.
May I love the ground on which I stand, as the leaf-mould and decay of
summer mulches the soil and strengthens roots.
May I hunker down, curled up like a hedgehog, in dark peace of quiet.
May my wholesome table bulge with roasted earth fruits, steaming pies and
warming drink, fuelling my body for the wintry days.
Let me celebrate the sacred vigour of dying as I welcome this autumn day.

✿ Opening Out
O Living One,
bring comfort in the warm damp drizzly days
when the copper glow of autumn is colourless and grey.
For it is summer's end and all is put away,
hidden in the unknown darkness,
like our fears of womb and tomb that we do not willingly invite,
until they interrupt our day-to-day and reckon with our real time.
Be with all this day living in that slow moment-by-moment capsule
of birth and grief

Protect our fragility when we are sealed in by shock,
and help us to honour the special gift of tenderness at that time.

☾ Thanksgiving
As I end this day in your safe-keeping
I count three blessings before my sleeping

☾ Night Shielding
Spirit of God, surround and sustain me as I lie down to sleep.
Outside, the nights thicken and the streets empty,
peopled only by shift workers and the drunk.
Root me in the dark safety of your love
where I may deepen and grow.
Be with all who need to be hidden in your love this night

Protect us from all that harms and restore our souls with sleep.
Bless my body to my rest at the ending of this day.

Blessing
Treasure of my soul, as the light glints with topaz and amber,
And you gild the season and crown the trees
bejewel my time with moments when your presence shines through.
✿ Bless me with your precious love as I set out this day.
☾ Bless me with your precious love as I lie down this night.

SUNDAY Silence

On Rising/Resting
Blessed be you Love at the centre of the Silence,
love when I doubt your presence, love when I know you are there.
☼ Still my heart like the quiet of dawn this morning
☾ Still my heart like the quiet of the darkest hours this night

Praising
Praise to you Heart of all that is,
I welcome you with me and within me.
I welcome the silence outside me and inside me.
I welcome each sound I hear.
I welcome the feel of my body on the surface where I sit.
I welcome the rising and sinking of my chest as I attend to my breath.
I welcome your grace within my heart.
For the daily miracle of your love,
praise to you.

In Stillness
Be still in the silence and aware of the Love with and within…………….

☼ Morning Invocation
Beloved One, let me be aware of you in silence this day.
Let me attend to the gift of each part of my body.
Let me trust your presence in the nothingness.
Let me not be distracted by the clamour of every thought
but let my heart be still, my mind unlearned,
my face unmasked.
Empty me of all I think I can offer.
Let me not be afraid of all I know I cannot be.
Let me trust that I am enough,
that just to be here is enough,
Just as I am.
And to trust that you look on me, my Beloved,
with eyes that see
and eyes that love.
Love.

✿ Opening Out

Still-point of the turning world, from which all life comes,
hold me in your love when the noise of busyness is hushed.
After the gunfire of war, the silence of the fallen.
After the crying of the baby, the contentment of sleep.
After the gossiping tongues, the heart of the one that is maligned.
After laughter with friends, the silence of solitude.
After the hymns have been sung, the prayerfulness of an empty church.
After the loved voice of one dear to me, the silence when they have gone.
Be with those who are afraid of the stillness this day

Assure us of your peace, for from love's silence did we come
and to the same shall we return.

☾ Thanksgiving

As I end this day in your safe-keeping
I count three blessings before my sleeping

☾ Night Shielding

Spirit of God, centre me
as I breathe you in and breathe you out,
in the silence that falls across this place with the dark.
Guard me from fears of the hollow of this night.
Absorb me in your Divine Mystery
not that I might know, but that I might trust the unknowing.
Keep all whom I met today and re-collect in quiet now

Settle us as we go to sleep this night in the peace of your eternal love.

Blessing

By the blessing of God, may I trust this day/night
that in the nothingness is everything,
in the absence is your presence,
in the silence is the still small voice,
in the stillness is the life of your love,
that keeps me this day/night and always.

NOVEMBER

INTRODUCTION TO NOVEMBER

November is seen as the beginning of winter. With the clocks gone back, the darkness falls noticeably earlier and begins to encroach into the middle of the afternoon as the month wears on. For many this lowers spirits, but for others November is the best winter month. The darkness is still novel and November does not carry the stress of Christmas or the feeling of on-going gloom that can hover over January and February. As global warming increases, November will be less crisp and wintry than in our memories. With the first frosts though, the animals that hibernate will begin their deep sleep and plants that will not survive are taken in. It is a quieter month for wildlife but a lovely sight in November is the skeins of geese or the wild geese in their traditional "V" flying overhead. They are migrating from the far north to Britain, which even in winter, is warmer than Iceland or Siberia. For the Celts, November was sometimes referred to as "Blod-monath" or "blood month" as the livestock that would not survive the winter were slaughtered and eaten. Bede[13] records that in pre-Christian times, some of these would have been offered to the gods in a ritual. We have no sense of this now but November is a month packed with other rituals and festivals. All Saints, All Souls, Bonfire Night and Remembrance Day, make November the month for remembering. It is as if, with the darkness, our memory, our dreaming, our shadow selves and the whole cast of our inner life, comes out to play. At the end, the Christian calendar officially begins again with the first Sunday of Advent. This will be considered in the Introduction to December.

All Saints and All Souls

All Saints or All Hallows falls on November 1. A feast to commemorate the Christian martyrs was already held in the fourth century. However, it became All Saints and moved to November 1 by AD 800 in England and Germany. All Souls, which falls on November 2 and is the day we remember our dead loved ones, came later. In AD 998, Odilo, Abbot of Cluny held a mass for all dead souls and it soon became established. It was put next to All Saints so that the saints could intercede on behalf of the dead loved ones. By the end of the Middle Ages, Hallowtide or the feast of the dead was a significant and popular festival.

To understand the customs of Hallowtide it is important to understand the beliefs about the dead. It was thought that the dead went to Purgatory and that the living could help their relatives in order to ensure they went to heaven.

They would pray for them and used to do this by ringing bells. The bell-ringers would be paid for this. After the Reformation, the church stopped this practice as they did not believe that this could change the state of the dead. However the custom was extremely popular and it continued long after it had been banned.

Before Christians, pagans also believed in life after death. In the Iron Age, people were buried with the possessions they were likely to need in the after-life like drinking horns, jewels and weapons. There was not so much separation between the invisible and visible for the pre-Christian Celts, so they felt much closer to their dead than we do. A belief shared by Christians and pre-Christian Celts was that the dead return to their former homes and partake in the food of the living. On All Souls, people used to light a hearth fire and leave food and wine for them. The Irish used to leave the entrances to their burial mounds open and light the interiors until cockcrow so that the dead could find their way. Flowers and candles would be taken and put on the graves. The Hallowe'en fires from the Reformation onwards were lit to pray for and comfort the souls in purgatory. People stood in a circle round them and held burning straw up high.

It was on this night that the custom of "souling" happened and seems a predecessor to the later Hallowe'en custom of trick or treating (see Introduction to October). Groups of people went house to house singing songs like,

"Soul, soul, for a soul cake!
I pray good missis, for a soul cake!
An apple or pear, a plum or a cherry,
any good thing to make us merry"[14].

A soul cake was a flat round biscuit-like cake, lightly spiced. The soulers made requests for ale and wished the donor good health. Pranks also ensued on refusal. It is not entirely clear whether the soul cakes and the prayers were for the dead or the living.

All Souls and All Saints lost some momentum with the Reformation but were celebrated again with the Anglo-Catholic revival of the nineteenth century and both are now standard feasts in the more sacramental churches. All Souls is a sombre ceremony and the names of the departed are read out. All Saints, is spectacular and colourful and lists of Saints are invoked. The reading often used at All Saints is Jesus' words from the Sermon on the Mount called the Beatitudes. The Beatitudes are regarded as some of the most profound of Jesus' words.

> "Blessed are the poor in spirit,
>> for theirs is the commonwealth of heaven.
> Blessed are those who mourn,
>> for they will be comforted.
> Blessed are the meek,
>> for they will inherit the earth.
> Blessed are those who hunger and thirst for righteousness,
>> for they will be filled.
> Blessed are the merciful,
>> for they will be shown mercy.
> Blessed are the pure in heart,
>> for they will see God.
> Blessed are the peacemakers,
>> for they will be called the children of God.
> Blessed are those who are persecuted because of righteousness,
>> for theirs is the commonwealth of heaven.
> - Matthew 5.3-10

Bonfire Night

"When the curfew is sounded throughout Nature" so wrote Thomas Hardy in *The Return of the Native,* 1878, "a spontaneous Promethean rebelliousness rises up in us to light a fire against the darkness and chaos."[15] It has often been thought that we took to celebrating Guy Fawkes' attempt to blow up Parliament in 1605 so readily, because it followed a tradition of lighting bonfires at the beginning of winter. Folk-lorists made a link between ancient funeral pyres to Druid rites to Hallowe'en fires to the Gunpowder plot. However, there is no evidence of this link or of the widespread nature of bonfire lighting in November. Within twenty years of Guy Fawkes' failed attempt, November 5 was designated Bonfire Night in Britain and the celebration has never waned. At first there was a statute ordering everyone to go to church where prayers of thanksgiving were said and the clergy had to read out an Act of Parliament which continued to denounce Catholic worship. Guy Fawkes was Catholic and not only Guys but effigies of the Pope and the Devil were burned on top of the fire. Boys in the twentieth century would go house to house for wood or money for food or drink, with the rhyme, "Remember

remember, the fifth of November, gunpowder, treason and plot". [16] By the 1920s their begging cry was "penny for the guy". From the seventeenth century to the present day, fireworks were part of the celebration. In some areas there were spectacular processions with men carrying burning tar barrels. This continues to this day in Ottery St Mary, Devon. The bonfire became much more significant than the anti-Catholic feeling that began the celebrations. Today there is more sensitivity to the Catholic aspect but the bonfire and fireworks show no sign of declining in popularity. A huge part of their appeal must be, as Thomas Hardy said, a primitive need to light a bonfire to guard against the darkness.

Remembrance Day

Remembrance Day is November 11 (the eleventh month) and a two-minute silence is held at 11am to commemorate the end of fighting in the First World War in 1918. Remembrance Sunday is the Sunday nearest to it. It is kept in most towns and villages at local war memorials. Ex-servicemen and women and civic dignitaries, uniformed youth organizations and military cadets gather to lay a wreath. In London the Queen does this at the Cenotaph on Whitehall. A gun is fired at the beginning and end of the silence and the Royal Marines buglers play the Last Post. The Royal British Legion which is an organization that looks after the ex-servicemen and women, organize marches with veterans who lay their own wreaths. It is the British Legion who also organizes the poppies that people wear in their lapels as a sign of remembrance.

Services are held in churches on Remembrance Sunday and the two-minute silence is kept. During the ceremonies at memorials or in church, Laurence Binyon's moving words from his poem "For the Fallen" are spoken,

"They shall not grow old, as we that are left grow old:
Age shall not weary them, nor the years condemn.
At the going down of the sun and in the morning,
we will remember them."

Poppies were chosen because they grow in the wild in Western Europe in areas where the earth is disturbed. In the nineteenth century, after the Napoleonic wars, there was so much killing on bare land that the fields became full of red poppies growing around the bodies of fallen soldiers. In 1914, the fields of Northern France and Flanders once more became fields of blood. Poppies became symbolic of the blood that was shed and the untellable sacrifice made by those who lost their lives in the First World War and then in later conflicts.

In 1933, the Women's Co-operative Guild introduced the white poppy as a symbol of peace and an end to all war. Many people, especially the Royal British Legion were seriously upset because they felt it did not honour the sacrifice the veterans had made. Red poppies are worn extensively today, over sixty years after the end of the Second World War. White poppies are growing in popularity especially as more recent military action has caused anger among many British people.

In the Bible, the prophet Micah in the Old Testament, speaks words, believed to be given by God, describing a vision of a world where all can live peaceably with each other and with God,

"And they shall beat their swords into ploughshares
and their spears into pruning hooks;
nation shall not lift up sword against nation,
neither shall they learn war any more;
but they shall sit every one under the vine
and under the tree and none shall make them afraid"
- Micah 4.3-4.

It is similar to the desires that people expressed in 2000, for what they would most hope for in the third millennium. These were collated into a millenium "prayer" that could be said by as many people as possible, regardless of their background,

"Let there be respect for the earth, peace for its people, love in our lives, delight in the good, forgiveness for past wrong, and from now on, a new start".

Thanksgiving

In 1620, one hundred and two English Puritans, later called Pilgrims, seeking a better life, set sail on the Mayflower ship. They landed at Plymouth Rock in America. Their first winter was harsh and they lost forty six of their company. The harvest of 1621 was a good one, and being devout, they decided to celebrate with a feast. Thanksgiving was originally just prayers in thankfulness for the harvest and not the great occasion for feasting and celebration that it has become in the United States today. At the first Thanksgiving there were ninety one native Americans, the Wampanoag, who had helped the Pilgrims to survive and to find food.

That first Thanksgiving was not the beginning of a long tradition though. It took until 1863 when President Lincoln proclaimed the last Thursday in November a national day of Thanksgiving. Sadly, the goodwill between the native Americans and the colonists did not last either. Even by 1676, a Thanksgiving was held, partly to celebrate victory in fighting the native peoples.

Nowadays, in North America, Thanksgiving is a one-day holiday on the fourth Thursday of November. People often come home for it. There is a Thanksgiving Parade in some cities, football is played and also there is a wonderful feast. Traditionally, the Thanksgiving meal is roast turkey, cranberry sauce, stuffing and gravy. There can be sweet potatoes, mashed potatoes, corn on the cob, beans and carrots. Puddings are traditionally pies made from pumpkin, apple, sweet potato or pecans. These were thought to be the original foodstuffs that the Wampanoag gave to the Pilgrims for the first Thanksgiving meal. It is more likely that the feast included fish, berries, watercress, lobster, dried fruit, clams, venison, and plums.

The Friday after Thanksgiving is seen as the beginning of the winter season in North America when Christmas shopping can begin.

Saint Andrew

St Andrew is the patron saint of Scotland and his feast is November 30. He is the only one of the four patron saints of Britain who is Biblical. He followed John the Baptist originally and then, along with Peter his brother, was chosen by Jesus to be one of the twelve disciples. Both were fishermen in Galilee and so he is associated with fish and the sea and is the patron saint of fishermen. It is said that St Andrew spread Christianity through Asia Minor and Greece and was crucified by the Romans in Greece on a saltire which is a diagonal cross. St Andrew's association with Scotland is because his relics were taken to the place on the east coast of Scotland that is now called St Andrews. One story says they were taken there by St Regulus in the sixth century. He was told in a dream to take them to the ends of the earth and his boat got shipwrecked there. Alternatively, Acca, the Bishop of Hexham asked for them to be brought to Scotland in AD 733. The relics were kept in a chapel built for them which was re-built as the Cathedral of St. Andrews in 1160. This became a pilgrimage site and is now a ruin.

The story of the Scottish flag is told that the Pictish King Angus was praying for guidance when a large invading army was approaching. He saw a white cloud in the shape of a saltire cross set against the blue sky above him. He won the battle and decreed that Andrew would be the patron saint of his country. St Andrew officially became the patron saint of Scotland after Robert Bruce's victory at the Battle of Bannockburn in 1314. The Saltire became the national flag of Scotland in 1385.

St Andrew's Day was very popular in Scotland. Farm workers and labourers used to go "St Andra'ing." They would catch rabbits and hares and have a great feast in the evening. Other meals included fish, or any traditional Scottish food and of course, plenty of whisky and bagpipe music. It declined in widespread popularity especially with the success of Burns Night on January 25 which is a great feast of Scottishness. However, in recent times, and increasingly since the Scottish Parliament began in 1999, St Andrew's Day is enjoying revival and some would like to see it a national holiday.

So November is the month of remembering, of gathering inward and gathering in communities in the darkness. The human spirit is drawn to the colour and light of fires and fireworks but the darkness of grief, of war, of tyranny emerges in our memories and in public acts of remembering. As the month draws on, the beginning of the Christmas season gathers, acting like a national "full-stop" to the year, and so November ends with a different feel than it started with at the beginning of the month.

MONDAY All Saints

On Rising/Resting

Blessed be you from the heavenly realm,
who touched ordinary lives until they were extraordinary.
☼ Inspire me this day to live a life less ordinary.
☾ Inspire me as I lie down this night to live a life less ordinary.

Praising

Praise you Source of all Love,
surrounded by those who have uncommonly loved
and rest now from their labours.
Hallowed be for the light they left behind
that continues to blaze here and sparks generations of little lights,
making all the difference in this dark world.
Praise you that your love can never be put out.

In Stillness

Be still in the silence and aware of the Love with and within...............

☼ Morning Invocation

As I rise up this morning, I invoke the spirit of the saints.
I invoke Desmond Tutu and Nelson Mandela that I might fight for freedom.
I invoke poor Francis and fiery Hildegard that I might honour the earth.
I invoke Martin Luther King and Rosa Parks that I might dream of justice.
I invoke Brother Roger and Mahatma Gandhi that I might seek to reconcile.
I invoke Mother Teresa and Jean Vanier that I might live with compassion.
I invoke the unnamed ones who have shown love to loveless children.
I invoke the small acts of kindness, the pots of stew left on doorstep,
the welcome of the different one, the lone voice who dares to speak out.
I invoke the devotion of unsung men and women to their fellow human
beings.
I invoke the prophetic action of those who do not count the cost.
I invoke the faithfulness of those who have prayed in their little rooms
day in and day out, with no fame or fuss, and kept the world turning.
Surrounded by so great a cloud of witnesses I invoke the Holy Spirit,
for without love, my life will be as nothing this day.

✿ Opening Out

Blessed are the poor in spirit for they can be real with you.
Blessed are those who mourn for they are thrown on your love.
Blessed are those who are gentle for they have nothing to prove.
Blessed are those who hunger and thirst for what is right
for their courageous hearts lead them to your love for the world.
Blessed are those who know my need of mercy for they must know their own.
Blessed are the pure in heart for with no guile they can see you.
Blessed are the peacemakers who would rather play as children on the shared
earth, than fight for your crown.
Blessed are those who are persecuted in the cause of right
for the ripples of their radicalism have brought heaven to many on earth.
Blessed One, be with those who do not know their need of you this day

☾ Thanksgiving

As I end this day in your safe-keeping
I count three blessings before my sleeping

☾ Night Shielding

O Holy Ones beyond us now, completed in love's resting place,
send your angels to guard me
Stream your beaded light upon me like dew upon a web,
so I may glimpse how my trudge and dreary might glisten with love.
May the same Spirit who enfolds you now show me how to unfold my heart,
lay my burdens down, and see beyond the day with thankfulness.
I offer all who need your tending this night

Show us your mercy as we lie down to sleep
and bring us the peace of the place where you now reside.

Blessing

Hallowed be for your blessing that falls on saints and sinners alike.
✿ May the blessing of the prophets, angels and saints, fall on me this day
☾ May the blessing of the prophets, angels and saints, fall on me this night
til I rest with them, my toil done, safe in the love they helped me to know.

TUESDAY All Souls

On Rising/Resting

Blessed be you deep Peace beyond my understanding.
The mystery of this short life is written into everything,
the story of how I cannot love, unless I can let go.
✿ Give me grace to love with open hand this day.
☾ Touch my folded hands and closed lids with your grace this night.

Praising

Praise to you Keeper of those I love and can no longer see.
I have entrusted to you the care that was mine once to give,
the embrace that was mine once to feel,
the story that was mine once to share.
Praise you for the love that I can never be separated from.
For even with the last leaf fallen and the flowers gone,
those I have loved are not under the earth,
they are here in my heart, they are here.

In Stillness

Be still in the silence and aware of the Love with and within...............

✿ Morning Invocation

As I rise up this morning I remember the love that I lost.
I remember their laughter and smile, their quirks and silly moments.
I remember the place they always sat and the things that they once said.
I remember that old thing they used to wear that carried their smell,
and I remember burying my head in it and weeping.
I remember with sorrow the words left unspoken, the plans forever shelved.
And I remember the first birthdays and the first seasons without them,
the wrongness of them leaving me here, as the world kept turning.
And November remembers, in the vapours and mists,
the brownness of decay, the intractable darkness in the afternoons.
But though I can no longer touch, time cannot undo or unravel their mark,
And I weave their love as I wend my way, plaiting it with new love.
They are never far, in the lash of the wind, in the birds that keep song,
in the lamp-lit streets at night, and in the quiet of my prayer this morn,
for though the summer has gone now, I know that spring will come.

✿ Opening Out

Tender God who knows our griefs, comfort all who mourn this day.
Be with those whose loved ones returned in their dreams
and who on waking must remember again.
Be with them when the world feels large and harsh and cruel;
when people still get on buses and go to work in the morning,
and the news plays the same theme at six o'clock in the evening.
Contain them when their longing feels too vast be held within,
and the sky does not feel large enough to rage at.
Meet us where we hurt this day

Bear our pain and anger, our tears and our loneliness.
Bear the questions that have no answers and in our darkness, give us hope.

☾ Thanksgiving

As I end this day in your safe-keeping
I count three blessings before my sleeping

☾ Night Shielding

Source of all love,
from whom every soul has come and to whom every soul will return,
come to me this night, as you did when morning woke me.
For you alone know me in the stillness before sleep overtakes,
and fleeting shades of memory dapple my spirit,
when those I loved and lost visit or death's certainty frightens me.
Make your love known to all who are afraid this night

May we have faith tonight for we see only dimly now, dear God.
Give me hope until I see you face to face and only love remains.

Blessing

The love of God who makes the leaves to curl and the sun to go down
Bless this heart of mine as I love here, this winter's day.
The joy of God who shot the whole earth through with the gold of home
Bless this life of mine with the golden joy of those I see no longer.
The peace of God who holds my loved ones in the everlasting arms
Bless this journey of mine until I reach the deep peace of my homecoming.

WEDNESDAY Vocation

On Rising/Resting
Blessed be you Caller into being, who breaks into my daily doing
and speaks my name within the heart.
☼ Let me hear your voice as I rise up and follow the Spirit this day.
☾ Let me hear your voice as I lie down and rest in your Spirit this night.

Praising
Praise to you Living One.
As the branches bare and blacken in the greyness of day
you stand on the edge of my life and beckon me forward
until I come to see you are at the centre.
Give me courage to put out into deep water
and to trust your blessing.
Praise to you

In Stillness
Be still in the silence and aware of the Love with and within………..

☼ Morning Invocation
You who are my Maker,
you knew my name at the beginning
and long to draw me into becoming who I fully am.
Guide me by your Holy Spirit as I go about this day.
Guide my hands to find the work that only I can do.
Guide my feet so I may go where I am meant to be.
Guide my eyes that I may see your love in the face of friend and stranger.
Guide my words that I may speak with integrity.
Guide my heart towards your loving gaze that I may live free from fear.
Guide my understanding that I may find my true place in the world.
Guide my vision so I may not doubt your call even when it leads to troubles.
Guide my uncertainty when I do not know the way to go.
Let my good faith delight you more than the way itself.
Guide me deeper into life as I set out this day.
Guide me deeper into you.

☼ Opening Out
Love-Bringer you hold my story as I glimpse our meaning.
I delight in the randomness of the things I see:
the wind that makes a plastic bag to dance,
the serendipitous meeting with a friend.
But the chaos frightens me too:
the one who only took that bus the morning of the bomb,
the wards of tiny babies where some return to heaven, others go home.
Be with all this day who cannot make sense of what is happening.

Hold us when we question your presence this day.
Lead us gently to discern your loving pattern.

☾ Thanksgiving
As I end this day in your safe-keeping
I count three blessings before my sleeping

☾ Night Shielding
Navigating Spirit
who draws me into faith's adventure, from the first small "yes"
when you boarded the boat of my life
and I found yours were the sea and the waves.
Settle me as I lie down this night
when storms overwhelm me and I feel alone.
Let me know your presence with me.
Let me know your peace.
Be with all who need your comfort now

As the stars shine above, keep us in safety this night.
Keep me on course and give me rest until the light of morning wakes.

Blessing
Bless my boat and bless the sea
for the water is deep and wide,
but not as deep and wide as your love for me.
I have not wings but bless me with the eyes of faith
and keep me all my voyage through
until I reach the heavenly shore and rest in your eternal peace.

THURSDAY Thanksgiving

On Rising/Resting
Blessed be you Inspirer of pilgrim hearts,
for your Holy Spirit who breaks through conventions
and leads me on to new places.
☼ Lead me onwards as I set out this day.
☾ Lead me onwards as I lie down this night.

Praising
Praise to you Freedom-Giver,
for giving hope when all around has lost sight of precious things,
for giving grace to dare to live a different life,
for giving courage to leave security behind,
for giving strength on stormy waters,
for giving conviction when choices do not bring immediate rewards,
for giving faith to endure the danger of the road less travelled.
Praise to you.

In Stillness
Be still in the silence and aware of the Love with and within...............

☼ Morning Invocation
O Holy One
who never took the easy path and knows how we can spoil goodness,
indwell my feet with adventure but let me not walk over others.
Indwell my hands with purposeful work but let me not be grasping.
Indwell my words with your spirit of love
but let me not turn in different company.
Indwell my belly with passion for a better way
but let my ears listen to others.
Indwell my heart with belief but save me from arrogance.
Indwell my insight with mercy but let me see my need for mercy first.
Indwell me with gratitude for all that you have given
as I set out this day.

☼ Opening Out
Divine Presence whose justice extends to the ends of the earth,

who sees to the heart and favours no tribe.
I lament with you the oppression caused by white-skinned people
in lands not their own.
I lament the blindness to native ways.
I lament the inability to learn from those who know better.
I lament the use of freedom that takes the freedom of another.
I lament the conflict that believing can lead to.
I lament every trail of tears that every invasion has caused, including

Call all of us to repentance in whose name, violation happens.
Comfort all who have lost loved ones, homes and livelihoods this day.

☽ Thanksgiving
As I end this day in your safe-keeping
I count three blessings before my sleeping

☽ Night Shielding
Spirit of God,
anchor my pilgrim heart in your love this night
wherever I have landed in my journey this season.
Give me the grace to accept the welcome of strangers
and gratitude for the faithfulness of friends.
For all I have received this day
and all whom I have met and remember before you now

Give us your peace as we take our rest now.
Give me the generosity and humility I lack to live peaceably.
Anchor me in your love as I lie down this night.

Blessing
I offer this thanksgiving for the feast of food you provide
I offer this thanksgiving for friends with whom to share
I offer this thanksgiving for the kindness of the earth.
I remember those who struggle to survive this day
and ask your blessing on us all.
✿ Settle me in the Spirit as I travel my road this day.
☽ Settle me in the Spirit as I lay down my travelling this night.

FRIDAY Re-membering

On Rising/Resting
Blessed be you O Holy Shadowmancer
flickering through our memory and desire, reverie and twilight moments
when we know we are not alone.
✿ Let me glimpse you as the veil moves in the split-seconds of my day.
☾ Let me glimpse you as the veil moves when I lie down to sleep this night.

Praising
Lover of all I have known here,
look tenderly on those times that make me re-coil and shrink,
times when I felt like a different person but I was not.
Help me to know that just as hindsight can make fools of us all,
your compassion turns us into kings and queens of our stories,
for there is no crack or crevice or shadow of our lives
that is not beloved by you.
Praise you.

In Stillness
Be still in the silence and aware of the Love with and within............

✿ Morning Invocation
Holder of all my moments in the palm of your hands,
breathe your warm transforming Spirit over my story.
Breathe over my eyes as I awaken to the old and the new this day.
Breathe over my nostrils as I inhale the crisp November air
and know the sweet fragrance of your gifts in the present.
Be the breath carrying the leaves as they twizzle and float to the ground.
Breathe over my feet as I kick my way through them,
containing the child-like glee I once expressed freely.
Breathe through my replaying memory stuttering like black and white images
from a reel-to-reel: the loved ones no longer here; the war happened;
my family are who they are; times were different then.
Breathe wisdom through my desire as I seek to sever or connect the past.
Breathe your warm transforming Spirit over my time this day.

☼ Opening Out

Merciful One, bring your comfort this day,
and release us from our sorrow, regret and despair.
Be with the sorrowful who have lost.
Be with the regretful who wish for their time again.
Be with those who have given up hope of change.

Pour out your grace which helps us move on.
May we respect the things that happened,
and honour the deep struggles of our bodies minds and souls as we passed
through those times.

☾ Thanksgiving

As I end this day in your safe-keeping
I count three blessings before my sleeping

☾ Night Shielding

Weaving Spirit, surround and sustain me this night
for you alone see the theatre of my dreams:
the stories that arise from my memory,
from the vasty deep oceanic store-house long forgotten;
the characters that appear, some familiar and some that seem new,
the phantoms and fantasies that cause me fear and shame,
and those that bring me peace and make me smile.
Be with all who feel haunted and frightened this night

Weave in and around our dreams and memories with your mercy's yarn
to create our unique patterns beloved by you.
Tuck in the threads of this spent day and guard my many-coloured dreams.

Blessing

May God's countenance shine on the story of my life.
May God's mercy earth the roots of my life.
May God's embrace meet the yearning of my life
☼ as I take another step on my journey's road this day.
☾ as I lie down to rest after another day on my journey's road this night.

SATURDAY Fire

On Rising/Resting
Blessed be you Holy Flame
for taking the fire of love into the heart of darkness.
☼ Stir up your fire in me this day.
☾ Warm me with your fire at the ending of this day.

Praising
Praise to you Kindler of our spirits.
As communities gather to light a fire in the dark
give us faith to trust that your light can never be put out.
As the sun's power withers and wanes,
give us faith to light a candle rather than curse the darkness
that together, we might light up this suffering world
and see your love reflected in the glow of each face.

In Stillness
Be still in the silence and aware of the Love with and within............

☼ Morning Invocation
Holy Spirit, Sacred Fire within,
you crackle with life when winter settles in.
As plants are taken in from the cold, wood is chopped for the hearth,
and leaves are swept beneath unclad trees,
enflame me as I move around my world this day.
Enflame my conversations with genuine meeting.
Enflame my spirits when poor health overtakes my body.
Enflame my love for those dearest to me.
Enflame my perceptions with your searing justice.
Enflame my vision with your wisdom.
Enflame my task and toil with your overflowing generosity.
Enflame my heart with warmth for another.
And when my energy merely smoulders with stress and strain,
stoke the embers, with your courage and your hope.
Ignite my soul again with dancing flame,
the flaming dance of your Spirit, that I might tread with joyful step
through all the places that I find myself in this day.

✿ Opening Out

Holy Life-Light, brighten my discernment as I set out this cold day
The ducks on the pond with their beaks tucked in
remind me of my need for protection.
The Christmas adverts that beguile with their promise
remind me of my need to find my security in lasting things.
Protect me from all that douses love's energy.
Comfort all those who have lost their spark at this time.
Cup your hands over the dimming flame and flare their passion gently.

Warm our spirits so love may not grow cold.
and do not extinguish the fire of your Spirit in this dark world.

☾ Thanksgiving

As I end this day in your safe-keeping
I count three blessings before my sleeping

☾ Night Shielding

Imperishable One, I lie down this night
under whiteness of moon against the clear blue night sky.
Some nights the fireworks explode into a thousand neon fragments,
reminding me of those who live about.
Some nights all is quiet and there is just me and the silence.
Be with all this night who feel content or troubled by their aloneness.

May our flame burn strong and unflickering in crowds or on our own.
And may your imperishable love not dim as the light disappears from this day

Blessing

Unquenchable Flame, Source of all love,
keep me on every side and glow within,
that when the cold winds blow and dark times come,
I may know the warmth of your blessing.
✿ Kindle your blessing as the sun rises on the world this day.
☾ Kindle your blessing as the sun goes down on the world this night.

SUNDAY Poppies

On Rising/Resting

Blessed be you O Sacred Peace-maker who longs for harmony
and weeps over the things we do to each other.
✿ Indwell your spirit of peace in all I do this day.
☾ Indwell your spirit of peace as I lie down this night.

Praising

Praise to you Suffering God.
You know the wounding by metal of skin that was made to love.
Your prophets spoke long ago of melting down weapons and bombs
to make machines for hospitals and farms,
of using the money and intelligence spent studying war
on housing all and finding cures.
Praise to you for not abandoning us
but remaining with us in the darkest derelictions of our choice.

In Stillness

Be still in the silence and aware of the Love with and within.............

✿ Morning Invocation

Giver of peace, I pray for an end to war
but there can be none without living for peace.
I pray for peace in the world
but there can be none without peace in the nations.
I pray for peace in the nations
but there can be none without peace in the communities.
I pray for peace in the communities
but there can be none without peace between neighbours.
I pray for peace between neighbours
but there can be none without peace in the home.
I pray for peace in the home
but there can be none without peace in the heart.
Give peace in my heart this day O God
and when the fighting of this world overwhelms me,
let me know that peace begins with me.

✿ Opening Out

O Holy One who came in peace, your blood fell on dusty ground
like scarlet poppies in golden fields, standing erect as graves,
for every father, son and brother; for every woman too;
row on row of unmarked stone, indecently clean and straight
belying the messy stain that can never be erased from our story now.
As age shall not weary them may despair not overcome me.
I will not cover the spectre of terror with forgetfulness.
I will remember them.

For all the war studied and all the lessons never learnt,
I offer my contrite heart and my sadness and place it into your hands.

☾ Thanksgiving

As I end this day in your safe-keeping
I count three blessings before my sleeping

☾ Night Shielding

Source of peace beyond all understanding,
peace which the world cannot give,
as I lie down this night, I survey all the day has brought.
I recall with sorrow, all those things I have thought or said or done
which did not make for peace.
I recall all those I have met today, who do not have peace within.
I bring before you those places in the world where there is no peace.

Give me grace to change what I can.
And for all beyond my reach, hear my prayer as I lie down this night.

Blessing

May God's dream of peace bless the world.
May every gun be dropped so every mouth be fed
May every plan of war be torn up so every person go to school
May every fist raised become a tender hand towards child
May all God's people sit in the shade of a tree, without fear.
✿ Be present in my choices this day and use me in your dream of peace.
☾ Let me rest with my choices this night and use me in your dream of peace

DECEMBER

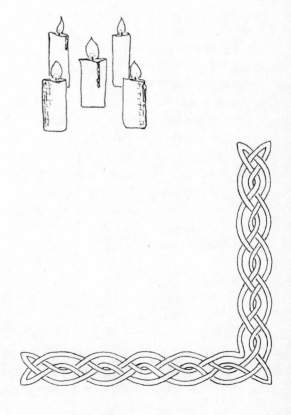

INTRODUCTION TO DECEMBER

December may be short on flowers and wildlife, and may have increasingly shorter days, but it has its own peculiar beauty that makes it wonderful to walk in, and is even lovelier when it is colder. The dusky light can give the month a mystical sheen. For the birds and creatures that are still awake and about and trying to survive, there are only seven or eight hours of daylight in the south of the British Isles and even less farther north. December can be fairly mild and surprisingly, urban foxes may start their courting already, with their frightening-sounding scream. Some birds may start singing for a mate and building nests. Global warming has affected all our seasons but it seems particularly wrong to see blossom before Christmas, and hedgehogs still scurrying about, as can happen now. In popular imagination though, December is cold, quiet and misty and there is always the hope of a white Christmas. In reality, snow is more common in January and February. However, the frost defining the stark features of leafless trees or spider-webs in white is one of winter's most uplifting sights.

The wintering birds, particularly starlings and pied wagtails, ducks, geese and waders gather in large roosts at night from December through to the spring. They do this to keep warm and safe. They gather at dusk, a few at first, maybe up to hundreds or even thousands until the last birds are in and then they go to sleep. The birds that either live here or that have migrated from colder climates like Scandinavia or Iceland feed on the remaining red and orange berries. Holly berries are actually poisonous and birds do not like them though the leaves are good to eat, as are ivy berries. Interestingly, although the robin has been associated with Christmas since the eighteenth century, the reason is unknown. They just have always been beloved by British people. It is easy to see why the red of the berries and the green of the evergreens became the Christmas colours (see below). The robins' breasts have that in their favour.

The Season to be Jolly

It is interesting that the word "jolly" may derive from the same root word as "Yule". The evidence shows for the last two millennia, and suggests for earlier times, that at midwinter there has always been a need to have festivities. This is the longest Introduction because the history of the midwinter feast is so long and enduring and has passed through many different phases, losing and acquiring and re-acquiring customs on the way. Whilst the pre-Christian religious beliefs are not fully known, the season we call Christmas has always been based on a variety of traditions. So the Christian spiritual content of Christmas has always been but a fraction of what we celebrate at Christmas. Indeed Christmas could be viewed as a sacrament of society's hopes and fears. Charles Dickens so cleverly illustrated this in his book, *A Christmas Carol,* which was to play such a large part in defining the modern Christmas. In a society as diverse as ours is now, Christmas will therefore never express everybody's views or priorities and its connection to the baby Jesus, after whom the festival is named, may be at best complex and often, tenuous. For this reason, like Samhain/All Hallows (see Introductions to October and November), the layering of pre-Christian, Christian and secular rituals and customs is immensely complicated. In truth, they cannot be divided, but for simplicity's sake and to honour the difference that is there, they are separated under several headings here.

Winter Solstice

The earth's equatorial plane changes in relation to the sun, as it travels round the sun each year. Because the earth is tilted, around December 21 and 22, the northern hemisphere is leaning furthest away from the sun, giving us the shortest day and longest night. The sun is furthest south and appears to "stand still." So there is the curious paradox that at the darkest point of the year, we can begin to celebrate the return of the light.

As long as three thousand years before Christ, some of the standing stones in our isles were clearly built aligned to the solstices. Most spectacularly for the sunrise of the winter solstice is the Newgrange grave passage in Ireland. The sun not only shines down to the chamber, but lights up the exquisite spirals carved on the stone. No-one knows exactly what the spirals represent, but our spirits respond to them as spiritual symbols that seem to describe the inner journey, as well as being symbolic of the sun and the eternal cycle. Stonehenge which was built around 2100 BC is aligned to the midsummer sunrise but was possibly used for the midwinter sunset as well. It must be said that most of our stone circles are not aligned to the solstices and that we can not be sure what kind of religious activity took place at them. We also have no literary sources that confirm pagan celebrations of midwinter. However, there is enough evidence to suggest that there was a major pre-Christian festival which marked the beginning of the year, and this was around the time of the winter solstice.

Yule

Some of the strongest evidence for a midwinter feast is from Scandinavia where "Yule" was celebrated. Another notion of the word's meaning is that it might be related to the Anglo-Saxon word for "wheel." This has remained a popular notion because the sun is clearly at such a significant moment in the wheel of the year. One early source says that Yule lasted three nights from the solstice to New Year (with a different calendar). It was a solstice festival and originally a feast of the dead, and many of the ceremonies, as at Samhain, were about the spirits and devils and most particularly Odin and his night-riders (see under Father Christmas below). Odin was the god of intoxicating drink and ecstasy as well as of death and there may have been a link between his sacrificial beer and the blessed Christmas ale of the Wassail (see below). In Scandinavia, they left fresh food and drink on the table after the feasting to feed the roaming Yuletide spirits of the dead. So the Viking invasion of the eleventh century restored pagan celebrations despite the church's attempts to quell them. Along with the revelry there was much divination for the New Year. However, the church's denunciation of both the sorcery and the festivities, did not subdue the peoples' enthusiasm.

Yule Candles

In Germany and Scandinavia, candles at midwinter were lit to welcome back the light or the sun. In Scotland and Ireland this evolved into lighting big candles for Christmas, called Christmas candles and Yule candles. Yule candles, which were coloured, were lit on Christmas eve to mark the movement from the ordinary daily world to the magical time of Christmas. They were placed in every window like a light for Mary and Joseph to give them a warm welcome as they had found no room.

Yule Log

In the nineteenth century, they revived the older Northern European tradition of the Yule log, which had notions of "bringing home the sun". It was burnt on Christmas Day, and large enough to burn for the whole day and to need several people to haul it in and onto the hearth. It was brought into the house with music and merriment and lit with some ceremony. In older times it was decorated with greenery and a libation of cider poured on it. It was customary not to burn all of it, but to save some to kindle the Yule log the following year, as a token that the sun was always going to return. In Scotland some people called it the Cailleach or Old Woman of Yule. The idea was that she had swallowed up the light and so she had to be burnt to set the light free. For some, the log was believed to bring protection and in Wales, they saved the ashes to scatter on the land with the spring sowing for luck and fertility. This was one of several "saining" or purifying rituals performed around New Year time, as at other times of the year.

Bringing the Outside In
The Holly and the Ivy

Decking the halls with holly and ivy is a custom that pre-dates Christianity and derives from a need to bring greenery into the house when there is little green or light or warmth outside. It is a celebration that the green world cannot die. Holly and ivy represented masculine and feminine respectively in pre-Christian thinking. The red of the holly berries was symbolic of the fire of the sun and later the blood of Christ. The wreaths on the door came to Britain from the United States in the nineteenth century, but in Northern European countries they were much earlier and symbolized the sacred and eternal wheel of life. People adorn the holly, ivy, laurel, bay, yew and other greenery with pinecones, oranges, nuts and bundles of cinnamon and cloves.

Mistletoe

Mistletoe is a parasitic plant that grows in balls with its roots attached to the trunk of deciduous trees like apple, hawthorn, lime or willow. The seeds of the mistletoe are spread by birds who eat the sticky berries and then either wipe their beaks or leave dung on another tree. It is not mentioned as frequently as holly and ivy and is harder to come by, but there is the delightful recording of a single incident by Pliny in the first century. He tells of how mistletoe was regarded by the Gauls as an antidote to poison and a bringer of fertility to animals. The Druids found it especially magical when it was growing on oak, which is rare. He said, at such times, it was ritually gathered on the sixth day of the moon. To this day, mistletoe retains a special reputation, even without the picture of Druids in white robes climbing trees by moonlight with golden sickles. Kissing under mistletoe was a custom from Saturnalia. In Scandinavia, mistletoe was a plant of peace, which evolved into part of its meaning when it became popular in England in the late eighteenth century. They made elaborate "kissing boughs". Sometimes this was just mistletoe and sometimes other greenery was entwined around a structure made in a basin shape of two to four crossed hoops in a sphere, sometimes several feet wide. As well as mistletoe there might be holly, apples, oranges, oat ears, dolls, can-

dles, coloured paper and ribbons. As now, people kissed under it in a romantic and light-hearted way, but it had a deeper meaning too. Sometimes a little
Christ child was placed in it. As a bough of peace the idea was not to let anyone over the threshold without forgiving and forgetting any enmity that had
ensued in the year.

Christmas

The Romans may not have been entirely sure when the winter solstice was,
but in their calendar they marked this period as the turn of the year. The calendar of Julius Caesar put the solstice on December 25. The pagan Roman
customs celebrated Saturnalia for a few days starting December 17 and then
Kalendae, the New Year celebrations from January 1-3. Saturnalia involved
much merry-making and misrule, and gifts of light were exchanged.

In the Roman empire in the second and third centuries there had been an
early cult of the Unconquered Sun. In AD 274, this became a more official
feast and celebrated in December, but only until AD 323 when Constantine
converted to Christianity. Everyone would agree that it would be impossible
to identify the real date of Christ's birth, so celebrating the Nativity on
December 25 was a deliberate attempt to transfer the people's allegiance from
worship of the birth of the Sun, to worship of the birth of the Son. The first
certain record of it being celebrated on that day was AD 354 in Rome.

A cluster of Christian festivals emerged or re-emerged over the next
couple of centuries, including St Stephen's Day on December 26, (he was the
first Christian martyr) St John the Evangelist, (Christ's beloved disciple) on
December 27, Holy Innocents on December 28, (remembering King Herod's
slaughter of the baby boys at the time of Christ's birth), Christ's circumcision
on January 1, the Baptism of Christ by John the Baptist on January 6, and
most popularly, on the same day, the Visit of the Magi/Wise Men, which we
call Epiphany. Thus in AD 567 at the Council of Tours, the Twelve Days was
officially declared the festal period, commencing on December 25, including
January 1 and ending on January 6. In the Eastern Christian countries, Easter
remained the more important feast, but in the northern colder countries
like our own, the human need to celebrate the light in the darkness, and
especially when not much work on the land could take place, Christmas
became the principal festival of the year.

The Mediaeval period was a rich period for Christmas. There was
feasting, Christmas liturgies in churches, the singing of carols, pageants with
plays and music and hospitality in homes all across the Twelve Days.

Landowners and nobles would provide sumptuous feasts for workers. Plays were put on in local churches. Guisers or mummers (see Introduction to January) who were players wearing festive masks, animal skins, bells and disguises were popular, from the royal court to the pubs. However, crime and disorder were also associated with them, for they also went from house to house playing and singing funny songs. These practices enabled poorer people to both entertain the wealthier classes by poking fun at them and earn money from so doing. The notion of misrule at Christmas and the reversal of norms have a long tradition. We have retained it only in mild form in the Christmas pantomime, where men and women are dressed as each other, and the "underdog" wins. The Christmas cracker invented by a nineteenth century confectioner means that at Christmas, we all get to wear crowns, even if they are only paper.

Christmas from the beginning had been a time of "giving to the poor." Although the tradition of the grand feast at the landowner's house on Christmas day died out in the nineteenth century as less people were employed on the land and farms became smaller enterprises, the notion of charity at Christmas remained. There were many begging customs around December and January, but suffice it to mention "Thomasing" or "gooding," which took place on December 21, St Thomas' day. Groups of older women, often widows, would go from house to house begging food or money with a rhyme such as this:

"Well a day, well a day,
St Thomas goes too soon away,
Then your gooding we do pray
For a good time will not stay.
St Thomas gray, St Thomas gray,
The longest night and shortest day
Please to remember St Thomas's day."[17]

This interestingly combines a Christian saint's day, the solstice, and the idea of charity at a particular time of goodwill.

The custom of carrying the wassailing bowl from house to house and singing wassail songs, was common from the Mediaeval times until the nineteenth century. (See Introduction to January). The bowl or cup was decorated with greenery and ribbons, full of warm ale, apples and toast.

"Our Wassail we do fill
With apples and with spice,
Then grant us your good will
To taste here once or twice
Of our good Wassail......"[18]

Of course the custom that remains with us today, is carolling or carol-singing, which still earns money for charity. Carols were banned in the Reformation and not widely resurrected until the nineteenth century. However, in the Middle Ages, the gates of the walled cities were guarded by watchmen called "waits." They had to sound the hours by blowing a single note or tune on an instrument like a horn. Some of them became good musicians and played at official occasions wearing their bright smart uniforms. With the development of the police force in the nineteenth century the waits died out, but it became the name for any groups of people singing carols and popular songs unaccompanied or with harps, fiddles or pipes. They collected drinks or money.

One of the lovely traditions in Wales was the "plygain" which was a candle-lit assembly in the church in the early hours of Christmas day, where carols would be sung and coloured candles lit. The Reformation put an end to such sacred gatherings but the Methodist "watch-night" from Christmas Eve to Christmas morn in the eighteenth century and the Midnight Mass in the twentieth century, which we know today, had a precedent.

From the Reformation in the sixteenth century to the Restoration in the seventeenth century, Christmas was denounced by the church as Papist, and particularly by the Scottish Kirk, though the Catholic highlands and islands remained festive. Christmas was legally abolished in 1644, although the new government in England in 1660 overturned all the laws since 1642. Ironically, this Puritan backlash against Christmas services only served to heighten the enthusiasm for secular celebrations in the middle of winter. People's need for festivities in the middle of the dark months and especially in Scotland where the days were shorter, did not wane throughout this period. In Scotland, much of the revelry and feasting transferred to Hogmanay, or New Year. Thus the Kirk's attempts to ban festivals resulted in the fulsome celebration of a feast closer in spirit to the pagan Vikings and Saxons and maybe the pre-Christian British.

Ireland continued to celebrate the Twelve Days from Big Christmas on December 25 to Little Christmas on January 6. It was thought that the gates of heaven were open (thus bypassing purgatory) to anyone who died during that time, and people were open to the sacred and generous qualities of both human and divine love. Country people would go to the big markets in the towns to "bring home the Christmas" and people gave gifts. Shopkeepers gave Christmas boxes, normally fruitcake and drink, as still happens between a few employers and employees today.

It is well known that the Victorians are largely responsible for inventing or re-inventing the plethora of traditions that make up our modern Christmas. Industrialization had served to divide and de-stabilize Britain, and so people welcomed the harking back to the past, seeing it as a more harmonized and ordered society. At the beginning of the nineteenth century, Christmas was not kept with enthusiasm in all places to the extent that when, of the Twelve Days, only Christmas Day was officially declared a holiday, there was little resistance. The huge change brought by industrialization made people's fears crystallize in particular desires – a fear of the widening gap between rich and poor, a stronger emphasis on family, a desire to protect children from the world, and this yearning for safer pre-industrial times. It is easy to see how Christmas, with its emphasis on piety, charity and family time, became a focus for those desires. Into this mix in 1843, Charles Dickens wrote *A Christmas Carol,* which did much to cement the refinding of Christmas and continues to influence Christmas as we know it today. He saw Christmas with the family and charity beyond as the palliative to the ills of society. One of the other factors was the Oxford Movement in the Church of England, which revived the more catholic part of the church with its enthusiasm for ritual, seasons and decoration. This nostalgia also emerged in a renewed interest in Paganism, some of which was integrated into the new customs. However, there were many scientific developments in the nineteenth century, most notably the evolutionary theories of Charles Darwin, and so amidst the piety and romanticism was the rise of rationalism and a questioning of religion. All of these factors contributed to the welcome of many customs that were popularized in Victorian times, and have endured until the present.

The origin of the modern Christmas customs
The Christmas tree

By the mid-nineteenth century, the Christmas tree was already part of Christmas in Scandinavia, the Netherlands and the United States. It had been popular in Germany, at least from the early sixteenth century, and came with German settlers to Britain, but after the German Prince Albert erected one in Windsor Castle, the custom spread quickly. It was decorated with little candles (until electric lights in the 1890s) and tiny toys and musical instruments, real fruit painted with gold leaf, fake fruit and all kinds of edible surprises. The Germans also gave us the blown-glass tree ornaments. It took a hundred years, until the 1950s, for nearly every household to have one.

Christmas cards

The Christmas card also started during the mid-nineteenth century. Originally, it was a way, amongst wealthy people, of sending a decorated card and poem with New Year's blessings and good wishes. By the end of the century, they were being manufactured and widely used. Religious themes were never as common as natural and jolly ones. They most commonly depicted holly, mistletoe and robins or Christmas pudding, Father Christmas, bells and the Christmas tree.

The Christmas present

The idea of giving presents also originated in New Year. It took some time for the custom of giving at Christmas rather than New Year to spread from the middle-classes to the upper and working classes. The stronger emphasis on family and charity contributed to the greater focus being on the Nativity. Interestingly, the greater separation of children from their parents, with the advent of nurseries and nannies, meant they had to be occupied, hence the huge upsurge in new toys and games in the Victorian period. By the 1880s market forces and the press were responding, and so even in the nineteenth century shopping adverts were appearing in November! It took a bit longer for them to start in late September but the fact remains that the marketing of toys and other Christmas goods has been a reality for well over a century.

Christmas dinner

Until the late eighteenth century the traditional Christmas dinner had been beef, but the Americans introduced turkey, whilst poorer families had the cheaper goose. By the twentieth century, turkey was the tradition across the board. Plum pudding became the dessert in Victorian times and the cake complete with coins inside transferred to Christmas from Twelfth Night.

The Christmas stocking and Father Christmas including Saint Nicholas December 6

The Christmas stocking also came to Britain from Germany, and after it had been established, in other parts of Europe. Originally it was the Christ-child that was thought to fill it on Christmas Eve, but this did not last long as the United States brought us the rotund red-coated, white-haired gentleman that became so ubiquitously loved. Most people are aware that Father Christmas derives from Santa Claus or Saint Nicholas. He was popular with the Dutch who still keep his day on December 6. Saint Nicholas is the patron saint of children and associated with charitable giving. Dutch, and some German, children would put a shoe, or later a stocking, out on the eve of December 6. This is where the origin of only receiving if the child had been good came from. There is a legend of Saint Nicholas that he knew a man with three daughters. He was a poor a man and could not afford their dowries. They were destined for prostitution and each night over a period of time, as they came of age, Saint Nicholas would secretly throw a bag of gold into the house through the window. In one version, the man wants to see who is helping them and to avoid being seen, Saint Nicholas climbs onto the roof and throws the last one down the chimney. Saint Nicholas is the patron saint of pawn-brokers, for his aid to the poor and the three balls of the pawnbroker are sometimes attributed to the three bags of gold.

Some commentators say that the Saint Nicholas tradition can be linked to the Germanic god Odin. In the Dutch and Flemish tradition, Saint Nicholas rides a horse over the rooftops, which may have been connected to Odin riding through the sky. Saint Nicholas is indeed always portrayed bearded, in a red robe, his Bishop's robe, flying through the December night on his grey horse with his sack of presents for children.

There were Dutch settlers in New York, then called New Amsterdam, who brought the tradition of Saint Nicholas with them. It died out but it was described by a New York writer Washington Irving in the early nineteenth century. This may have been the inspiration for Clement Clark Moore, an academic and a poet to write a poem "A Visit from Saint Nicholas", often known as "The Night Before Christmas", for his children in 1822. It was printed publicly without permission and later illustrated, and was staggeringly popular. Moore's Santa Claus was not exactly the same as the Dutch image. He had taken the figure on into his imagination. He became a magical northern midwinter spirit with a beard and fur clothes. He travelled through the sky with his sack of presents, on a sleigh drawn by reindeer, delivering children's presents down the chimneys for their stockings on Christmas Eve. Susan and Ann Warner introduced him and the stocking to England in 1854, in their book "The Christmas Stocking". After the Coca-Cola campaign at Christmas in 1931 in Britain, he came to be represented in the red and white fur trimmed suit and hood that we recognize today. In England there was already a personification of Christmas called Father Christmas, so he became more popularly known by that name. He was established as a tradition of Christmas by the 1880s, embodying, as he so perfectly did, the ideas already abroad about children, bounty and charity.

Christmas carols

Both the Evangelicals and the Anglo-Catholics were determined to revive hymn-singing and carolling, and some attractive carol collections were published, most notably "Christmas Carols Old and New" in 1871 by two Oxford academics from Magdalen College. In 1880 a future archbishop, Edward Benson instituted the "Festival of Nine Lessons and Carols." Both school and church services of carol singing ensued effortlessly and has continued to the present day. All the carols that would be sung now were mostly written, and a few revived, at that time.

The nativity play

In 1920s and 1930s, the primary school nativity play became popular and has not waned. Indeed it is now normally viewed ducking and dipping the parental camcorder in front. As now, this was not a religious activity but the Holy Family (despite it's abnormality and Jesus being illegitimate), is a potent symbol used to emphasize the importance of family at times when this is required. It will be interesting to see how the rise of civil partnerships and the different configurations of family now will affect the "festival of the family" notion of Christmas.

Christmas in the public arena

From 1950s onwards, Christmas became social and patriotic more than religious. Huge civic Christmas trees had been appearing in public places since the second world war. Public money began to be spent on lights in cities and the lighting up time has gone further back into November. Increased affluence has also extended the number of weeks and the amount of money we spend Christmas shopping. The arrival of the television in most households by the 1970s has increased the pressure to buy certain products, especially amongst children.

In Scotland, the Protestants relaxed their ban on Christmas and in 1958 it became a national holiday. Likewise, England adopted New Year as a holiday and a time for celebration with adult friends rather than the emphasis on family. It is now commonplace to have a nine-day holiday from Christmas Eve until New Years' Day. There are new complaints of stress at Christmas time and commercialism obscuring the "true spirit of Christmas," but from the beginning, Christmas has always been a mix of cultural, political and religious traditions. It seems that feasting and celebrating in the midwinter will never die, so human is the need, but the meaning and customs of Christmas may well evolve over the next few decades as notions of religion, family and society change, and as the backlash against materialism increases.

Spiritual significance of the Winter Solstice

There are deities associated with the solstice though not everyone who keeps the solstice necessarily invokes the deities. The waxing sun overcomes the waning sun and this is symbolized by the struggle between the Oak King and the Holly King. The Holly King represents the death aspect of the God and the Oak King is the Divine Child, the rebirth. The Holly that "of all the trees that are in the wood, bears the crown," is a wonderful syncretistic Pagan reference in "The Holly and the Ivy". It is curious and delightful that the carol survived the protestant ban on carols. The version we know is credited to Cecil Sharp, the folklore revivalist, in 1911.

As with the sun itself, it is a time to stop and people reflect back. It is a time to see what has been incubating in the darkest part of the year – from Samhain to the Solstice. People celebrate in different ways. Unlike Christmas there are not unifying and monolithic traditions. Some gather around standing stones for both the solstices for ceremony. In more informal and smaller gatherings, many light a bonfire at dusk, sometimes throwing on symbolic pieces of wood to represent the darkness and fears of the old and welcoming the hopes and dreams for the new year, still hidden in darkness, but in faith that they will emerge. It is a time of hope and new life and light emerging from the womb of darkness. There is a strong sense that the dark is necessary and that beyond the eye, the roots are growing, the buds are forming, the shoots from bulbs are soon to appear. Something old must die so that the new can be re-born.

Spiritual significance of Christmas

Whilst church-going is declining in Britain, at Christmas time, the churches become packed. There are many reasons why people come to church at Christmas. For some it is undoubtedly because it is part of the tradition, along with the turkey and the stocking and also because it re-creates childhood and touches wistful spirits. At the heart of it, over and over again, maybe people still come to hear the story and sing the carols. The story can be found and is read in all the Christmas services from the gospels. Matthew records it in chapters 1-3 and is the only gospel which tells the story of the visit of the wise men. He also gives us more insight into Joseph. Mark does not tell the birth of Christ but emphasizes the ministry of John the Baptist. Luke is known as the Gospel writer who writes for the underdog, so it is in Luke that we hear the story of women, in this case Mary, and of the shepherds in chapters 1-2. John has no narrative of the birth of Christ. Instead he gives us the wonderful prologue in chapter one (John 1.1-18).

"In the beginning was the Word, and the Word was with God, and the Word was God. The Word was with God in the beginning. All things were created by him, and apart from him not one thing was created that has been created. In him was life, and the life was the light of all people. And the light shines in the darkness, but the darkness has not overcome it."

- John 1.1-5

For Christians, the birth of Christ means that God became one of us, like us, a baby. We do not have to do all the reaching out to God. God in unimaginable love comes to be with us. The story of Jesus is not a story of a King born in a palace, but a story of struggle and difficulty, and literally mortal danger. An angel comes to Mary, a young girl, and says she is to have a baby though she is a virgin. Mary consents to this, and Joseph to whom she is betrothed, is told in a dream by God to stand by her. They have to go to Bethlehem to be registered in the final month of Mary's pregnancy. There are so many people there that they cannot find a room and so she gives birth in a stable amongst the animals. Angels appear to ordinary shepherds in the fields telling them to go and see the baby Jesus, born to be the Saviour of the world and the bringer of peace, "goodwill to all people." It is common to conflate the story of the wise men into the nativity, though it is believed to have happened later. Astrologers come from the East following a star. En route they go to King Herod, who is furious that this star which signifies kingship, hangs over another, not himself. The wise men come to Jesus with their gifts and do not return to Herod. Herod issues a decree to kill all the baby boys under two years old so that his kingship is not threatened. Joseph is warned in a dream not to return home, and so they make for safety in Egypt, in fear for Jesus' life.

The story has a universal quality. It is about good people with no wealth or status who are touched by God and who overcome personal struggle and terrifying evil in the world. There is a moving relationship between Mary, Joseph and Jesus in the story. They protect each other in this difficult and dangerous world that they move through. Some of the traditions of Christmas may seem far-fetched, irrelevant or downright hideous, but most of them have emanations from the glow of this strange story, which people still come to church to hear, regardless of belief. It can hold people's hopes and fears. It is about hoping for God or good things amidst a difficult world, and the belief that it can happen to us, ordinary people. It is also a triumph of human relatedness and love, over evil. From this, we evolve rituals and customs about being with people you love, bringing gifts, welcoming the stranger, celebrating in the middle of darkness, trying to be more charitable, offering prayers for the world and for our own protection.

Advent

For many practising Christians, Advent is a special time and a time of spiritual preparation before the clamour of Christmas. Advent means "coming" and anticipates the coming of Christ. It lasts for four Sundays before Christmas. It starts on the Sunday closest to November 30 and ends on Christmas Day. Advent may last between twenty two to twenty eight days, depending on which day of the week Christmas falls. The liturgical colour of Advent is the same as for Lent and funerals, which is purple or occasionally, midnight blue. Purple is the mournful colour and also the royal colour so combines the contemplative waiting and repenting of Lent with the joy of the coming Saviour.

In the fourth and fifth centuries, Advent was the preparation for Epiphany rather than Christmas. It was also a time for new Christians to be baptized and welcomed into the church. Originally it was a fasting period and had the sombre overtones of Lent. It lasted for forty days from St Martin's Day on November 12. In sixth century Rome, the focus of Advent was the second coming of Christ, but in the Middle Ages, it became about anticipating Christ's birth as well. Nowadays it is not regarded as a fast, and is a joyful waiting for the God who is to come, and preparing our hearts for that event. However, it is also a serious time with a focus on John the Baptist's radical and uncompromising call to repentance and there is a reckoning with the difficulties of the world. The Second Coming remains an Advent theme and is a time when Christ is believed to come again in judgment and with justice. The Advent carols like "O Come O Come Emmanuel" are not like Christmas carols musically or lyrically. They have a longing and a deep dark edge to their hopeful waiting.

Both in homes and in churches, there is an Advent wreath. This originated in Germany from the idea of the Yule candles (see above). There are five Advent candles, normally four in the outer ring and one in the centre. The four represent the four weeks of Advent and are lit each Sunday, and the fifth is the light of Christ lit on Christmas day. They represent the Advent themes which go with the readings for each week. The first is for Abraham and the Patriarchs who put their trust in God's promises. The second is for Isaiah and the prophets who foretold the coming of the Messiah. The third is for John the Baptist who prepared the people through repentance and faith. The fourth is for Mary who was chosen to bear the Christ child. Traditionally, they were purple and the third was pink for Gaudete Sunday when the fast was relaxed. Gaudete means "Rejoice" and was the first word from the introit to the Mass.

There was a special period of Advent, called the Octave, before Christmas lasting from December 17th to the 23rd. During that time at Vespers (Evening Prayer), just before the Magnificat (the song of Mary), monastic houses would chant the seven O Antiphons. Each one is a name for the Messiah and refers to Isaiah's prophecy of the coming of the Messiah. They are "O Wisdom", "O Lord", "O Root of Jesse", "O Key of David", "O Rising Sun", "O Ruler of the Nations" and "O Emmanuel" (Emmanuel means "God with us"). They were an evocative part of the liturgy that heralded the coming of the Christ, and like all of Advent, looked back to the Scriptural story of God, before Jesus, in the Old Testament, and forward to God's coming to us now, and at the Second Coming of Christ.

Of all the Old Testament prophets who spoke of the coming of the Messiah, Isaiah is the most meditated over in Advent. Here are a sample of some of the passages read in Advent:

"The wilderness and the dry land shall be glad,
the desert shall rejoice and blossom,
like a crocus it shall blossom abundantly
and rejoice with joy and singing" 35.1-2a

"A shoot shall come out from the stock of Jesse,
and a branch shall grow out of his roots.
The spirit of the Lord shall rest on him,
The spirit of wisdom and understanding,

the spirit of counsel and might,
the spirit of knowledge and the fear of the Lord......
the wolf shall live with the lamb,
the leopard shall lie down with the kid,
the calf and the lion and the fatling together
and a little child shall lead them." 11.1-2,6

"Here is my servant whom I uphold,
my chosen, in whom my soul delights........
He will not cry or lift up his voice,
or make it heard in the street;
a bruised reed he will not break
and a dimly burning wick he will not quench,
he will faithfully bring forth justice." 42.1-3

For most people though, the weeks of Advent are extremely stressful buying presents for Christmas, sending cards, completing jobs at work, getting ready for entertaining or feeding extra people. For children, December is a time of intense excitement, helped only by the Advent Calendar which has a window to open each day until Christmas Eve. The first Advent Calendar was published in Germany in 1903 and depicted the Christ child's garden. Each 'door' opened to reveal a religious text. It did not come to Britain until the 1950s. After the earlier ones, the windows revealed Christmas pictures and now, many contain chocolates.

So the themes of December are about waiting and watching in the darkest part of the year. It is celebrating hope, and the return of the light amidst the bleakness of the natural world and the struggles of the human world. There is a focus on the little and ordinary holding the truths of life and the need for love, both of those nearest and dearest to us and those whom we do not know. For some this hope is located symbolically by offering intentions before the movement of the sun, and for others it is found in the arrival of a tiny baby.

MONDAY Waiting

On Rising/Resting

Blessed be you Gracious One, who waits with our world,
who never departs but longs to be invited,
who never insists but comes when least expected.
☼ Be in my waiting and watching as I make my way this day.
☾ Be in my waiting and watching as I lie down this night to sleep.

Praising

Praise to you Ground of my Longing. You see my restless heart and offer rest.
You see my sense of incompleteness and offer wholeness.
You see my prayers for a better world and offer redemption.
You see my waiting and know the terror of dreams that never come true,
but still you wait with me.
For you embrace my deepest desire
Ground of my Longing,
praise to you.

Stilling

Be still in the silence and aware of the Love with and within........

☼ Morning Invocation

As I arise today in the shrouded morning light
with the waning rays of sun, the leafless trees,
come O Bringer of the New to this worn and weary season.
Come to my hardiness of effort while the land is waiting to be reborn.
Come to my sleepy eyes while my vision waits to be renewed.
Come to my sluggardly limbs while I wait for a time to rest awhile.
Come to my busy hands that I might learn to tend and take care.
Come to my anxious heart that I might not be overwhelmed.
Come to my soul in stillness Advent God,
that I may discern the work that I must do to get ready,
the work that I can let go, and the work of prayer that I might be attentive.
Let me learn from the earth's quiet so I may relax in each moment
and enjoy my task for now, untroubled by tasks for later,
Let me receive the peace of your blessing as I wait and watch with you.

☼ Opening Out

Defender of the deep down hidden things,
you see the yearnings that are invisible to others,
the waiting in the darkness for a springtime bud that never came,
the waiting for a baby for year upon year,
the waiting for a true love who never appeared,
the waiting for a vocation never found or fulfilled,
the waiting for healing from the long ago hurt.
Defend all who wait and wait

Thank you that you do not see us as fools but cherish our heart's desire.
Encircle us with dignity and teach us to live without bitterness,
and to discover the true meaning of hope.

☾ Thanksgiving

As I end this day in your safe-keeping
I count three blessings before my sleeping

☾ Night Shielding

Outrageous One, who comes in the night, ready or not,
who surprises with your arrival in the darkest moonless places.
For you did not wait til we were ready.
You did not wait til every child was loved, and every mouth fed;
til our lives were spotless and the fighting had ceased.
You come just as we are.
Come to me this night dear God and to all who need your peace.

Watch and wait with us in the darkness until the light of justice dawns.
Bring me safely to tomorrow as I lie down this night.

Blessing

May I wait this day/night and not lose hope
that every wound may be bound, the broken-hearted comforted,
the oppressed become free,
that peace will come and goodwill for all the earth's people.
☼ Bless me with the grace to live with incompleteness this day.
☾ Bless me with the grace to live with incompleteness as I lie down this night.

TUESDAY Coming Home for Christmas

On Rising/Resting

Blessed be you Deep Home inside myself,

In whom all my wanderings return.

✻ Be the hearth of my heart burning within as I walk out this cold day.

☾ Be the hearth of my heart burning within as I lie down to sleep this night

Praising

Praise to you Dweller among us,

for your family extends beyond your kin

and knows no boundary of blood or race.

You made and shelter all under this wondrous same sky,

roof of stars and angels declaring your presence

and whispering "Peace".

Praise to you.

In the Stillness

Be still in the silence and aware of the Love with and within…………..

✻ Morning Invocation

God of all unholy families, from whom we all come,

preserve me this December day as the immoveable feast comes round again.

Preserve my hands and my heart with love as I consider the giving of gifts.

Preserve my feet with peace as I navigate through shops bringing home the Christmas.

Preserve my home-making with joy as I bring the outside in.

Preserve my mind from overwhelming as I complete my work.

Preserve my celebration from pretence.

Preserve my deep home within where you reside.

Preserve my access to it when Christmas grows over the path.

Preserve my hopes from false expectations of happy families.

Preserve me from homesickness for all that once was or all that never has been.

Preserve my spirit with your grounding that I may be generous and true.

Preserve my wounds with your mercy that my Christmas home may accommodate them.

Preserve me this day with your newness that I might make the old ways new

✿ Opening Out

O Holy Spirit, on whom doors are shut with cries of "no room".
Rest this Christmas time upon
all who have not chosen to be alone,
all who miss their loved ones,
all whose family causes heartbreak,
all who have taken different paths and feel excluded,
all who look through lit windows and feel out in the cold

Unwelcomed One who dwells among us,
bring us in to the warmth of your shelter
that I may keep my door open to your mercy and love.

☾ Thanksgiving

As I end this day in your safe-keeping
I count three blessings before my sleeping

☾ Night Shielding

Ripe-bellied God, waiting to bring forth heaven,
you do not come to the brightest and best,
the happiest, the most secure so be born in me this quiet night.
With the busyness hushed, the people of my day gone now,
do not just visit the part where I find it easy to love.
Come to my fear and loneliness, my struggle and grieving.
Come to my yearning for a life that could have been different.
Come to all whose hurts cannot find a home at Christmas

Be born in us this night O Love Divine that we may come home this Christmas.
Rest me in quietness as I lie down this night.

Blessing

May the joy of the Homeless One bless my home,
May the love of the Unbegotten One bless my family,
May the peace of the Newborn One bless our strife,
   ✿ as I set out this Christmas season.
   ☾ as I lie down this Christmas season.

WEDNESDAY The Shortest Day, the Longest Night

On Resting/Rising
Blessed be you Sun Maker, Orb Turner,
you know the wisdom of the rhythms.
✷ Teach me the health of resting time as I walk out this short day.
☽ Teach me the health of resting time as I lie down this long night.

Praising
Praise to you Undiminished One,
whose light the darkness can never put out;
whose growth is nurtured in hiddeness;
whose faithfulness never stands still or waxes cold;
whose life is the light of all that lives;
in whom love, honour, thanksgiving, prayer
and praise, to you.

In the Stillness
Be still in the silence and aware of the Love with and within...............

✷ Morning Invocation
From the rising of the midwinter sun to its setting,
scatter the darkness with the light of your love, O Shining One.
Make me short on mean thoughts, long on offering words of comfort.
Make me short on being driven, long on paying attention.
Make me short on focussing only on my own, long on looking beyond.
Make me short on obsessive lists, long on spontaneous acts of kindness.
Make me short on mindless activity, long on time to reflect.
Make me short on tradition as habit, long on re-discovery and re-owning.
Make me short on rushing and tiring, long on walking and wondering.
Make me short on false festive jollity, long on stilling and rooted joy.
Make me short on guilt, long on being merciful to myself.
Make me short on being overwhelmed, long on peaceableness as I set forth
this day.

✷ Opening Out
Bright Mystery,
at this solstice time, where we leave a space to look back and look forward,

your mercy covers more than the white frosty sparkle on leafless trees.
Your love burnishes more than the scarlet sheen of hips and berries.
Your Spirit of life rejoices more than the confidence of green needles and leaves.
Be with all who wish to leave behind their years with the dying things

Cover with your mercy, burnish with your love and rejoice with new life,
as we lay down the year we cannot change,
and offer our hopes and fears for the next.

☾ Thanksgiving

As I end this day in your safe-keeping
I count three blessings before my sleeping

☾ Night Shielding

This is the long night,
where I kindle the flame of your presence O Faithful One.
with firelight without, and candle flickering on sill within,
with crackling log on hearth within and starglow without,
I welcome you to my house and heart.
Give me grace to cherish the darkness that I may know my need of light.
Visit all who need to feel the beam of your hope lengthen this long night.

Give us courage to meet the fiends and foes of our night fears,
so when the new day comes I may awake with gratitude and praise.

Blessing

Like the moon stippling on the face of dark waters,
like the Spirit hovering over my deep,
like a seed needing the dark to grow in the light,
like the darkest hour coming just before the dawn,
like the new life ready within the womb,
may God's face shine upon me as I wait in hope for the returning light
☼ in the dusky daylight hours of this short day.
☾ in the deep dark hours of this long night.

THURSDAY O Come, O Come

On Rising/Resting

Blessed be you Eternal Unfleeting One,
Source of all desiring, your peace eludes.
☼ I seek your presence as I wake up this morning.
☾ I seek your presence as I give thanks for this day that you have given.

Praising

Praise to you God-with-us, for coming as we prepare for you,
for creeping into the gatherings,
midst the chatter and laughter and the spices warming;
for passing through the late night shoppers
midst the dimly lit anxiety;
for wandering into the churches
midst the hopes and fears felt by the orange glow of crib.
Praise to you.

In the Stillness

Be still in the silence and aware of the Love with and within...........

☼ Morning Invocation

O Rising Sun, come like the radiant dawn breaking through the darkest hour
as I awake this morning.
O Green Shoot come, when all seemed fallow and dead.
O Key-holder come, unlock the cell-door of my fears.
O Snowflake come, unique and tiny, miraculous and quiet.
O Returning Wanderer come, when all was lost and beyond believing.
O Robin Redbreast come, ordinary and cheering, constant and true.
O Fool come, appear where I least expect you and crease up my seriousness.
O Holly come, with your extrovert green and scarlet brightening the brown.
O Friend come, where I can share and be received in safety.
O Dancer come, express your joy with your whole body.
O Most Mis-shapen and Most Misunderstood come, mirror my crookedness
and my sorrow.
O Bells come, ring out news of peace across all the cities and hills.
O quickly come, and begin in my heart as I set forth this morning.

☼ Opening Out

O Peace beyond our understanding come to our world this morning I pray.
O Wisdom come, whisper your earthed truth where opinion shrieks and power is shrill.
O Child come, walk into the rooms where men plan war.
O Celtic knot come, with no beginning or end, when nothing seems to last.
O Loving Eyes come, see every child's unheard cry.
O Gift come, ungraspable yet longed for.
Come to every place where there is no peace this day

Let me work in your ways of justice as wait for peace to come.

☾ Thanksgiving

As I end this day in your safe-keeping
I count three blessings before my sleeping

☾ Night Shielding

O Holy One who looks out for me, I take my rest this night.
Like the wintering birds swarming to roost across the evening sky,
you will not rest til all are safely gathered in.
Gather us in, the famous and the overlooked,
the dream-livers and the broken-hearted,
the assured and the lost, the friendsome and the lonely

Have mercy on the struggling soul in each one of us.
Yet will I offer thankfulness as I close my eyes this night.

Blessing

Come O Hope-Bringer,
bless me with patience when the world still weeps.
Bless me with courage to never give up believing in peace.
Bless me with work that I may do my part.
Bless me with prayer as I light my candle against the darkness.
☼ Love come down to my little day this morning.
☾ Love come down to my little room as I go to sleep this night.

FRIDAY Crocus in the desert

On Rising/Resting
Blessed be you who appears like a crocus in the wilderness,
like a quiet stream in the desert,
when all seemed broken and beyond repair.
✿ Blossom in tiny sweetness within me this day.
☽ I welcome your sweetness that has blossomed within me this day.

Praising
Praise to you Hope Bringer,
for not coming with clash of cymbals and a chariot
but for meeting me in the small.
Praise for the vulnerable purple petal,
for the delicate frost on spider's web,
for the cluster of cells in the womb,
for the child's hand reaching for mine to lead me.
Praise to you.

In the Stillness
Be still in the silence and aware of the Love with and within…………..

✿ Morning Invocation
O Gentle One with spirit upon you
who would not break a bruised reed or quench a dimly burning wick,
gather me up this dark morning, however you find me.
Gather my feet and touch them with quiet purpose.
Gather my hands and touch them with mindful attentiveness.
Gather my chest and touch all I do with strength of heart.
Gather my voice and touch it with tenderness, without need to be loud.
Gather my judgment and touch it with wisdom beyond what the eye can see.
Gather my heart and touch it with faithfulness.
Gather my words and touch them with truthfulness.
Gather my eyes and touch them with joy.
Gather my face, touch it with your love and set it towards your world.
Gather me up as I rise this morning and touch me with your peace.

☼ Opening Out

Sacred the Weakness reaching out to the weak.
Thank you that you do not overwhelm the broken with your strength
like the mighty dispensing charity to the unfortunate.
You do not offer painlessness but bind our wounds with mercy.
You stand with us in our need that you may protest alongside us.
Be with all who feel fragile and small and skinless this day.

Sacred the sign of crocus hope for the hopeless in the long desert,
the ridiculous presence, letting us know we are not alone.

☾ Thanksgiving

As I end this day in your safe-keeping
I count three blessings before my sleeping

☾ Night Shielding

O Holy One, soft of foot,
keep vigil with me as I lie down this December night,
against the deep, broad pregnant sky.
For in this dark and lonely place, only stillness will do
so I may know how silently the gift is given,
so I may feel the joy that raises me when I cannot raise myself,
so I may sleep in the peace that you are here.
Keep vigil with all who need your presence this night

Watch with us, the slow and the suffering, the little and the lost.
Keep with sleepless eye through this long night til light is come again.

Blessing

Before the first snowflake, before the first glimpse of green,
before the sun pulls back further the dark drapes of day,
here, in this day/night, give sign of your blessing
☼ that I may trust the new thing happening, little by little, this day.
☾ that I may trust the new thing happening, little by little, this night.

SATURDAY Yule

On Resting/Rising
Blessed be you O Oneness shining in midwinter,
your love more constant than evergreen
the light of hope more transforming than the sun.
✿ Radiate your love and hope in the world that I walk in this day.
☾ Radiate your love and hope in the world that I lie down in this night.

Praising
Praise to you Still Small Voice, for though you are all around,
praise for the moments when I can hear you better,
as I leave the bustle and the market-place
and walk awhile with you in the short day-light hours.
Praise for the land and the trees hushed as if with snow,
with barely a soul except for the deep of my call, echoing yours.
Praise to you.

In the Stillness
Be still in the silence and aware of the Love with and within...............

✿ Morning Invocation
Beautiful One, on this wintry morning,
as the earth is still and so is the sun, so may I stop awhile.
As last years ashes grow cold on the hearth I give thanks for your keeping
through all.
Warm my remembering with gratitude, and my pain with your mercy.
Warm my body that I might be free and open to the world today.
Warm my hands with creativity as I make and do and touch.
Warm my enthusiasm with childlike delight when I bring in the tree
from outside, and dress it with trinkets and sweets.
Warm my spirit with generosity so I may not shrink from another in cold.
Warm my heart with wonder as my eye alights on all that you have made.
Warm my meanness with humility that I might know my need of kindness.
Warm my house and soul with welcome and my solitude with your peace.
Warm me with the fire of your love as I set forth this day.

☼ Opening Out

O Heavenly Maker of the earth,
I offer in sorrow, the damage I have helped to cause,
the blossom when branches should be bare,
the leaves and creatures still around.
Green my spirit with wisdom and long-sightedness.
May I discern the carbon footprint I have left behind me
that I may know how to lessen it in the year ahead.
I lament with you the care we have not shown

Deepen our understanding of the One life we share together
given by you, flowing through all, by your Spirit, entrusted to us to take care.

☾ Thanksgiving

As I end this day in your safe-keeping
I count three blessings before my sleeping

☾ Night Shielding

Sweet Giver of Gifts even whilst I sleep,
thank you that your visit to me this night
depends not on whether I have been bad or good,
for your love is far broader and deeper than that.
For in the starlit darkness you let heaven in,
giving us night visions of a world that could be different.
And in the quiet of the midnight blue,
as the white moon glistens with clarity behind the stark black tree,
show me what old must die to make space for the new.
Visit all who need heaven on earth this night.

Fill our dreams with love and our hearts with fresh purpose.

Blessing

As the sun rises over the woods and sets upon the same,
bring your Yule blessings of good cheer.
As the fire rises on the hearth,
bless all with the warmth of your love.
As the gift is given in the quiet of darkness
bless me and all I know with surprise of your nearness.

SUNDAY Gaudete (Rejoice)

On Rising/Resting
Blessed be you Source of deepest Joy,
for whom Creation waits on tip-toe.
✿ Let me set forth with joy as I welcome this new day.
☾ Let me lie down with joy this night, for this day that you have given.

Praising
Praise to you Real Presence, whom heaven cannot hold.
For you cannot be found in dogma and doctrine
but come with tiny finger-print,
like the mark left on all that is made,
like the touch as tears are wiped away.
Praise to you for the glimpse of heaven here.

In Stillness
Be still in the silence and aware of the Love with and within.............

✿ Morning Invocation
As the morning stars sing together, I rejoice this day.
I rejoice for satsumas and nuts, chocolate coins and sugar mice.
I rejoice for cinnamon and nutmeg, ginger and cloves.
I rejoice for the spiced scent of mulled wine warming on the stove.
I rejoice for the hoarfrost, the midwinter light, the wind and the cold.
I rejoice for candles on sills welcoming strangers in homes.
I rejoice for wreaths on the doors, fairy-lit trees and pine-cones.
I rejoice for holly and ivy decking halls and logs on the fire.
I rejoice for the mysterious mistletoe and the kisses it bestows.
I rejoice for carols in the church and the Christmas songs on radio.
I rejoice for Christmas street lighting and Salvation army bands.
I rejoice for advent calendars and stockings and the magic that they bring.
I rejoice for curry on Christmas day, bad television and one drink too many.
I rejoice for families trying to be family despite all that's happened.
I rejoice for people's generosity of giving and the delight of receiving.
I rejoice for people's praying for an end to all the pain.
I rejoice for being human and that as a person you came.
I rejoice that I am able to be tender towards Christmas this day.

☼ Opening Out
O Divine Storyteller,
not for you pious platitudes or round-robins keeping distance,
but love beyond imagining for the stories of each and all;
not edited high-lights and main events that do not tell the truth,
but the stories of real lives in their daily, busy, ordinariness,
like your story waiting to be discovered and re-discovered.
Tell all who need to hear this day the old, old story
of your great love for us in every detail of our lives.

For you alone know the part when……. and what happened next……
and love with compassion and rejoicing.

☾ Thanksgiving
As I end this day in your safe-keeping
I count three blessings before my sleeping

☾ Night Shielding
Spirit of God, be with me as I rest this silent night
with the clamour quietened, the day's doing still now.
Help me to make a space in the darkest part of the year,
to leave it open so I may discover
how to welcome your light and the way of peace,
as dependent on me,
as fragile, as precious
as a tiny baby.
Be with all who need that light, that peace and that care

May we go to sleep with peace this night
and wake with joy for your presence among us.
May I go to sleep with peace.

Blessing
May the joy of the angels in heaven,
the love of the human heart
and the peace of God bless me
☼ as I walk out into the world this morning.
☾ as I lie down to sleep this night.

REFERENCES IN INTRODUCTIONS AND PRAYERS

Introduction

[1] Oddie B. *How to Watch Wildlife* Harper Collins 2005

Hutton R. *Stations of the Sun* Oxford University Press 1996

Kindred G. *Sacred Celebrations* Gothic Image Publications 2001

Freeman M. *Kindling the Celtic Spirit* Harper Collins/ San Francisco 2001

Neu D. L *Return Blessings* Pilgrim Press 2002/Wild Goose Publications 2004

Glennon K. *Heartbeat of the Seasons. Earth Rituals for the Celtic Year.* Columba Press 2005

Eds. Lawrence KT, Cather Weaver J, Wedell R. *Imaging the Word An Arts and Lectionary Resource.* Volumes 1-3 United Church Press/Pilgrim Press 1994

Campanelli P. *Wheel of the Year. Living the Magical Life* Llewellyn Publications 2000

Palmer G. and Lloyd N. *A Year of Festivals* Warne 1972

Day B. *The Celtic Calendar* CW Daniel Co. Ltd. 2003

Self D. *Highdays and Holidays. Celebrating the Christian Year.* Lion 1993

[2] p119 Bradley I. *The Celtic Way* Dartman Longman and Todd 1993

[3] Cunliffe B. *The Celts. A Very Short Introduction* Oxford University Press 2003

Green M. *Exploring the World of the Druids* Thames and Hudson 1997

I am also indebted to the historian Ronald Hutton who is in much agreement with the archaeologists:

Hutton R. ibid.

[4] www.druidnetwork.org. Emma Restall Orr, head of the International Druid Network runs courses about druidry today and has written helpful books for example

Restall Orr E. *Living Druidry. Magical Spirituality for the Wild Soul* Piatkus 2004

[5] Frazer J. *The Golden Bough:A Study in Magic and Religion* Touchstone 1995

[6] p426 Hutton R. ibid

[7] From p111, Bradley I. ibid

[8] Matthews C. *Celtic Devotional* Godsfield Press 1996

[9] Kindred G. ibid
[10]

mail@othona-bb.org.uk
The Othona Community
Coast Road
Burton Bradstock
BRIDPORT
Dorset DT6 4RN
UK
Tel: 01308 897130
www.othona-bb.org.uk

enquiries@findhorn.org
Tel: +44 (0)1309 690311
Findhorn Foundation
The Park
Forres
Scotland
IV36 3TZ
www.findhorn.org/home_new.php

admin@theabbeysc.demon.co.uk
The Abbey
Sutton Courtenay
Abingdon
Oxon
OX14 4AF
Tel: 01235 847401
www.theabbey.uk.com

greenfir@midcoast.com
Greenfire
329 Wallston Road
Tenants Harbor, Maine 04860
Tel: 207-372-6442
www.greenfireretreat.org

[11] bspace@btconnect.com

28 Abbotts Rd
New Barnet
Herts EN5 5DP
Tel: 020 8441 8903 / 020 8441 2809
www.breeathingspacearts.co.uk

[12] Untraceable quote from an interview with Maya Angelou in a Sunday newspaper
[13] attributed to St Patrick, AD 433
[14] Newell J. P. *Sounds of the Eternal* Canterbury 2002
[15] I am indebted to Bradley (ibid.) and also to other theologians for this part of the introduction:
Newell P. *Listening for the Heartbeat of God* SPCK 1997
Wessels A. *Europe: Was it Ever Really Christian?* SCM 1994
Ed. Cross F.L. *The Oxford Dictionary of the Christian Church* Oxford University Press 2005
[16] From p6 Bradley I. ibid
[17] From p155 Matthews C. *The Way of the Celtic Tradition* Element 1989
[18] Carmichael A. *Carmina Gadelica* Floris Books 1992
[19] Can be found in the music books of the Wild Goose Resource Group (Iona Community) and in many modern hymnals.
For example, Bell J.L. and Maule G. *Heaven Cannot Wait. Wild Goose Songs Vol 1* Wild Goose Publications 1987
[20] Many including Adam D. *The Cry of the Deer – Meditations on the Hymn of St Patrick* Triangle/SPCK 1987
[21] Newell P. *Celtic Benediction* Canterbury 2000
[22] de Waal E. *The Celtic Way of Prayer* Doubleday 1997
[23] Anything by Cotter J. for example *Prayer at Night's Approaching* Cairns Publications 2001
[24] Particularly Morley J. *All Desires Known* SPCK 1992/Morehouse publishing 2006

INTRODUCTION TO JANUARY
[1] p66 Hutton, R. *The Stations of the Sun* Oxford University Press 1996
[2] p47,ibid.

January
Bible references and other sources within the prayers
Monday: Morning Invocation. See Isaiah 6.6-8
Tuesday: Opening Out. See Isaiah 60.1
Friday: Opening Out. See Matthew 8.20
Saturday: On Rising/Resting. See Proverbs 8.27 and 30
Sunday: Night Shielding. See spirituality of Julian of Norwich, for example in *Enfolded in Love: Daily Readings with Julian of Norwich* ed. Llewelyn R. Darton, Longman and Todd 2004.
See the Magnificat in Luke 1.46-55

February
Bible references and other sources within the prayers
Monday: On Rising/Resting. See John 1.5
Praising. See Psalm 139.12
Morning Invocation. See Isaiah 43.2
Tuesday: Morning Invocation. See *For People With Bodies,* Taplin K. Flarestack 1997. Used with permission from Kim.
Wednesday: Morning Invocation. See Psalm 139.13 and 2-3. Genesis 3.19.
Opening Out. See Genesis 32.23-32.
Night Shielding. See Genesis 28.16
Blessing. See Job 1.21
Thursday: Night Shielding. See John 3.8
Blessing. See Romans 8.38-9
Friday: Morning Invocation. See Isaiah 43.19
Night Shielding. See Isaiah 49.15. For notion of the greening Spirit of God see spirituality of Hildegard of Bingen for example in *Hildegard von Bingen's Mystical Visions,* St Hildegard. Bear and Co. 1995
Saturday: Night Shielding. See *All Desires Known,* Morley J. SPCK 1992. I am indebted to the superior prayer on p85.
Blessing. See Psalm 51.11
Sunday: Blessing. See Numbers 6.24-6

March
Bible references and other sources within the prayers
Tuesday: Praising. See Psalm 6.3
Wednesday: Praising. See Philippians 2.6 and Matthew 10.42
Opening Out. See John 8.6. See many but at least Luke 6.12

See many but at least Mark 10.13-14 See many but at least John 4.7-30 and John 12.1-8 See John 21.12.

Blessing. See Lamentations 3.22-3

Thursday: Opening Out. See Matthew 13.3-9

Friday: Morning Invocation and Night Shielding. In honour of CF Alexander's hymn of St Patrick's breastplate, adapted from the Irish. Originally from *Poems* London 1896 p.59-62, but now found in most standard hymn books.

Saturday: Blessing. See Matthew 3.17

Sunday: On Rising/Resting. See Genesis 1.1-2

Blessing: I Corinthians 13.11

April
Bible references and other sources within the prayers

Monday: Morning Invocation. See Matthew 10.34

Praising. See Psalm 42.7

Blessing. See Micah 6.8

Tuesday: Opening Out. See Matthew 13.45 and 6:20

Wednesday: Praising. See 1 Corinthians 1.25

Opening Out. See Psalm 84.5-6 and Luke 1.53

Thursday: On Rising/Resting. See Romans 12.15

Sunday: Morning Invocation. See John 20.1-18, John 20.24-28, John 21.9-14, Luke 24.31-32, John 21.4-8, John 20.16-18, Luke 24.13-35

Opening Out. See Genesis 3.3 and John 20.17

Blessing. See John 20.1-18, Matthew 28.16-20, John 21.4-14, John 20.19-29

INTRODUCTION TO MAY

[3] from a Cornish May Song p149, Freeman M. *Kindling the Celtic Spirit* 2001 Harper San Francisco

[4] Frazer J. *The Golden Bough:A Study in Magic and Religion* Touchstone 1995

May
Bible references and other sources within the prayers

Tuesday: On Rising/Resting and Night Shielding. For idea of God dwelling within us like an underground stream see spirituality of St John of the Cross, for example in *John of the Cross: Selections from the Dark Night and other Writings* (Western Spiritual Classics). Harper Collins/ San Francisco 2004

Wednesday: On Rising/Resting. See John 1.48
Praising. See Song of Songs 2.10-12
Thursday: Morning Invocation. See Galatians 5.22
Friday: Opening Out. See Genesis 1.27
Saturday: Praising. See John 3.8
Morning Invocation. See Acts 1.11
Sunday: Blessing. See Isaiah 55.11

INTRODUCTION TO JUNE
[5] p186 Freeman M. *Kindling the Celtic Spirit* Harper San Francisco 2001

June
Bible references and other sources within the prayers
Tuesday: On Rising/Resting. See Psalm 84.1
Praising. See Mark 1.11
Thanksgiving. See Genesis 1.2
Wednesday: Praising. See Job 38.4-11
Opening out. See Genesis 1.2, Psalm 8, Matthew 9.20, Romans 8.38-9
Thursday: Morning Invocation. See Matthew 11.28
Opening Out. See Matthew 5.3-6
Blessing. See Psalm 23
Friday: Morning Invocation. See Psalm 23 and Matthew 18.12-14
Sunday: Morning Invocation. See Luke 15.11-32

July
Bible references and other sources within the prayers
Monday: Opening Out. See Psalm 133.1
Tuesday: Morning Invocation. See Exodus 17.6
Night Shielding. See Psalm 137
Wednesday: Opening Out. See Genesis 9.2-17
Night Shielding. See John 1.5, Ps 139
Friday: Blessing. See Psalm 98 or 150
Sunday: On Rising/Resting. See Mark 6.31

INTRODUCTION TO AUGUST
[6] Maire MacNeill *The Festival of Lughnasah* Oxford 1962
[7] Carmichael A. *The Carmina Gadelica* Floris Books 1992
[8] p196-7 ibid.

August
Bible references and other sources within the prayers
Monday: Morning Invocation. See John 6.35-40, Matthew 6.11 or the Lord's Prayer.
Opening Out. See Psalm 126
Wednesday: Opening Out and Blessing. See John 21.4
Night Shielding. See Genesis 1.1-2 and Numbers 6.24-26
Thursday: Night Shielding. See Matthew 5.9
Friday: Praising. See Genesis 3.8
Saturday: Morning Invocation and Opening Out. See Psalm 121
Sunday: On Rising/Resting. See Genesis 2.2
Blessing. See Psalm 121

INTRODUCTION TO SEPTEMBER
[9] p.342 Hutton R. *Stations of the Sun* Oxford 1996
[10] p86 Self D. *Highdays and Holidays* Lion 1993
[11] p333 as quoted from Hutton R. ibid.

September
Bible references and other sources within the prayers
Thursday: On Rising/Resting and Praising. See Proverbs 8
Opening Out. See Genesis 3 and Matthew 10.13
Night Shielding. See Sirach 24.17-19
Saturday: Praising. See Genesis 28.12
Sunday: Praising. See John 12.24

INTRODUCTION TO OCTOBER
[12] p335 Jung C. from "The Philosophical Tree" 1945 in *Collected Works 13: Alchemical Studies*, Ed. Hubert Read, Routledge and Kegan Paul 1967

October
Bible references and other sources within the prayers
Monday: Night Shielding. See Psalm 119.105
Tuesday: Praising. See Gandhi for example in The Wit and Wisdom of Gandhi ed. Gandhi Mohandas and Homer A. Jack, Dover publications 2005
Thursday: Blessing. Echoes the great prayer by Dag Hammerskold: "For all that has been, 'Thanks'. For all that shall be, 'Yes'".
Friday: Morning Invocation. See 1 Kings 19.13

INTRODUCTION TO NOVEMBER

[13] p333 as quoted from Hutton R. ibid.
[14] p80 Palmer and Lloyd, *A Year of British Calendar Customs*
[15] from p393 Hutton R. ibid.
[16] p403, Hutton R. ibid.

November
Bible references and other sources within the prayers

Monday: Praising. See hymn, "For all the saints".
Morning Invocation. See Hebrews 12.1
Tuesday: Night Shielding. See 1Corinthians 13
Wednesday: Praising. See Luke 5.4
Saturday: Praising. See Chinese Proverb, "it is better to light a candle than to curse the darkness"
Sunday: Praising. See Isaiah 2.4, Micah 4.3
Morning Invocation. See sayings of Lao Tsu.
Night Shielding. John 14.27

INTRODUCTION TO DECEMBER

[17] P58 Hutton R. "Stations of the Sun" 1996 Oxford
[18] p62 ibid

December
Bible references and other sources within the prayers

Monday: Blessing. See Luke 4.18-19 Opening Out. Resonant with "God's Grandeur". Manley Hopkins G. *The Major Works (Oxford World's Classics)* Oxford University Press 2002.
Friday: On Rising/Resting. See Isaiah 35.1-2a,6-7
Praising. See Isaiah 11.6
Morning Invocation. See Isiaiah 42.3
Night Shielding. See O Little Town of Bethlehem. The phrase "The slow and the suffering" is borrowed from an older prayer "God of the watching ones".
Saturday: Praising. See Psalm 42.7
Sunday: On Rising/Resting. See Romans 8.19
Morning Invocation. See Job 38.7, which is the origin of the line in O little Town of Bethlehem.

BOOKS

O books
O is a symbol of the world, of oneness and unity. In different cultures it also means the "eye", symbolizing knowledge and insight, and in Old English it means "place of love or home". O books explores the many paths of understanding which different traditions have developed down the ages, particularly those today that express respect for the planet and all of life.

For more information on the full list of over 300 titles please visit our website
www.O-books.net

myspiritradio is an exciting web, internet, podcast and mobile phone global broadcast network for all those interested in teaching and learning in the fields of body, mind, spirit and self development. Listeners can hear the show online via computer or mobile phone, and even download their favourite shows to listen to on MP3 players whilst driving, working, or relaxing.

Feed your mind, change your life with O Books,
The O Books radio programme carries interviews with most authors, sharing their wisdom on life, the universe and everything...e mail questions and co-create the show with O Books and myspiritradio.

Just visit **www.myspiritradio.com** for more information.

Daughters of the Earth
Cheryl Straffon

In her new book Cheryl combines legend, landscape and women's ceremonies to create a wonderful mixture of Goddess experience in the present day. Her knowledge ranges from the paleolithic and neolithic eras to modern times as we follow her explorations of sacred sites from the Cave of the Bear in Crete to the Cave of Cats at Rathcroghan in Ireland. A feast of information, ideas, facts and visions. **Kathy Jones**, co-founder of the Glastonbury Goddess Conference and author of *The Ancient British Goddess*.
1846940168 240pp **£11.99 $21.95**

The Gods Within
An interactive guide to archetypal therapy
Peter Lemesurier

Whether you enjoy analyzing your family and friends or looking for ways to explain or excuse your own strengths and weaknesses, this book provides a whole new slant. It can be read just for fun, but there is an uncanny ring of truth to it. Peter Lemesurier combines scholarship with wry humour, a compulsive mixture. **Anna Corser**, Physiotherapy Manager.
1905047991 260pp 30 b/w photos **£14.99 $24.95**

Maiden, Mother, Crone
Voices of the Goddess
Claire Hamilton

Written in the first person, these provocative and surprising renderings of Celtic tales take us on a challenging journey in which the twelve most ancient and extraordinary goddesses of the land reveal their light and dark faces. In bringing their symbolism to life for today they restore our earlier understanding of war, sex and death.
1905047398 240pp **£12.99 $24.95**

Savage Breast
One man's search for the goddess
Tim Ward

An epic, elegant, scholarly search for the goddess, weaving together travel, Greek mythology, and personal autobiographic relationships into a remarkable exploration of the Western World's culture and sexual history. It is also entertainingly human, as we listen and learn from this accomplished person and the challenging mate he wooed. If you ever travel to Greece, take Savage Breast along with you. **Harold Schulman**, Professor of Gynaecology at Winthrop University Hospital, and author of *An Intimate History of the Vagina.*
1905047584 400pp colour section +100 b/w photos **£12.99 $19.95**

Tales of the Celtic Bards
With CD
Claire Hamilton

An original and compelling retelling of some wonderful stories by an accomplished mistress of the bardic art. Unusual and refreshing, the book provides within its covers the variety and colour of a complete bardic festival. **Ronald Hutton**, Professor of History, University of Bristol.
1903816548 320pp with CD 230/152mm **£16.99 $24.95** cl.

The Virgin and the Pentacle
The Freemasonic plot to destroy the Church
Alan Butler

The author unfolds the history of the tensions between Freemasonry and the Catholic Church, which he sees as reflecting that between patriarchal and matriarchal views of the godhead. It is essentially a power struggle that continues to this day. He marshals considerable evidence to make his case, which is a valuable contribution to the relationship between inner and outer history. **Scientific and Medical Network Review**
1905047320 208pp 230/153mm **£12.99 $17.95** pb

Way of the Druid
The renaissance of a Celtic religion and its relevance for today
Graeme K. Talboys

Enjoyable and revelatory...goes into closely argued debate on the nature of belief, religion and the Celtic metaphysic. Should be on library shelves-public and academic-and on the personal shelves of all those who already call themselves Druid. **Liz Murray**, Liaison officer, Council of British Druid Orders
1905047231 304pp 230/153mm **£17.99 $29.95**

The Creative Christian
God and us; Partners in Creation
Adrian B. Smith

Enlivening and stimulating, the author presents a new approach to Jesus and the Kingdom he spoke of, in the context of the evolution of our Universe. He reveals its meaning for us of the 21st century. **Hans Schrenk**, Lecturer in Holy Scripture and Biblical Languages, Middlesex University.
1905047754 160pp **£11.99 $24.95**

The Gospel of Falling Down
Mark Townsend

This little book is tackling one of the biggest and deepest questions which, unexpectedly, brings us to the foundation of the Christian faith. Mark has discovered this through his own experience of falling down, or failure. **Bishop Stephen Verney**
1846940095 144pp **£9.99 $16.95**

I Still Haven't Found What I'm Looking For
Paul Walker

Traditional understandings of Christianity may not be credible perhaps they can still speak to us in a different way. Perhaps they point to something which we can still sense. Something we need in our lives. Something not just to make us decent, or responsible, but happy and fulfilled. Paul Walker, former *Times* preacher of the year, does not give answers, but rejoices in the search. 1905047762 144pp **£9.99 $16.95**

An Introduction to Radical Theology
The death and resurrection of God
Trevor Greenfield

This is a clearly written and scholarly introduction to radical theology that, at the same time, provides a contextualised and much needed survey of the movement. At times and in turns Greenfield is passionate, ironical, polemical and acerbic. An underlying wit surfaces in images that punctuate the text. This work is a significant and valuable addition to the literature available not only on theological writing but also cultural change. **Journal of Beliefs and Values**
1905047606 208pp **£12.99 $29.95**

Tomorrow's Christian
A new framework for Christian living
Adrian B. Smith

This is a vision of a radically new kind of Christianity. While many of the ideas here have been accepted by radical Christians and liberal theologians for some time, this presents them as an accessible, coherent package: a faith you can imagine living out with integrity in the real world. And even if you already see yourself as a "progressive Christian" or whatever label you choose to adopt, you'll find ideas in both books that challenge and surprise you. Highly recommended. **Movement**
1903816971 176pp **£9.99 $15.95**

Back to the Truth
5,000 years of Advaita
Dennis Waite

A wonderful book. Encyclopedic in nature, and destined to become a classic. **James Braha**
   Absolutely brilliant...an ease of writing with a water-tight argument out-

lining the great universal truths. *This book will become a modern classic. A milestone in the history of Advaita.* **Paula Marvelly**
1905047614 500pp **£19.95 $29.95**

Beyond Photography
Encounters with orbs, angels and mysterious light forms
Katie Hall and John Pickering

The authors invite you to join them on a fascinating quest; a voyage of discovery into the nature of a phenomenon, manifestations of which are shown as being historical and global as well as contemporary and intently personal.

At journey's end you may find yourself a believer, a doubter or simply an intrigued wonderer... Whatever the outcome, the process of journeying is likely prove provocative and stimulating and - as with the mysterious images fleetingly captured by the authors' cameras - inspiring and potentially enlightening. **Brian Sibley**, author and broadcaster.
1905047908 272pp 50 b/w photos +8pp colour insert **£12.99 $24.95**

Don't Get MAD Get Wise
Why no one ever makes you angry, ever!
Mike George

There is a journey we all need to make, from anger, to peace, to forgiveness. Anger always destroys, peace always restores, and forgiveness always heals. This explains the journey, the steps you can take to make it happen for you.
1905047827 160pp **£7.99 $14.95**

IF You Fall...
It's a new beginning
Karen Darke

Karen Darke's story is about the indomitability of spirit, from one of life's cruel vagaries of fortune to what is insight and inspiration. She has overcome the limitations of paralysis and discovered a life of challenge and adventure that many of us only dream about. It is all about the mind, the spirit and the desire that some of us find, but which all of us possess. **Joe Simpson**, mountaineer and author of *Touching the Void*
1905047886 240pp **£9.99 $19.95**

Love, Healing and Happiness
Spiritual wisdom for a post-secular era
Larry Culliford

This will become a classic book on spirituality. It is immensely practical and grounded. It mirrors the author's compassion and lays the foundation for a higher understanding of human suffering and hope. **Reinhard Kowalski** Consultant Clinical Psychologist
1905047916 304pp **£10.99 $19.95**

A Map to God
Awakening Spiritual Integrity
Susie Anthony

This describes an ancient hermetic pathway, representing a golden thread running through many traditions, which offers all we need to understand and do to actually become our best selves.
1846940443 260pp **£10.99 $21.95**

Punk Science
Inside the mind of God
Manjir Samanta-Laughton

Wow! Punk Science is an extraordinary journey from the microcosm of the atom to the macrocosm of the Universe and all stops in between. Manjir Samanta-Laughton's synthesis of cosmology and consciousness is sheer genius. It is elegant, simple and, as an added bonus, makes great reading.
Dr Bruce H. Lipton, author of *The Biology of Belief*
1905047932 320pp **£12.95 $22.95**

Rosslyn Revealed
A secret library in stone
Alan Butler

Rosslyn Revealed gets to the bottom of the mystery of the chapel featured in the Da Vinci Code. The results of a lifetime of careful research and study demonstrate that truth really is stranger than fiction; a library of

philosophical ideas and mystery rites, that were heresy in their time, have been disguised in the extraordinarily elaborate stone carvings.
1905047924 260pp b/w + colour illustrations **£19.95 $29.95** cl

The Way of Thomas
Nine Insights for Enlightened Living from the Secret Sayings of Jesus
John R. Mabry

What is the real story of early Christianity? Can we find a Jesus that is relevant as a spiritual guide for people today?
These and many other questions are addressed in this popular presentation of the teachings of this mystical Christian text. Includes a reader-friendly version of the gospel.
1846940303 196pp **£10.99 $19.95**

The Way Things Are
A Living Approach to Buddhism
Lama Ole Nydahl

An up-to-date and revised edition of a seminal work in the Diamond Way Buddhist tradition (three times the original length), that makes the timeless wisdom of Buddhism accessible to western audiences. Lama Ole has established more than 450 centres in 43 countries.
1846940427 240pp **£9.99 $19.95**

The 7 Ahas! of Highly Enlightened Souls
How to free yourself from ALL forms of stress
Mike George
7th printing

A very profound, self empowering book. Each page bursting with wisdom and insight. One you will need to read and reread over and over again! Paradigm Shift. I totally love this book, a wonderful nugget of inspiration. **PlanetStarz**
1903816319 128pp 190/135mm **£5.99 $11.95**

God Calling
A Devotional Diary
A. J. Russell

46th printing
"When supply seems to have failed, you must know that it has not done so. But you must look around to see what you can give away. Give away something." One of the best-selling devotional books of all time, with over 6 million copies sold.
1905047428 280pp 135/95mm **£7.99** cl.
US rights sold

The Goddess, the Grail and the Lodge
The Da Vinci code and the real origins of religion
Alan Butler

5th printing
This book rings through with the integrity of sharing time-honoured revelations. As a historical detective, following a golden thread from the great Megalithic cultures, Alan Butler vividly presents a compelling picture of the fight for life of a great secret and one that we simply can't afford to ignore.
Lynn Picknett & Clive Prince
1903816696 360pp 230/152mm **£12.99 $19.95**

The Heart of Tantric Sex
A unique guide to love and sexual fulfilment
Diana Richardson

3rd printing
The art of keeping love fresh and new long after the honeymoon is over. Tantra for modern Western lovers adapted in a practical, refreshing and sympathetic way.

One of the most revolutionary books on sexuality ever written. **Ruth Ostrow**, News Ltd.
1903816378 256pp **£9.99 $14.95**

I Am With You
The best-selling modern inspirational classic
John Woolley

14th printing hardback
Will bring peace and consolation to all who read it. **Cardinal Cormac Murphy-O'Connor**
0853053413 280pp 150x100mm **£9.99** cl
4th printing paperback
1903816998 280pp 150/100mm **£6.99 $12.95**

In the Light of Meditation
The art and practice of meditation in 10 lessons
Mike George

2nd printing
A classy book. A gentle yet satisfying pace and is beautifully illustrated. Complete with a CD or guided meditation commentaries, this is a true gem among meditation guides. **Brainwave**
   In-depth approach, accessible and clearly written, a convincing map of the overall territory and a practical path for the journey. **The Light**
1903816610 224pp 235/165mm full colour throughout +CD **£11.99 $19.95**

The Instant Astrologer
A revolutionary new book and software package for the astrological seeker
Lyn Birkbeck

2nd printing
The brilliant Lyn Birkbeck's new book and CD package, The Instant Astrologer, combines modern technology and the wisdom of the ancients, creating an invitation to enlightenment for the masses, just when we need it most!
Astrologer **Jenny Lynch**, Host of NYC's StarPower Astrology Television Show
1903816491 628pp full colour throughout with CD ROM 240/180 **£39 $69** cl

Is There An Afterlife?
A comprehensive overview of the evidence, from east and west
David Fontana

2nd printing
An extensive, authoritative and detailed survey of the best of the evidence supporting survival after death. It will surely become a classic not only of parapsychology literature in general but also of survival literature in particular. **Universalist**
1903816904 496pp 230/153mm **£14.99 $24.95**

The Reiki Sourcebook
Bronwen and Frans Stiene

5th printing
It captures everything a Reiki practitioner will ever need to know about the ancient art. This book is hailed by most Reiki professionals as the best guide to Reiki. For an average reader, it's also highly enjoyable and a good way to learn to understand Buddhism, therapy and healing. **Michelle Bakar**, Beauty magazine
1903816556 384pp **£12.99 $19.95**

Soul Power
The transformation that happens when you know
Nikki de Carteret

4th printing
One of the finest books in its genre today. Using scenes from her own life and growth, Nikki de Carteret weaves wisdom about soul growth and the power of love and transcendent wisdom gleaned from the writings of the mystics. This is a book that I will read gain and again as a reference for my own soul growth. **Barnes and Noble review**
190381636X 240pp **£9.99 $15.95**